Contents

Acknowledgments

We wrote this book because we saw that the world needs to recognize that true heroes are those men and women who live every day with compassionate awareness, bringing fulfillment to their lives and others'. Creating the book has certainly been a hero's journey for both of us; we could not have completed it without the caring, wisdom, and living heroic examples of many allies along our path.

We owe a great deal to our students at Stanford University, at Sonoma State University, and in many workshops for inspiring, using, and critiquing our material. We thank M. Scott Peck for writing a foreword that gave us a new perspective on our work. We join in sending love to Rochelle Myers, a hero of the first rank, for her leadership and inspiration in the creativity course at Stanford. And Sylvia Lorton's magic made the impossible possible as we revised endless versions of the manuscript. We each thank our parents (who, strangely, become more and more heroic as we grow older) for planting the seeds of our everyday heroism and for being role models in meeting challenges.

Lorna expresses gratitude to Jean Houston, Athena incarnate, for inspiration from her essential and transformational work on the hero's journey, and to the spirit of Joseph Campbell, for his awe-provoking teaching at Esalen in the early years. The creative spirit of her husband, soulmate, and helpmate, Bruce Robinson, is alive in these pages in the form of hundreds of hours of TLC, computer consulting, editing, and other reminders of the path to Mount Olympus. A slobbery kiss and happy giggles are given to little Trickster, Amber Catford-Robinson, for effortlessly creating challenge and inspiration at the same time.

Michael's work is due to the grace of Gurumayi Chidvilasa-nanda. How can one ever thank her? What can be better than trying? He has no greater example of an everyday hero than his wife, Sarah. She mixes courage, wisdom, love, and true friendship in a way that makes their life together a joyful adventure. His love for her is more than tongues can tell and then some. He also thanks their daughter, Sandy, for showing how herohood can grow and how challenges can be met with style.

The team at our publisher, Jeremy P. Tarcher, Inc., were the proverbial guardians of the threshold, providing mythic assistance and direction. Where else can you find editors and production people who research multiple versions of stories to make sure of your inter-pretations? Our editor, Rick Benzel, encouraged and motivated us with intelligence, wit, and caring. Jeremy himself poked and prodded every aspect of the book with zest. Jennifer Boynton in production somehow got the book out after all of us pushed her beyond her deadlines.

Finally, we thank you for using this book. It comes from our hearts, but without you to translate it into your reality, it would re-main only our dream.

Thank you, thank you, and thank you.

Foreword

On the surface this might appear as another deceptively simple self-help book. It is not. In reality it is profound and possibly earth shattering.

Earth shattering? The earth, on its current course, is in grave jeopardy from humanity. Something needs shattering to save it—specifically, certain human illusions.

If you think about it for a moment, you will realize that the title of this book alone is itself shattering. One of our human illusions is that heroes are most extraordinary people living lives of rare glory. Yet right off the bat we are introduced to a new, far more realistic concept: that of the everyday hero.

Along with a thousand others, one of the authors, Michael Ray, and I are deeply involved in the work of The Foundation for Community Encouragement (FCE). This nonprofit, public, educational foundation educates primarily through experiential workshops where people learn how to communicate with each other at an ever more authentic level. They are painful workshops. People do not "get real" easily. But I keep doing this painful work because it is paradoxically so joyful. One of the roots of my joy is that at these workshops I have the privilege of witnessing what I have come to call "the routine heroism of human beings."

What happens when people become authentic with each other is that as their masks drop, their real stories emerge. They are stories of abuse and wounds, of terror and grief, of loneliness and isolation. They are also stories of accomplishment. Sometimes the accomplishment is nothing more and nothing less than the fact that the people are *there,* in the process of actually overcoming their fear and isolation. They are stories of survival—of wisdom learned despite the darkness, of reaching out despite the rejections, of power assumed despite the oppression, of love discovered despite the wounds. Gradually, it emerges that these are stories of more than survival, of healing beyond expectation, of growth against the odds. The stranger begins to be seen as the hero. And, finally, women and men, who had previously thought of themselves as average at best, even begin to see themselves as heroes.

So what? Just this: while the man (or woman) in the street is probably more heroic than he thinks, he is not heroic enough. The world, so in need of saving, desperately needs even more heroism. Not Napoleons, but the kind of everyday heroism to balance the budget; the kind of heroism required to love at the very moment you are feeling tired and irritable; the kind of heroism to proclaim that the emperor has no clothes even when every TV network is proclaiming otherwise.

Beyond a certain point we cannot become even more heroic until we realize that we are heroes, that we are already on the hero's journey. It is not enough to be unconscious heroes. In order to more vigorously exercise our capacity for heroism, we must first accept that we already possess that capacity. In other words, we must consciously identify ourselves as heroes. And that is the second thing that is so earth shattering (read earth-saving) about this book: it not only opens our eyes to the reality of everyday heroism, but it calls upon us to accept our identities as heroes.

Such acceptance does not come easily. Humans seem to have an inherent desire to want others to be heroes for them, rather than to want to be heroes themselves. I suppose it is because of the work involved. In many ways it is so much eaiser to think of ourselves as merely ordinary. Then we can't be expected, can we, to speak out when such speaking is so unpopular? To remember when it is less painful to forget? To pick up a burden which others ignore? To pick up a burden when someone else (some *real* hero, perhaps) might pick it up?

Let me illustrate the problem by recounting an experience that comes from my own Christian tradition. I suspect people from other traditions have had analogous experiences. In any case, not long ago I was one of six hundred attendees—virtually all of whom were Christian authors, clergy, theologians, or therapists—at a professional conference on spirituality and healing where the Harvard theologian Harvey Cox was speaking. He was providing us with a brilliant interpretation of one of the most powerful healing stories of the New Testament. In it Jesus is asked by a very wealthy but worried man to come and heal his seriously ill daughter. On the way to do so, however, a poor woman emerges from the crowd and sneaks up behind Jesus to touch his robe so that she might be healed of chronic hemorrhaging. Instead of being angry at her, Jesus stops to both heal and praise her. Then he proceeds to the wealthy man's house where the family is wailing because Jesus did not come in time and the daughter is dead. Jesus orders the family to shut up and leave him and the girl alone. When they are gone he commands the girl to awake, and she does, whereupon he hands her over to the family with the suggestion that they give her something to eat.

In the midst of his talk, Professor Cox requested those members of the audience to stand up who identified with characters in the story. Dozens upon dozens each identified with the bleeding woman, the worried father, the little girl. But, when asked, only six (including myself) acknowledged ourselves as identifying with Jesus.

Something is seriously wrong here. I know there were another few who did not stand because they felt it would look arrogant for them to do so. But that itself is misguided when people don't want to appear arrogant for doing the very thing their religion tells them they ought to do. When Christ is supposedly their hero, when one of the most famous classics of Christianity is entitled *The Imitation of Christ,* how is it that only one in a hundred people designating themselves as Christians are willing to publicly identify with Christ? Isn't identification with Christ much of what Christianity is supposed to be all about? The problem is not, as I see it, a failure so much of Christians, per se, as it is a human problem. It is simply easier to look up to heroes than to imitate them.

Also, whatever your tradition, this book is shattering not only because it proposes the reality of everyday heroism but goes on to frighteningly encourage us to accept this reality—to overcome our humanly reluctance to be empowered and assume our true identity as heroes. And, finally, it is shattering because it blesses a certain kind of suffering.

Yes, another idol shattered. Hopefully. Indeed, the authors are courageous heroes themselves for doing something so outrageous in our pain-avoiding culture as to bless any kind of suffering whatsoever.

Neither the authors nor I are pain freaks. If I have a headache, the first thing I'm likely to do when I have an opportunity is to go into the kitchen to get myself two super strength uncapsulized Tylenols. I see no virtue inherent in that headache per se for me or for the person in my office I am trying to attend to. As a physician, unnecessary pain—unconstructive suffering—in myself as well as others is my enemy. But note the qualifiers—some suffering is necessary and constructive.

Throughout this book you will see a U-shaped figure. It is terribly simple. The upper arms of the U symbolize the high ground, the places where either out of innocence or wisdom we feel good, where life seems easy. But in between them there is this steep bow to the bottom. What does it symbolize? The pits. Time and again it is graphically displayed that to get from here to there we go through pits.

The pits are different each go-around. They may last a few hours, a few days or weeks, sometimes even months or years. Sometimes they are deeper or steeper than at others. (If they are too deep or prolonged, you should suspect that you may be stuck and need some professional help getting out—some of the pain is likely unnecessary. It is not helpful to revel in the pits.) They may be nothing more than acknowledging a mistake. Or they may look like a mid-life crisis. Or something else. But they are the pits. They always hurt. There is always some degree of depression.

What the authors are doing here is dignifying crisis and dignifying depression. They are an essential, normal, necessary, *healthy* part of the hero's journey. This may seem like Bad News to those who labor under the American illusion that life should be easy, that mental health is characterized by an absence of crises and that something must be wrong with you if you're even slightly depressed. But it will be Good News to those more realistic who may question their own sanity for believing that there might just be a little more to life than being unfailingly happy, placidly comfortable, and self-righteously rich in spirit. It will also be Good News for at least some of those who are in the pits. It might lead them to correctly suspect that their particular dark night may be part of a psychospiritual growth spurt—that something is shaking and moving in their soul.

Which is Good News for all of us. The supply of heroes will never be equal to the demand, and the demand seems particularly acute at the moment. You are important. Come join the journey. You are wanted and needed far more than you can even imagine.

M. Scott Peck, M.D.

PART ONE

LIVING AS A HERO

The Path of the Everyday Hero

Does your life seem to be successful, and yet sometimes you have a secret feeling that it could be more deeply fulfilling? Do you ever yearn for a greater sense of flow or harmony, or have a hunch that there's more to journeying from birth to death on this planet than what you have yet experienced?

Do you ever feel trapped in a life that just isn't working out the way you imagined it would? Do you ever wish you could find the magic wand that would transform your daily frustrations and conflicts into glorious heroic adventures with happy endings?

Or is your life going well for you, except in one specific area? Perhaps you ache inside for a meaningful relationship, or your work responsibilities threaten to destroy your personal life, or you haven't found a pursuit of true importance that makes your life feel worthwhile.

If you can identify with any of these very normal human situations, then you know the feeling that Peggy Lee once sang about: "Is that all there is?" You know that the glitter of a long-sought objective can tarnish once you achieve it. You know that life is more than reaching a particular goal; it is a journey to the tops of mountains, down into seemingly bottomless pits, and up again.

This book invites you to take a new path. It assumes that all of us are on a journey, charting a direction for our life, whether we are aware of this or not. By being conscious about your path rather than a specific destination or goal, you can live every day with greater joy, in-

I have found my hero and he is me.

George Sheehan

3

The dictionary is the only place where success comes before work.

Arthur Brisbane

tuition, will, strength, and compassion. *The Path of the Everyday Hero* shows how in each moment you can be a hero to yourself. And the secret is that if you can be a hero to yourself, then you can be of your greatest value to others and to the world.

Specifically, this book offers a personalized course for developing greater personal power and fulfillment and in using practical creativity to resolve five significant challenges of adult life. It assists you in seeing your challenges not as hindrances, problems, or failures, but as tests in the great school of life, opportunities to call on and use personal strengths and wisdom you may not yet know you have. This book offers the tools you need if, in the words of mythologist Joseph Campbell, you are to "follow your bliss [and] actually feel the rapture of being alive."

Heroes come in every shape and size
Making special sacrifices for others in their lives
No one gives them medals
The world don't know their names
But in someone's eyes they're heroes just the same.

Paul Overstreet

WHAT IT MEANS TO LIVE AS A HERO

When we talk about an everyday hero, we use the term *hero* to refer to a man or woman who, as defined in Webster's dictionary, is a "central personage taking an admirable part in any remarkable action or event." As we see it, the "remarkable action" is simply the ability to call on our creative spirit to guide us through life. Thus, everyday heroes are those men and women who have found and are manifesting their creative spirit. We believe that almost everyone can do this if they open their eyes and heart to the possibility.

Living as a hero is not without its ups and downs. This is the nature of the path of the everyday hero. In fact, it is in order to deal with these vacillations that you need to be heroic. But how do you learn to do this?

The secret is in the journey itself. With the hero's attitude towards resolving challenges, you can use everything that happens to you in life as a lesson to move you more deeply into the flow of creativity and all of its benefits.

The pioneering work of poet Robert Bly, of mythologist Joseph Campbell, of psychologist Jean Houston, and of others has shown how the pattern of the hero's journey as demonstrated in myths, fairy tales, and folk stories provides an archetypal map for transcending the barriers we find on our path. Their work acknowledges that humans are whole and complex beings, existing simultaneously in the external world of everyday responsibilities and also (even if we don't always pay attention to it) in the subtle inner dimensions of the human psyche. Living a creative life can be likened to the journey of the mythic hero, who might start out quite unheroic, but in the process of traveling down a road full of trials and having to attain new heights of sensitivity, skill, or wisdom, becomes transformed.

The hero's journey, as we will be using it here, refers to our inner transformation, and the subsequent transformation of our outer lives, when we learn to activate our hidden creative resources and connect with transcendent sources of support. As we become heroic, in this sense, we learn to view our challenges differently, and they subsequently lose their hold over us. Bly, Campbell, and Houston each emphasize the point that since metaphor and story are the language by which we understand our psyche and its relation to our practical, daily experience, there is tremendous value in thinking in terms of the hero's journey as we deal with our own challenge of living a creative life.

The true hero meets challenges in a special way. Being heroic is being passionately committed to some course of action. If you look at the high points in your life, you'll see that many of them came from situations that initially seemed impossible or even terrifying. Consider, for instance, your first date, first job, first high-dive, or the first time you were able to stay up on a bike. You made a commitment to do them. The heroic nature of that commitment draws support. As Goethe said:

> Concerning all acts of initiative and creation, there is one elemental truth—the ignorance of which kills countless ideas and splendid plans: that the moment one definitely commits oneself, the Providence moves, too. All sorts of things occur to help one that would never otherwise have occurred.

Being a hero is about being committed to the journey of life in the highest possible sense. It is about trusting that we can find a path that will take us beyond what seem to be bottomless pits to the top of Mount Olympus, the realm of the mythical gods. It is about discovering our human divinity—that powerful, creative source that we each have within us—and living by it.

Being a hero is not the same thing as being in conflict and competition with others. Instead, the hero of whom we speak is a peaceful warrior, embodying both the so-called feminine qualities of sensitivity and nurturance on one hand and the masculine ones of assertiveness and strength on the other. The path of the everyday hero is, as

*I shall be telling this with a
    sigh
Somewhere ages and ages
    hence:
Two roads diverged in a
    wood, and I—
I took the one less traveled by,
And that has made all the
    difference.*

Robert Frost

We shall not cease from exploration
And the end of all our exploring
Will be to arrive where we started
And know the place for the first time.

T. S. Eliot

one of our friends calls it, the path of detached involvement. When you travel it, you certainly revel in the challenges of life and the joy of the process, but you are not attached to the outcomes, not saddled with getting credit for them—even though you probably will get credit for more and more positive ones.

Having searched for and found his or her inner creativity, the hero can see it in others, and therefore is the ultimate team player. Community in the truest sense of the word comes about with people who are on this hero's journey in life.

In the last five years, more educators, psychologists, writers, and business consultants have brought the idea of life as a hero's journey into their work. It has proven time and again to be a catalyst for profound personal changes in those who've used it, resulting in increased self-fulfillment and mastery of personal and professional challenges. We have been working with this model for the last fifteen years with our students, clients, and ourselves. We have witnessed people experience tremendous shifts in attitude, confidence, and success when they begin to live their lives as a hero, particularily as they deal with the five major life challenges highlighted in this book. The book is organized so that your resolution of each of these challenges can be a smaller version of the hero's journey in itself.

WHAT IT MEANS TO LIVE CREATIVELY

If you are like many people, you might shy away from the word *creative* when it is applied to yourself. In this society we seem to use that word only for people who are geniuses or who are involved in the arts. But what we are talking about in this book is something you've already experienced many times in your life, even if you haven't experienced enough of it to feel it is a fundamental part of your journey. It is something everyday; something quite *ordinary*. It is the creativity of real life and real living.

You've experienced creativity if you've ever looked into the face of a newborn baby—particularly if you've raised that child. You've been creative when you've dealt successfully with a difficult client or found a perfect gift for someone you love. Creativity is what you experience when you hit a perfect golf or tennis shot—not because of where the ball lands, or whether you win, but because of the feeling and experience of hitting the shot.

You are being creative when you are in what psychologists call *flow* and athletes call the *zone*—so absorbed in what you are doing that, for the moment, everything outside the process you are engaged in disappears: the surfer on the wave, the skier on the slope, the singer in the song.

Creativity is waking up in the morning and being excited about what is ahead of you that day. You are being creative when you are making a contribution, serving the world in ways that are important to you, or when your work is something that you love so much that, even if you were being paid a great deal to do it, you would be secretly willing to pay for the privilege of doing it.

You've acted creatively in the past when you've made worries and fears disappear; when you've made appropriate decisions confidently; when you've been easily productive; when you've felt connection and interrelationship in communication with others; when your life has felt most meaningful and full of growth. These are the times when you have experienced the true rapture of life.

In sum, you are fully creative whenever you are operating from your soul, your self or your inner essence—from the highest, most complete part of you, the part you are thinking of when you sense you have much more potential than you have shown the world. This aspect of you can and does manifest infinite intuition, will, joy, strength, and compassion. Creativity is a gift that everyone receives at birth. We can show our gratitude for this gift by recognizing it and, therefore, increasing its power. Bringing out your own unique brand of creativity into your life and the world can be the most significant thing you'll ever do.

The journey in this book is the search for how this higher self of yours can be expressed in your day-to-day life. Right now, in this age of high tech, our machines, businesses, service professions, and the quality of life itself are all made what they are by humans. If we don't like what we have made, or feel we have much farther to go, we can only create a better life for ourselves and the rest of humanity by calling on our human resources to resolve these challenges. Like King Arthur's knights in their search for the Holy Grail, our journey is enlivened by the fact that the quest is never over and consists of endless adventures that can enrich us personally and deepen our understanding of life and ourselves. It is the only worthwhile path in today's world.

In the average man is curled
The hero stuff that rules the
world.

Sam Walter Foss

HOW TO USE THIS BOOK

Each chapter in this book is intended to inspire new ways of relating to life and the world. The first four chapters prepare you for the journey of self-development. In chapter 2 you will determine which of the five challenges of adult life is calling out to your hidden hero nature right now. In chapter 3, we describe what we mean by the idea of living creatively and, in chapter 4, we further explain the notion of the hero's journey. Each one of chapters 5 through 9 is a small hero's journey in itself, and addresses a particular major challenge of life using the language of myth and metaphor. We first retell a legend or story that captures the essence of how to resolve that particular challenge. Then you examine how characteristics of the story reflect aspects of your current situation. You practice living by a motto that sums up the key message of that chapter, and do activities and exercises to gain access to your hidden creative resources concerning that challenge. To chart your progress as you use this book, we encourage you to keep a log of your progress in resolving that challenge, before and after completing your journey through each chapter.

Here you will experience the hero's journey through some of the most profound tales of all time. The stories offer the same kind of insight and energy that the best kind of dreams can give you; they touch a deep wisdom and courage that you might not know you possess. They touch a truth that is beyond individual, time, or place. Even a story that you might know well, like Cinderella, can be illuminating when it is read and experienced from the perspective of dealing with a crucial life challenge. Once that energy is tapped, the exercises become adventures on your hero's journey to meet each challenge.

In chapter 4, the folk tale of Sleeping Beauty introduces you to the richness and usefulness of the hero's journey metaphor itself, and elements of the story illustrate different aspects of this universal journey.

In chapter 5 you will take the path of clarifying your purpose in life, using the Arthurian legend of Perceval and the Holy Grail. You will see what factors keep Perceval (representing yourself) from recognizing and pursuing his true purpose, and then observe his transformation as his self becomes more developed. As in all five of the later chapters, the exercises translate themes from the story into the context of your life.

In chapter 6, your work on the challenge of developing loving re-

The hero, therefore, is the man or woman who has been able to battle past his personal and local historical limitations.

Joseph Campbell

lationships begins with the story of Beauty and the Beast, in which you find that the title characters represent different aspects of yourself in your relationships. The exercises then encourage you to explore the symbolic meaning of each character and to consider new possibilities in how you create your relationships.

Your journey toward living stress-free in the here and now is initiated in chapter 7 with a less well-known story, The Peasant Who Married a Goddess. Through concentration, and reliance on both his inner creative resources and the transcendent grace that seemed to be carried through his wife, the peasant is able literally to move mountains. The exercises in this chapter offer you a variety of approaches to learn how to do this figuratively, in your own life.

To meet the challenge of balancing the personal and professional sides of your life, you will be helped along by the Greek myth of Theseus in chapter 8. You will see how to stay mindful about both aspects of your life, and the exercises offer several ways to do this.

In chapter 9, you'll be surprised how reflecting on the story of Cinderella can help you understand prosperity in a heroic way. After exploring the Cinderella and stepsister aspects of yourself, you will be prompted to consider what it is that truly gives you a rich sense of value in your life.

There are several ways you could use this book. You might like to read it cover-to-cover, and then do the activities for each challenge as a sort of psychological tune up. You might like to use it as a five-week home-study course. Or you may prefer to read the four introductory chapters and then go directly to the chapter that deals with the most important challenge for you right now. Do whichever seems to work best for you.

Whatever you do, we strongly recommend that you spend a week or more with each of the chapters on specific life-challenges so that you can assimilate the ideas, do the exercises, and have time to reflect on what you discover. You will get a lot more out of this than by simply reading a chapter quickly without doing the exercises. That's a bit like reading a recipe book without cooking and eating the food: the real satisfaction just isn't there.

A number of meditative exercises are also included. You could either read through each one several times to get to know it, and then put the book down and do it, or ask a friend to read the meditation to you. Alternately, many people make a tape recording of themselves

The unexamined life is not worth living.

Plato

9

reading the instructions at an appropriate pace, and then play it back. This is a particularly relaxing way to do the meditations, and it makes it easier for you to do them more than once.

If you find an exercise or type of activity that is particularly valuable for you, feel free to adapt it and apply it to other situations in your life. The premise of this book is to use it so that it works for you. Do what Jean Houston recommends: "Cheat, and make it meaningful for yourself."

You may also want to consider keeping a personal journal to record your responses to the activities. While the exercises can be done right in the book itself, a personal journal allows you the opportunity for extended reflection, writing, and drawing. With a journal of this sort, synergy begins to develop between the various things you put in it. A bound book that you maintain specifically for this purpose is better than just using the odd piece of paper when you want to do an exercise.

I never travel without my diary. One should always have something sensational to read in the train.

Oscar Wilde

ON BEING AN EVERYDAY HERO: A STORY

Before you begin, we believe it is important to add that to some degree, you are already on the path of the everyday hero, whether or not you realize it. You may see in others what M. Scott Peck calls "the routine heroism of human beings," but more than likely you have trouble seeing it in yourself. In fact, the more you recognize it in yourself, the more you'll see it in the world and the more you'll be able to live in this wonderful way. We've designed this book to help you journey with the recognition that you *are* an everyday hero and that you *can* meet life's challenges with all of your gifts and limitations.

We'll explain what we mean (as we do so often in the book) with a story. This story, often called "Both Here and There," is ancient, but, like the other stories in this book, it still has the potential to give insight in the present. We've read it and heard it told by several people, most recently by meditation master Gurumayi Chidvilasananda. But we've retold it here in our own way.

Both Here and There

It seems that in ancient times there was a king named Akbar, who had a brilliant and clever prime minister named Birbal. Akbar was always asking questions that he hoped would baffle Birbal, but Birbal was always able to answer, and so save his life and his ministership.

One day Akbar asked Birbal if he could bring him someone who was Here and not There. Birbal brought him a thief, saying, "This thief is only in the world trying to get money and goods to increase his wealth Here."

Then Akbar told Birbal, "Bring me someone who is There and not Here." Birbal responded by bringing a wandering ascetic—a sadhu or mendicant—and said, "He completely neglects all aspects of this world, including his body and his well being, to focus entirely on the world beyond."

"Very good," said Akbar. "Now bring me someone who is neither Here nor There." Birbal left for a while and then returned, presenting to the king a beggar, saying, "This man is neither Here nor There, because he is always envious of everyone else in the world. He's not participating in the world in any sense and, at the same time, has no concern for spiritual matters. Thus, he is in no way There either."

"Very good again," exclaimed a pleased Akbar. "Now, is it possible that there is anyone in the world who is both Here and There?"

"Yes, your majesty," answered Birbal, and brought forth an honest householder couple. "This man and woman work in the world and tend to their family, but do everything with God in their thoughts. Because they do the work of the world and allow their spiritual practices to carry them through both the good and the bad times, they are a man and woman who are both Here and There."

"Very good," said Akbar, and immediately began to think about the next challenge he would give Birbal.

As illustrated by the above story, we use the word *everyday* not just to indicate that you can be a hero all the time, but in the sense that it is ordinary—that it is the birthright of every man or woman to live his or her life heroically (although most of us ignore this possibility). We invite you to recognize that you can be all you can be, you can do all you can do, and you can have all you can have, in everything you do. On this kind of creative journey, you must set forth wholeheartedly, knowing that if you meet your challenges like the archetypal hero, you will overcome them, sometimes in unexpectedly easy ways, sometimes not. But because you are guided by larger forces, you can tap into enormous resources within that you seldom use.

We assume that each of us comes into the world with both a unique set of gifts and a unique set of limitations. The mystery of the soul, of our inner resources, is endless. We are all born with the god-given gift of creativity, but it is individual—each person has his or her distinct way of being creative and journeying through life. As one of

Come to the edge, he said.

They said: "We are afraid."

Come to the edge, he said.

They came.

He pushed them . . . And they

flew.

Guillaume Apollinaire

our course speakers said, "There has never been and never will be again the combination of molecules and atoms that is you. Your job in the world is to live out that potential."

That represents a good philosophy to have while using this book. Recognize and be grateful for your gifts and limitations. Every challenge gives you an opportunity to discover who you are and what you're made of. It also gives you an opportunity to connect with something greater than yourself.

You can take comfort in Goethe's statement (which we've cited above) that once you make a commitment, "Providence moves, too. All sorts of things occur to help one that would never otherwise have occurred." Some people say that God helps those who help themselves, or that you can depend on grace if you are willing to make the self-effort. When you are on a hero's journey to deal with one of the challenges in this book, it is powerful to recognize not only the creativity within you but also the larger forces of creativity around you that can guide you if you are open to them.

Don't forget your limitations. Life's challenges are usually not completely solved. Real peace comes from the discovery of those aspects of the challenges that you just have to let go. As the often-quoted prayer goes: "God grant me the serenity to know the things that I cannot change, the courage to change the things that I can change, and the wisdom to know the difference." The path of the everyday hero is one of this kind of serenity, courage, and wisdom that is more important than simply solving problems.

Now it's time to get on with your journey. As poet Guillaume Apollinaire reminds us in his poem in the margin, all you have to do is to take that first step, even though sometimes it is very hard. We hope this book will give you just the push you need.

How Goes Your Battle?

Now that you've embarked on this journey, you must recognize the most essential aspect of both creativity and of life itself: challenge. Out of challenge come all the higher aspects of life. The fuel of creativity is a special sort of battle.

What are you battling? Whatever stands in the way of leading a rich and fulfilling life.

Why are you battling? To be creative. To be your highest self.

Where is the battlefield? Everywhere.

When do battles occur? Every moment.

How do you battle? The hero battles not with aggression and competition but with honor, courage, compassion, and grace.

What weapons do you have? You have your inner essence with its qualities of intuition, will, joy, strength, and, most importantly, the wisdom of compassion, which affirms that you have this creative resource within you and allows you to see it in others.

In the traditional mythic journey, the hero is aided by magic. What "magic" can you employ? Have faith in your creativity, suspend negative judgment, practice precise observation, and ask penetrating questions.

What treasures do you seek on this path? Knowledge of your life's purpose, nourishing relationships, stress-free living, personal and professional balance, and true prosperity in your journey. The five challenges in life are your quests for these five treasures.

This chapter helps you assess how your battle is going. Answer each of the following questions in a sentence or two. Don't think about it; just write down what comes to mind. This will give you the best reading of what each challenge means to you right now as you begin this journey.

The creative artist and poet and saint must fight the actual (as contrasted to the ideal) gods of our society—the god of conformism as well as the gods of apathy, material success, and exploitative power.

Rollo May

Purpose: What activities give you a sense of meaning in your life?

In all the creative work I have done, what has come first is a problem, a puzzle involving discomfort. Then comes a concentrated voluntary application involving great effort. After this, a period without conscious thought, and finally a solution.

Bertrand Russell

Loving Relationships: With whom do you have mutually supportive, satisfying relationships?

Time and Stress: Do you have enough time to do what you want without being stressed out? What is your issue related to time and stress?

The best way out is always through.

Robert Frost

Balance: How content are you with the personal and professional sides of your life? Would would you change?

Prosperity: What makes you feel valuable? Why do you deserve prosperity?

Perhaps you're already seeing the five challenges in your life in a more heroic way than before. In the past, the battle to find one's purpose had to do with getting a job that paid well and had the approval of family, friends, and society. Now, people are looking for something different: work that is personally meaningful to *them*, no matter what others might say. As psychologist Jean Houston says in her seminars, the question is not, What is my work? (or job title). The question is, What is my Work? with capital W indicating a higher purpose in life.

Finding a satisfying relationship also used to be seen in terms of finding someone who meets the approval of family, friends, and society. But, as a hero, your challenge is to recognize that love emanates from you, not just from other people. As meditation master Gurumayi Chidvilasananda has said, "There is enough love in the individual human heart to fill the universe." Finding and thriving in a relationship starts with seeing this love in yourself. Then you can experience that connection with others as a way to live a creative life.

What use are cartridges in battle? I always carry chocolate instead.

George Bernard Shaw

The battle with time and stress used to be dealt with by learning time-management techniques. But now, even some of the most prominent proponents of those approaches acknowledge that they don't work in the long run. The new challenge is to live in the present moment in all you do. Instead of adding techniques, the battle is about stripping away worry, criticism, and the nattering of your mind so that the essence of your hero can come through.

In the past, people thought that achieving personal and professional balance meant allotting roughly equal amounts of time to the various parts of their lives. Now you recognize that certain aspects of your life will sometimes have more energy than others. Your battle is to find the dynamic synergy between competing parts of your life.

People used to think that prosperity was achieved by acquiring money and other external rewards such as power, status, or objects. Now you see that these outer goals can conflict with a rich, inner feeling of self-worth. This battle is to know that you deserve to experience this inner sense of prosperity in every moment of your life.

SELF-ASSESSMENT: WHAT CHALLENGES AM I DEALING WITH NOW?

The following two-part self-assessment will help you to become more deeply aware both of the challenges and of the calmer areas of your life. It will allow you to take stock of your life as you start the creative journey in this book. Once you have a clearer sense of where you are now, it will be easier to chart a path for where you want to go. You might also like to use this self-assessment as a before-and-after test for yourself. Do it now and then do it again when you have completed the book to get a stronger sense of the distance you've traveled.

Part One of the self-assessment uses a fairly typical quantitative approach. You circle the symbol that most accurately reflects your response to each of thirty statements, then score your responses to assess the relative importance of the five challenges in your life now. Part Two asks you to use a diagram representing the path of your creative journey and map where you are regarding the five challenges.

SELF-ASSESSMENT: PART 1

Circle the symbol that most closely represents your reaction to each statement below.

Code: –– Strongly disagree   + Agree

          – Disagree   + + Strongly agree

          * No opinion or Can't say

1. At the end of every workday I am exhausted.   ––   –   *   +   + +

2. For me, time seems to expand to make room for everything I have to do.   ––   –   *   +   + +

3. Given my training and experience, I should be much more successful.   ––   –   *   +   + +

4. I am bored with my life most of the time.   ––   –   *   +   + +

5. I really don't know what my true purpose is in life.   ––   –   *   +   + +

6. I don't mind doing the tedious tasks that go along with my real work.   ––   –   *   +   + +

7. I feel lonely a great deal of the time.   ––   –   *   +   + +

8. I feel wealthy in the quality of my life, no matter how much I earn.   ––   –   *   +   + +

9. I have at least one intimate friend with whom I can talk about anything.   ––   –   *   +   + +

10. I love my work and am doing exactly what I want to be doing.   ––   –   *   +   + +

11. I truly deserve to prosper in all areas of my life.   ––   –   *   +   + +

12. I wish I weren't such a workaholic.   ––   –   *   +   + +

13. I worry too much.   ––   –   *   +   + +

14. I would like to improve my communication with at least one person at work.   ––   –   *   +   + +

15. I often find myself choosing personal satisfaction at the expense of my work.   ––   –   *   +   + +

It is quite a three-pipe problem.

     Sir Arthur Conan Doyle

16. If I were to die tomorrow, at least I would have made a difference in the world.

      — —   –   * ⓛ + +

17. It is easy for me to take time for myself.

      — —   –   * Ⓐ + +

18. It is impossible to have it all, both a rewarding personal and professional life.

      — — Ⓢ* +   + +

19. It is narcissistic for people to spend their time doing what fulfills them.

     Ⓢ –   *   +   + +

It does not do to leave a live dragon out of your calculations, if you live near him.

J. R. R. Tolkien

20. Just being around certain people puts me in a bad mood.

      — — Ⓢ* +   + +

21. Mostly I feel lucky to have so much love in my life.

      — —   –   *   + Ⓐ

22. My personal life is great and I love my work.

      — —   –   * + Ⓐⓐ

23. My stress-management skills are excellent.

      — —   –   * Ⓐ + +

24. Overall, I am a pretty wonderful person.

      — —   –   * + Ⓐⓐ

25. People are generally easy to get along with.

      — —   –   * Ⓐ + +

26. Relaxation is a high priority for me.

      — —   –   * Ⓐ + +

27. Self-judgment is an issue for me.

      — —   –   * Ⓐ + +

28. To be successful in life, you first have to meet the expectations of others.

      — — Ⓢ * +   + +

29. When my life gets out of balance I make changes to correct it.

      — —   –   * Ⓐ + +

30. You cannot just live in the now; you always have to think of your future and your past.

      — Ⓢ   * +   + +

Scoring

The importance of each challenge is indicated by your responses to six of the thirty statements. You will have a score between 6 and 30 for each challenge. The higher the score, the more pressing the challenge. Find your scores by following these instructions.

      There are three boxes to fill out for scoring each challenge: two subtotal boxes and one total box. Each number on the left side of a subtotal box corresponds to a statement. Write down your score for each statement next to the number. Note that each column of subtotal boxes has a different scoring system. Then add your scores for each challenge and write the total in the total box on the right. Score each statement as follows:

		*	+	++		++	+	*	—	——
1	2	3	4	5		1	2	3	4	5

Life always gets harder towards the summit.

Friedrich Nietzsche

PURPOSE IN LIFE

Statement #	Score
4	2
5	2
19	1
Subtotal	5

+

Statement #	Score
6	2
10	1
16	1
Subtotal	5

=

PURPOSE IN LIFE TOTAL	10

LOVING RELATIONSHIPS

Statement #	Score
7	1
14	2
20	1
Subtotal	5

+

Statement #	Score
9	2
21	1
25	2
Subtotal	5

=

LOVING RELATIONSHIPS TOTAL	10

TIME AND STRESS

Statement #	Score
1	2
13	2
30	2
Subtotal	6

+

Statement #	Score
2	2
23	2
26	2
Subtotal	6

=

TIME AND STRESS TOTAL	12

PERSONAL AND PROFESSIONAL BALANCE

Statement #	Score
12	2
15	2
18	2
Subtotal	6

+

Statement #	Score
17	2
22	1
29	2
Subtotal	5

=

PERSONAL AND PROFESSIONAL BALANCE TOTAL	11

PROSPERITY

Statement #	Score
3	2
27	4
28	2
Subtotal	8

+

Statement #	Score
8	1
11	1
24	1
Subtotal	3

=

PROSPERITY TOTAL	11

Now look at your scores. In general, total scores over 24 suggest areas in your life in which you would like to see some changes. You might like to start your creative journey in this book with the chapter that addresses the challenge with your highest total. Total scores under 12 for any challenges indicate that you are fairly comfortable with these areas of your life right now. You might like to use the chapters that deal with these challenges as a refresher course, or an opportunity to deal with the one or two aspects of a challenge that you're concerned about.

Of course, a quiz like this only gives you a rough picture of the relative importance of each challenge. By contrasting the five challenges, it provides a starting point for the journey of self-exploration mapped out in these pages. Now, move on to part 2 of the self-assessment, which uses a more intuitive way of mapping where you are with the five challenges.

You must do the thing you think you cannot do.

Eleanor Roosevelt

SELF-ASSESSMENT: PART 2

Earlier, we talked of the idea that life is a journey, or even a series of journeys. The challenges you encounter make your life fulfilling by testing you. Can you rise to meet them? What previously hidden creative resources might you call on to meet them?

It is life's challenges that give it the feeling of ups and downs. You go along on the level quite happily until something happens to trip you up. You may stumble slightly, or you may fall heavily—that's the downside. Somehow you figure out how to meet the challenge with a flash of insight or perhaps a slow dawning of recognition—that's the up-side. You're back on the level again, but this time, because you have met your challenge, you are somehow richer or wiser, and the level is new or, metaphorically speaking, higher. Thus, a map of your journey looks something like this.

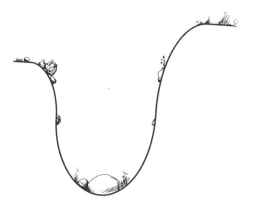

PURPOSE IN LIFE

In the margin is a series of maps that illustrate the basic paths toward resolving each of the five challenges. At a given point in time, you might be anywhere on each path—just starting to think about the issue, temporarily blocked, or in the middle of resolving it. Or perhaps it isn't an issue of all at that moment, and you're at a new level place, having worked things out pretty well. You likely feel differently about each of the challenges, leaping ahead on one, or at a standstill on another, or even turned upside down on a third. The stick figures below illustrate some ways you might depict your feelings about your challenges.

Now, take a few moments to shift gears from the analysis you just did in the first part of the self-assessment. Adopt a quiet state of mind in which you are not analyzing but are allowing yourself to sense what each of the challenges means to you right now. To do this, you might read over the following instructions first and then carry them out. Or, if you're using this book with someone else, you might have that person read the instructions slowly to you.

LOVING RELATIONSHIPS

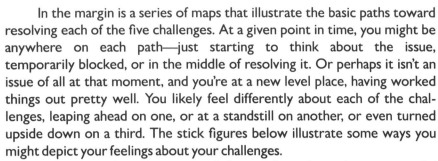

Make sure you're sitting comfortably, with your spine straight and supported. Uncross your arms and legs. You may want to close your eyes, or just look down towards the floor, not focusing on anything. Sit quietly like that for a few moments, noticing your breathing. Don't try to breathe differently: just pay attention to it so that your mind is not filled with thoughts. Let it be filled with attention to your breath, just quietly coming into you and then flowing out. In and out.

If you start thinking about the challenges, or discomfort in your body, or other thoughts, just let the thoughts drift by. Return your attention to your natural breathing. In and out.

After a few moments, look at the purpose map in the margin. It is a map for dealing with the challenge of having meaning in life. Where are you on this journey today?

Notice what images or sensations you have in your body right now. Notice how you feel when you ask yourself that question. Draw a little stick figure on the

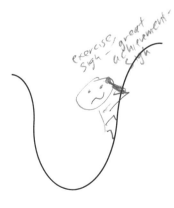

TIME AND STRESS

path, using its position on the curve and its body posture to represent where you are now on this quest. Do this without thinking or analyzing. Let your intuition rather than your mind decide how and where to draw the figure.

Now close your eyes for a few moments. Notice your breathing again. Clear all the thoughts out of your mind, and just be aware of your natural breathing. After about five breaths, open your eyes, look at the next map. Again, sense your images and feelings, and let your intuition tell you where to draw a little stick figure on that map. Do this for all five maps.

When you've finished, look at the five little figures you drew. See if they are positioned so as to represent where you feel you truly are on each of these journeys. If any need to be redrawn now that you see them all, draw them again.

The two self-assessments you have just completed are very different ways of exploring your journey. In part one, you were asked some questions, and we told you what your scores meant. In part two, you drew pictures and you had the final say regarding where you are with the five challenges.

Both activities are useful for clarifying the challenges you are now confronting and where you are right now in dealing with them. The first activity is more traditional. In it, you were asked to think, write, and then calculate scores. The second asked you to slow down and relax so you could focus your attention on what your deeper feelings might be telling you. It asked you to use your intuition. It also asked you to closely observe your feelings without judging them, to ask questions, and to have faith that you could produce an assessment in this manner.

Together, these activities allowed you to use several of your capacities for confronting challenges. The exercises throughout this book invite you to take a variety of approaches and use your full range of capacities for dealing with the five challenges of everyday life.

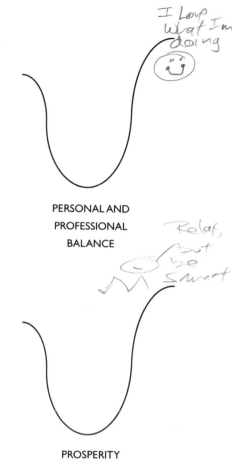

PERSONAL AND
PROFESSIONAL
BALANCE

PROSPERITY

The Everyday Hero
and the Creative Process

WHAT IS YOUR CREATIVE PROCESS?

Our aspirations are our possibilities.

Robert Browning

In chapter 2 you had an opportunity to evaluate where you are on your quest to meet the five major challenges of life. Before you actually set out on your path towards turning your aspirations into reality, reflect on how you've resolved challenges in the past. What is the nature of your own particular creativity?

Recall a creative experience you have had. It may be as recent as this morning, or it may have happened years ago. Think of a situation in which you were challenged and had to call on your inner resources to resolve it. The situation needn't be earth-shaking. For instance, you may have figured out a faster or more pleasant route to work, successfully dealt with a difficult customer, or found a way to enjoy a boring task. In fact, realizing that you can indeed be creative, even if you didn't end world hunger or paint the *Mona Lisa*, is an important step towards living from your true self. When you acknowledge this, it's easier to be creative at any time.

A student in one of our classes recently said he couldn't think of anything creative he had ever done. He told us he was extremely linear and rational. Then, after other people had described their creative experiences, he said, "Oh, I guess I thought that you meant *creative* like a great artist. I never thought of these everyday sorts of things as creative." It is exactly this kind of everyday creativity we are looking for here.

Let's look at your particular brand of creativity. Unless you have lived an extremely unusual life, you have probably confronted at least one situation where you weren't sure you could reach the goal to which you aspired. But, most likely, you eventually resolved the situation. Maybe it was a challenge of building a more efficient widget. Perhaps it was figuring out a plan to save money each month, or knowing what to say to that special person for whom you had more feeling than you dared show.

Take a few minutes now to recall some of your creative experiences. They can be deeply significant ones, or ones that are comparatively slight; it doesn't matter. Simply let them float through your mind. Sit back, relax, and imagine that you are watching a film documentary about all the creative experiences you've had. Let your memories free-associate, so that you can review several different types of creative experiences and remember many creative possibilities.

Notice an experience which seems to stay in your mind more than the others. Relive that experience in your mind's eye, remembering what led up to it, what happened, how you felt before and after you resolved it, and what you did. Now answer the following questions about your creative experience.

The action of the child inventing a new game with his playmates; Einstein formulating a theory of relativity; the housewife devising a new sauce for the meat; a young author writing his first novel; all of these are, in terms of our definition, creative, and there is no attempt to set them in some order of more or less creative.

Carl Rogers

What was the situation that challenged you?

How to present the content of the Unitio Workshop virtually – and to get it done on time.

How did you feel when you were first aware of this challenge? What was your first reaction?

Nonplussed – a feeling vacant, empty of ideas, unclear

What did you do first to try to meet the challenge?

Put it aside + not worry about – kept the deadline in mind – figured I'd clarify what was wanted as the deadline became ~~clearer~~ near

How did your idea for finally resolving the challenge come to you?

I thought about each slide + the flow in bed just after I woke up.

*When I am, as it were,
completely myself, entirely
alone, and of good cheer; it is
on such occasions that my
ideas flow best and most
abundantly.*

Wolfgang Amadeus Mozart

How did you feel when you got this idea?

Encouraged, excited, ready to dive in

What did you do? Was your idea implemented? How was your challenge finally resolved?

Set aside time and just started creating it.
Took advantage of smart chart features
+ Google images. Had Gretchen critique
final product which led to further improvements

What do you notice here? Did you have an initial feeling that you couldn't deal with the situation? When possibilities began to emerge did you feel excitement or relief? Were you surprised at the ease with which the solution or idea came to you? Did it seem to pop out of nowhere, or can you see specific steps that led up to your insight? Was there a pattern in your creative process?

While the specifics of your creative experience are yours and yours alone, there is a basic series of phases that most people go through in the creative process, whether they are painting a picture, drawing up a business plan, or solving a personal problem: 1) preparation; 2) frustration; 3) incubation, 4) strategizing; 5) illumination; and 6) verification.

Preparation

Success

Start

In the initial stage of the creative process you have an idea of where you are going or what you want. You gather the information to do what has to be done to get there. Things seem pretty clear, and you have the sense that you can accomplish your goal. You start, and are optimistic that you can reach success via a slightly uphill path, as the figure in the margin illustrates. This initial vision of creative possibility fuels you with confidence for your task.

In the creative experience that you reflected on in the previous exercise, did you feel this initial confidence of the preparation stage? To what extent?

Exactly. It's common for me. I wasn't
worried, but it was a familiar "Don't
have a clue" sensibility

Frustration

There is a catch in the creative process. Things don't always happen as planned. An unanticipated challenge almost invariably trips you up, and you feel as if you've either temporarily lost sight of your goal or even fallen into a bottomless pit. Sometimes the situation may seem hopeless.

Ultimately we know deeply that the other side of every fear is a freedom.

Marilyn Ferguson

However, this very challenge is a catalyst for your true creativity, because it forces you to find an alternative approach and discover your talents and strengths, which wait in reserve for emergency use. This is an important point about frustration; it is a *necessary* component of the creative process. Do not make the mistake of giving up on your aspiration if you encounter this impasse.

Was there a period of frustration in the creative experience you wrote about? If so, what was it like? Recall other creative experiences. What frustrations were associated with them?

I was going to address.
Not knowing the topic, trying to sort out what to provide students, worrying about time to get it done.

Incubation

The search for a new approach to your goal may take many forms. Sometimes you might give up on the challenge temporarily. You do something else, but the issue is still percolating in the back of your mind, even though you are not consciously doing anything about it. This is the process of incubation, which so many people describe as typifying creative insight.

But this idea of passive and mysterious incubation is not the whole story. If you truly have no control over the incubation, and just have to sit and wait for the Muses to visit you, that suggests that there's nothing you could do to encourage or develop your creativity. But what if the Muses never come? How long are you going to wait?

When you think about your own creative experience, did you simply sit and wait for inspiration, or was there anything you did that helped your solution come into focus?

Set aside time to deliberately think about it.

Strategizing

In an attempt to explore the mysteries of incubation, we asked sixty people facing challenges in their work to keep journals for a few weeks while each tried to resolve their particular challenge. At the end of this time period, each person was interviewed in depth, and their journals were analyzed.

We found that everyone developed a number of strategies for dealing with their challenge. There were intellectual strategies, such as listing pros and cons, making detailed plans, or mulling over the issues. There were emotional strategies, like asking for moral support, reflecting on one's own feelings in the situation, or using play or diversion to feel better. There were physical strategies, like exercising and relaxing. There were spiritual strategies such as meditating, visualizing, using dreams, or talking to an inner guide. Lastly, there were strategies that didn't fit neatly into one of those basic categories; for example, formal brainstorming for ideas, having insights in the shower, changing one's environment, or keeping a journal. And, even when people thought that their great idea had come unexpectedly, emerging out of incubation, its development could actually be traced in their journals.

The point is that those who met their challenges most creatively and effectively used a range of strategies to invite their creative breakthrough. They rose to the task like heroes; they didn't just sit passively and wait for inspiration to find them. In fact, sometimes they looped several times between strategizing and incubation in their particular creative process.

What did you do to bring about your solution to the challenge in your creative experience?

Set aside time to think about and not worry about it till then. Sent myself materials that would be helpful.

Illumination

The culmination of the incubation and strategizing is breakthrough—the illumination of an "Aha!" experience. Sometimes this is accompanied by a sense of excitement or amazement that you have found a way to meet your challenge. At other times it comes quietly, with a sense of, "This is *so* obvious!"

The truly creative individual stands ready to abandon the old classifications and to acknowledge that life, particularly his own unique life, is rich with new possibilities.

Frank Barron

Many of the serious criticisms of our culture and its trends may be best formulated in terms of a death of creativity.

Carl Rogers

What sort of feelings accompanied your illumination?

Satisfaction. Excitement. Energy, confidence,

Eureka! I have found it!

Archimedes

Verification

The last phase of the creative process is very important. This is when you test out your idea and make it real. You see how others react to it. In a sense, this is the part of the creative process that brings you back to level ground. Once again, things can go smoothly (until your next challenge), but this time you have a sense of newfound wisdom.

What was involved in the verification phase of your creative experience?

Had Gretchen critique it.

MAPPING THE PHASES OF THE CREATIVE PROCESS

When you see your creative process in these phases, you realize that the initial idea of a straight-line approach to meeting your challenge might be somewhat unrealistic. In fact, a map of the path that creativity takes most often looks more like the map of the path for dealing with challenges that you saw in the self-assessment in the last chapter. It looks something like the path in the margin.

You start out on solid ground, and then are tripped up by unexpected events that throw you temporarily into the bottomless pit.

In this in between space all sorts of things can happen. This is the secret darkness in which creative ideas germinate and then suddenly flower. Sometimes they emerge as a function of time, after a period of incubation. Or you may fertilize them along the way with your creative strategies.

THE FOUR TOOLS OF THE CREATIVE HERO

In addition to strategies that involve you intellectually, emotionally, physically, and spiritually, you may have used four tools to meet your challenge in the creative experience you recalled in the earlier exercise. The creative process virtually requires you to use them. They are: 1) having faith in your creativity; 2) suspending negative

27

judgment; 3) practicing precise observation; and 4) asking penetrating questions.

These tools were mentioned in chapter 2. We call them the *magic tools* of the hero. Just as the heroes of myth drew on powerful magic to assist them at crucial moments in their struggles, these tools can serve as *your* magic. You can use their power to help you break through creative blocks and resolve challenges of any sort. If you need creative illumination, simply remember to use these four tools and see how they uncover many possible solutions.

Having faith in your creativity can help you root out that annoying inner voice of criticism that is so pervasive: the voice of judgment. Once you suspend negative judgment you naturally become observant and ask questions. This leads to greater faith in your creativity and, therefore, an increased ability to use and reap the benefits of the other tools.

When you find yourself in the seemingly bottomless pit, you need to have faith in your creativity in order not to give up. Your faith has to be as strong as your faith that the sun rises and sets every day or that gravity will pull you down to earth after you jump. As Saint Paul said in his letter to the Hebrews, "[faith is] the evidence of things unseen, and the substance of things hoped for." This is the level of faith you need in your creativity. You need to know that you are creative and you will find your way to resolution. Knowing that the process naturally takes you through that unsettling experience of believing you're stuck can restore your faith in yourself. You are actually right on track. This is when you can recall Robert Browning's affirmation that "our aspirations are our possibilities."

Following the creative path requires you to *give up your judgments* and expectations that there is one right way to resolve the issue. By doing this, you open yourself up to all the other possibilities that you might find—to all manner of unexpected insights during the incubation. If you had believed the voice of judgment inside about what you couldn't, wouldn't, or shouldn't do, you'd probably never have had any creative experience at all.

In order to make sure you get back out of the pit and up to the new level on its other side, you need to *practice precise observation* to find out where you are. You need to notice what's happening and what the situation demands of you right now. You also need to explore yourself for clues about how to proceed. Do you feel tense? Excited? Afraid? Confident? What is your intuition saying?

No great thing is created suddenly.

Epictetus

And, of course, you need to *ask penetrating questions* all along to really get at what's going on. What do you know about the challenging situation? What else do you need to know? What do you not yet see? How do other people feel? Why are things the way they are? What are the beliefs and ideas of the key players? What would happen if you were to try something different?

Remember to use these four magic tools. Keep them with you on your journey and use them whenever you need to be creative in your approach to a challenge. Remember the map we drew of the creative process. By definition, you can't be creative if everything always goes smoothly; you'd just follow your formula for success. The creative process challenges you to use your hidden resources and to transform your challenges into rewarding adventures.

You are right if you are beginning to see that this creative process of preparation, frustration, incubation, strategizing, illumination, and verification is going on in your life all the time. In many small and large ways you step from the plain of preparation into the deep valley of frustration only to emerge at a new level of illumination and verification. This is the path of the everyday hero. You meet each creative challenge by using the four magic tools. And the more attention you pay to this process the more natural it becomes.

Faith is the choice of the nobler alternative.

Dean Inge

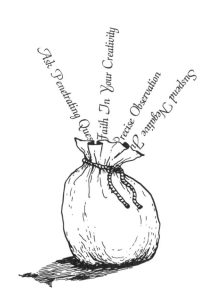

4

The Hero's Journey in Myth and Everyday Life

In any creative experience, you are like a hero on a path to adventure. Whether your path leads to developing more satisfying relationships or overcoming a sense of meaninglessness at work, there are some fairly predictable components of your journey to success. In this chapter we will look at these components.

HOW THE HERO'S JOURNEY PARALLELS YOUR LIFE

The hero's journey is a key theme in myths, fairy tales, and stories throughout time and throughout the world. The hero often doesn't seem particularly heroic at first. In the course of meeting a challenge that disrupts an initial state of innocence, the hero is initiated into a realm where grave danger lurks. With the assistance of allies, the hero breaks out of that world to successfully meet the challenge and return home with a gift of a treasure or wisdom. The hero's return is celebrated, and life is resumed—somehow transformed by the hero's journey.

In culture after culture, the same story emerges, with local variation, as a metaphor for some aspect of human development. The great storyteller Idries Shah notes that there are over three hundred and fifty variations of the story of Cinderella alone! What is it that keeps these tales alive for us?

As children, we love stories in which the protagonist overcomes some threatening force through courage, quick wits, luck, skill, or the help of others. Our childhood identification with the hero gives us a sense of our own autonomy, nobility, or creativity. In *The Uses of Enchantment*, Bruno Bettelheim states that we respond to fairy tales as children because they are metaphorical expressions of the challenges we are facing at that time. By consciously or unconsciously emulating the hero, we develop our latent capacities for creatively resolving these challenges.

As adults, these stories likewise stay with us—and endure in our culture for centuries—because there is more to them than the surface story line. They touch us and resonate on deep levels of our psyche. They impart profound truths that we can intuitively feel. In fact, at different times we might appreciate a story for its plot, its specific cultural context, its illustration of a universal psychological truth, or its very personal symbolic meaning for us at a particular moment. "Myths offer the multiplicity of meaning inherent in our lives," says Jungian psychologist James Hillman. "Myths do not tell us how. They simply give the invisible background which starts us imagining, questioning, going deeper."

Myths and stories are the reflection of the human soul. They remind us of our potential, of the divine possibilities of our existence. We see, in the language of imagery, the possibility of transforming our challenges and pain into gems of wisdom. Jean Houston notes that myths inspire us with the essence of the "great story," of incredible resolution of our challenges, when we are caught up in the details of our little "local story" full of struggle and pathos.

The great story is the archetypal myth of transformation. It is the completion of the hero's journey. In the great story, heroes are confronted with their mortality and, in the process of dealing with this, they discover their innate divinity. The apotheosis of the hero is an awakening; the hero transcends the mythical dragons and is elevated to the realm of the gods. The hero has learned compassion and strength. There is no "failure" in the great story. It is the story of healing and becoming whole. The great story is eternal, and is the blueprint from which folktales and myths are designed.

Our local story is our personal journey of transformation. However, we often find ourselves caught up in all the problems and chaos, and don't make it to the point of transcendence. In fact, we can be-

A hero ventures forth from the world of common day into a region of supernatural wonder: fabulous forces are there encountered and a decisive victory is won: the hero comes back from this mysterious adventure with the power to bestow boons on his fellow man.

Joseph Campbell

No coward soul is mine.

Emily Brontë

come so bogged down in the local story that we get stuck. We become myopic and forget that if we have faith in our path, it will lead us out of the darkness.

In short, the great story shows us the path to our human possibilities. This is why each of the five chapters on specific life challenges (chapters 5 through 9) starts with a story. You can read the story to gain insight about a particular challenge you are facing. In a sense, each story speaks to the hero that is hidden inside you. It calls to your inner wisdom and invites you on an adventure that goes beyond resolution of the challenge in your daily life to a deeper adventure of knowing and being your most creative self. You might say it asks you to recognize the "god" within you, as well as in the world surrounding you.

The hero's journey, then, is one of spiritual transformation. Whether we are talking about resolving the specific challenges in your life, or about the nature of the creative process, you can think of yourself as a kind of heroic alchemist finding a way to bring something rich and valuable out of what appears to be base. As the grandfather of psychology, William James, has said, "Believe that life is worth living and your belief will help create the fact." You may be able to do this simply by waving your metaphorical magic wand and changing your outlook so you see and experience an old situation in a different way. Or it may require a full frontal attack and a search through dangerous foreign lands. You may be conscious of your yearning for this transformation, or you may accidentally fall into it.

Whatever your particular hero's journey might be, mythologist Joseph Campbell describes it thus: "Whether small or great, and no matter what the stage or grade of life, the call rings up the curtain, always, on a mystery of transfiguration—a rite, or moment, or spiritual passage, which, when complete, amounts to a dying and a birth. The familiar life horizon has been outgrown; the old concepts, ideals, and emotional patterns no longer fit; the time for a passing of a threshold is at hand."

The path of the everyday hero takes you across that threshold. The hero's journey involves saying goodbye to your struggles and being receptive to new, often unexpected, insights and outlooks. When you realize that the journey you are on in your local story is mirrored in the metaphor of myth, you can find guidance from that great story.

It is apparent that to reach the breakthrough state we must make a fundamental shift in consciously and unconsciously held beliefs we all hold about our own limitations.

Willis Harman and
Howard Rheingold

*Afoot and light-hearted I take
to the open road,
Healthy, free, the world
before me.*

Walt Whitman

WITH WHICH HERO'S JOURNEY STORY
DO YOU IDENTIFY?

Bring to mind a hero's journey story that appeals to you. Be aware that the hero's journey doesn't have to take the form of an actual myth or folktale. It may be a movie, song, opera, novel, poem, or children's story. It could be based on biblical history, such as David and Goliath, or on life history, such as *The Miracle Worker* or *Sunrise at Compobello.* Also, these stories frequently portray only part of the overall hero's journey. It is by recognizing the limitations of the protagonist that you see, in contrast, what you might do to follow the path of the hero in your everyday life.

Consider the following titles and pick a story that you like. (It's okay if you are not familiar with all of them, or if you'd like to add one to the list.)

He was a verray parfit gentil knight.

Geoffrey Chaucer

By great story, I mean story that enables us to see patterns of connections, as well as symbols and metaphors to help us contain and understand our existence.

Jean Houston

Hansel and Grettel
"The Metamorphosis"
Puff, the Magic
   Dragon
Oedipus Rex
Alice in Wonderland
Eros and Psyche

Jonah and the
   Whale
Red Riding Hood
*The Little Engine
   That Could*
Peter Pan
Snow White

The Little Prince
Demeter and Persephone
Star Wars
The Velveteen Rabbit
Tristan and Isolde
The Odyssey

Other story _____

Now take a few minutes to reflect on the following questions.

Which story stands out for you?

Little engine that Could

What part of the story did you like best or find most fascinating?

Struggle + triumph — Not giving up

With which challenge or character did you most identify?

Little engine

How does this story relate to your life now?

Triumph following struggle

What direct or indirect clues does it give you about living your life as a hero's journey?

Persistence will be rewarded
Stay positive, even in the dark times

Don't give up!

Were you able to answer most of the questions? Notice how aspects of your life can be mirrored in a story and can suggest a wealth of imagery that speaks specifically to you.

SLEEPING BEAUTY: AN EXAMPLE OF THE HERO'S JOURNEY

On the surface, Sleeping Beauty is a very traditional "Prince and Princess" story. "Nice for children, but pretty mindless and horribly sexist," you might think. Don't be misled by appearances! This story exemplifies the great story of the hero's journey. It is the story of the quiet, receptive, traditionally feminine or *yin* way to power, and of the assertive, extraverted, traditionally masculine or *yang* way to the depths. It is a story in which each quality needs the other to complete itself and become whole, just as we need the sacred marriage of our heart and our mind if we are to meet the challenges in our lives. It is a story of the creative process, and of spiritual transformation. It is a metaphor for the path of the everyday hero. As you read the story of Sleeping Beauty, notice what is says to you about your life.

Sleeping Beauty

Once upon a time in a distant land beyond the sun and the clouds, a Princess was born who was more beautiful than the sun. The King and Queen invited all the people and all the fairy-folk to come and bless their new daughter.

But one fairy was not happy for the daughter; she was jealous of her beauty. When everyone else had given their blessing, she tiptoed to the cradle.

"Oh, royal Princess, let me add my wish," she cackled. "On your sixteenth birthday, my pretty rose, may you prick your finger on the spindle of a spinning wheel . . . and die!"

The heroine's journey begins with "separation from the feminine" and ends with "integration of masculine and feminine."

Maureen Murdock

I will act as if what I do makes a difference.

William James

She laughed a wicked laugh, spun around, and in the silence of the stunned crowd she strode out of the hall.

The King and Queen were beside themselves with grief. Suddenly there was a rustling noise, and a small, pretty fairy floated into the middle of the room. She was out of breath.

"Forgive me for being so late," she gasped. "I was weaving spells to make the flowers grow, and didn't mean to miss the Princess's blessings." She looked around. "But why such sadness on such a happy day?"

They told her about the wicked fairy's curse.

"Well, I can't undo the spell, but I can change it. The Princess won't die when she pricks her finger; she will only fall asleep—but she will sleep for one hundred years."

The King and Queen stopped weeping. "We can surely wake her up if she's only asleep," said the Queen. Nevertheless, all needles and spindles were banished from the kingdom, and it was announced that the Princess was never to leave the palace grounds until after she was sixteen years of age.

The Princess grew into a happy, beautiful, and intelligent girl, who was very much loved. By and by it was her sixteenth birthday, and a great celebration was planned. This was her passage into womanhood, and her time to leave the palace grounds and explore the rest of the kingdom.

While the festivities were being prepared, the Princess wandered around the palace. Suddenly, she came upon a doorway she had never noticed before. "How strange," she thought. "I've lived here for sixteen years and haven't seen this door. I wonder what's behind it."

She pushed it open, and there inside was a old woman bent over a wheel, spinning fleece into yarn. Of course, the Princess did not know what the old woman was doing, because she had never seen a spinning wheel before.

"Would you like to try this, my dear?" asked the old woman, handing the Princess the spindle.

The Princess reached out for it, and suddenly the old woman (who was really the wicked fairy) thrust it into her hand so that it pricked the Princess's white skin.

"Oh!" cried the Princess. "What has happened?" And, growing suddenly afraid of the old woman, she ran out of the room.

But just as she emerged into the hallway, she was overcome with fatigue, and fell to the ground in a deep, deep sleep.

The King and Queen and all the palace servants were unable to revive her, so they put her in a bed in a room at the far end of the palace. And then, miraculously, the King and Queen, the servants, and all the people in the kingdom fell into a deep sleep immediately, not to wake unless the Princess did. The country fell into a state of decay. Roses grew up all over the palace walls. Nothing stirred within the palace. The roses grew and grew.

A hundred years later, in another land, far away beyond the moon and the stars, a young Prince reached his sixteenth birthday.

"It's time for you to go forth and become a man," said his father, the King. And so the Prince saddled up his best steed, and set out to seek adventure.

For many weeks the Prince traveled through the rugged countryside. He encountered demons and dragons, vanquishing all of them and saving many lives. One day there was rustling noise, and a small, pretty fairy floated in front of him. She was out of breath.

"Forgive me for being so late," she gasped. "I was weaving spells to make the flowers grow, and didn't mean to miss your adventures. You have been doing manly things, and have saved hundreds of villagers from demons and dragons. But you have been called by another to complete one more task."

"What is that?" asked the Prince.

"Far away in a land beyond the sun and the clouds there is a palace, hidden by roses grown so thick that no one has ever made it through them. You must find a way through the thorn bushes and enter the palace. A great treasure awaits you there. Your sword is not the weapon you will need. This will serve you better." She handed him a small wooden whistle and disappeared.

The Prince was rather startled; even more so to discover that his sword had disappeared, also. However, he started on his way to search for the palace covered with roses. He rode for one hundred days and nights, through unfamiliar lands, keeping his spirits up by playing tunes on the whistle.

Finally he found the roses: an immense mountain of thorns and flowers. He tried to break off some branches, but they pricked his hands terribly, and wherever he broke off a branch, seven more immediately grew in its place.

"How will I ever get through them without my sword?" he wondered. And he sat down and stared at them in despair.

To cheer himself up, he pulled out his whistle, and started to play a lilting air rich with harmonies that were indescribably beautiful. There was a rustling, and then, magically, the rose bushes started bending back. He jumped up and walked to the opening in the roses and, as he did so, more branches bent back. He took another step, and still more bent back. He kept walking down the path they were forming for him, never taking his lips away from the flute, never breaking the melody that trilled out of the wooden pipe.

The path led to a great wooden door, which opened as he approached. Once inside the silent dusty palace, more doors opened and the Prince whistled his way through them. The last door creaked open and the Prince stepped through—and gasped.

There, asleep under a delicate mantle of cobwebs, was the most beautiful young woman he had ever seen! How could she be here in this ancient dusty palace?

So taken was he with her beauty that the Prince felt as if he were melting. He bent down and kissed her. "My Sleeping Beauty," he murmured. "Oh that you could come with me and be my bride."

And then an amazing thing happened. The Princess's eyes fluttered open and she blinked, as if she were awakening from a dream. "Oh my Prince," she sighed. "I dreamed for one hundred years that you would come." And she returned his kiss, ever so sweetly and passionately.

They took hands, and the Prince whistled them back down the path and to his horse. They rode together to his country, where they were married the next day. At the end of the ceremony came a rustling noise, and the small, pretty fairy floated into the middle of the great hall. She was out of breath.

"Forgive me for being so late," she gasped. "I was weaving spells to make the flowers grow, and didn't mean to miss the wedding. Princess, by kissing the Prince you have broken the spell that has been over your land for one hundred years. It has woken up and is alive and happy. You will be Queen of your land beyond the clouds and the sun."

In time, the Princess and the Prince became Queen and King, and their countries were joined together. They ruled long and well and happily together.

SLEEPING BEAUTY AS AN ARCHETYPAL HERO'S JOURNEY

Like the creative process, the hero's journey consists of six phases. We will describe each phase in general terms, show how it manifests itself in the Sleeping Beauty story, and remind you of the parallel phase of the creative process. As you read the descriptions, think not only of this story, but of yourself and your life. Be conscious of the challenges you are facing and have faced. Notice how you, too, have journeyed through the six phases described below. After each description, take a few minutes to reflect on the questions. This will help you identify the many manifestations of the hero's journey in your own life.

1. Innocence

The archetypal hero starts out in a state of innocence, relatively naive, and happy with the status quo. There's no hint of the challenges to come. All appears well in the Princess's land; the good King and Queen have given birth to a beautiful baby. The Prince has been developing into a healthy youth, just as he should.

This phase parallels the initial *preparation* in the creative process in which any thoughts of accomplishing something are in terms of the easy A to B straight line. There is a sense that all's well with the world.

Think of a state of innocence in your life. When have you felt things were easy, safe, or at least comfortably familiar?

High School
First years at MR

If a person follows the heroic principle of integrity and faith, when caught in a conflict, the potentiality of some unexpected inner help is quite real. An intuition, a dream, a creative solution, an instinctual "gut-level" response or a change in attitude arises to aid the situation.

Jean Shinoda Bolen

2. The Call to Adventure

Paradise can't last. Something disrupts the familiar patterns and challenges the incipient hero to be put to the test. The call to adventure presents a threshold, the crossing of which heralds the beginning of the journey. It may come as a crisis demanding immediate resolution, or it may be the subtle ticking of a hidden clock, signaling the need to mature. The call addresses the secret yearning in all of us to grow, to be all that we can. To not answer the call is to retreat back to innocence and safety. There is no hero's journey when this happens. If the hero answers the call, it may be dangerous, and there will be no turning back. To answer the call is to take on the challenge, to risk leaping into the unknown.

The wicked fairy calls the Sleeping Beauty to adventure with her curse of death at age sixteen. The Prince's call is less dramatic; it is simply time for him to become a man, as his father tells him.

This phase parallels *frustration* in the creative process. It ushers in the realization that things are going to be tougher than they seemed at first glance. There is a sense of do or die.

Whatever you can do or dream you can, begin it. Boldness has genius, power, and magic in it.

Goethe

What circumstances have recently called you to adventure? Did you answer the call? If so, what happened? If not, what do you need in order to take that leap of faith?

leaving PAIAt
Starting @ TBRA

3. Initiation

Once the hero accepts the call, the journey is under way. It starts with an initiation into strange other worlds; a journey of maturation and transformation in which the hero is confronted with the possibility of annihilation or death. It may take many forms. One is that of high drama, in which the hero faces almost certain death, and is truly put to the test to draw on previously unrecognized strengths or wisdom for survival. This is the sort of adventure we see in Western stories of chivalry and knightly adventure. The other is one in which the hero is somehow mindless, or falls asleep, or is taken to the underworld; the maturing continues in the mysterious depths but is invisible on the outside. Jonah in the belly of the whale, Rip Van Winkle, and many tales from Eastern philosophical traditions illustrate this more invisible path to transformation.

The Prince's use of his sword to battle the demons and dragons as he sets out on his typical quest exemplifies the first sort of journey, while his learning the soft power of the flute illustrates the second. The Princess's sleep and dream of the Prince exemplifies the second. Notice that each had not just one adventure, but a series of mini-adventures within the great journey: the Prince had his encounters with the dragons, and there were sixteen years of attempts to prevent Sleeping Beauty's awful fate.

This phase parallels *incubation* in that the hero has entered the realm of the bottomless pit, where secret strengths germinate. It is the experience of not knowing how or if the situation will ever be resolved. There is a sense of giving up, of realization that the situation cannot be dealt with by normal means. It is this surrender (the Prince to the flute, the Princess to the spindle's sleep) that allows for the transformation.

In what ways are you truly on a heroic journey of initiation right now? What are the dangers? What form does your surrender take?

drifting

Asking the bar question about a compelling future not forcing the answer

4. Allies

The hero receives assistance from allies on the journey. Sometimes they appear at the initial threshold and provide protective amulets or advice. Other times, allies appear at the moment of crisis and provide

It is not the critic who counts; not the man who points out how the strong man stumbled, or where the doer of deeds could have done them better. The credit belongs to the man who is actually in the arena.

Theodore Roosevelt

the wisdom for resolution and transformation. It is at the point of surrender that the allies usually appear: when the hero realizes that this journey cannot be completed within the known framework of previous journeys. While the allies may take the form of other characters or objects, they represent the deep well of wisdom that the hero has in reserve and learns to tap into at this time. Many religious people refer to the intervention of allies in their lives as "grace."

Sleeping Beauty's ally appears at the initial threshold as the good fairy who softens the wicked fairy's spell. She appears as an ally for the Prince when he is at the bottom of the pit, directing him to give up the machismo of the typical masculine adventure and to try a gentler approach. She reappears at the wedding to remind Sleeping Beauty of her power and to cement their union.

This phase parallels *strategizing* in the creative process, since the ally provides the hero the means to bring about the essential transformation necessary for the story to be a successful hero's journey. Just as incubation and strategizing nourish each other in the creative process, and both phases may be visited several times, so too do allies and initiation weave together in the hero's journey. The allies bring a sense of trust that there is a way out of the underworld.

Who or what are your allies as you face the challenges in your life right now?

5. Breakthrough

The allies provide the way for successful resolution of the initiation and completion of the task that makes the hero truly heroic. But this breakthrough can only come about as a result of the hero's transformation and new abilities. The point at which the hero recognizes or expresses this deepening understanding signals the crossing of the return threshold, out of the underworld back to the so-called ordinary world.

While Sleeping Beauty appears at first to be the passive recipient of the Prince's kiss—just as she was the passive victim of the wicked fairy's curse—we see that she has conjured up her own destiny by dreaming of the Prince. Thus, the breakthrough kiss is as much her doing as his. The Prince's breakthrough was only possible after he had exchanged his sword for the whistle, and had attacked the roses in a harmonious way rather than a confrontational one.

This parallels *illumination* in the creative process, in which a new level of awareness or way of being is attained; the sense of "Aha! This is it!"

What do you imagine the breakthrough of your current major challenge might be like? What is your ideal resolution?

An opening, a door, not a destination

The important thing is this: To be able at any moment to sacrifice what we are for what we could become.

Charles Du Bois

6. Celebration

The journey ends with the return of the hero, bringing gifts or wisdom back to those who had remained. The hero is acknowledged as wiser, deeper, or even divine. The returning hero is not the same person who left, something often represented by a marriage or change from child to adult or from mortal to god. The successful hero's journey benefits many people, not just the hero.

The Prince and Princess have become King and Queen. Their marriage represents the essential sacred union of the symbolic masculine and feminine. The good fairy pops up again to remind us that the two countries are one; they are not very different or far apart after all.

This parallels the *verification* phase of the creative process, where the new awareness is made tangible in the real world—except that the real world, although it is back on the level again, is at a higher or richer level than before. A new status quo is established, paving the way for the next hero's journey, the next level of transformation.

Imagine the celebration of your heroic completion of your current journey. How will you be different? What will life be like?

Confident, caring creative — like today, only moreso

This, then, is the hero's journey. You can see how the story illuminates the creative process. If you were thinking about your life as you read, you can probably see how the approach you take to your challenges reflects your own hero's journey.

If you mapped out the path of the hero, it would look something like the path in the margin.

If you are more analytical, you may prefer to think of the relationship as the following:

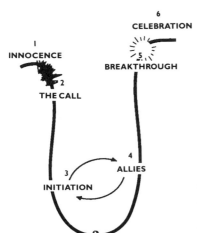

Creative Process	Hero's Journey
Preparation	Innocence
Frustration	Call to Adventure
Incubation	Initiation
Strategizing	Allies
Illumination	Breakthrough
Verification	Celebration

WHAT IS THE PLOT OF YOUR HERO'S JOURNEY?

When you consider the parallels between the creative process and the hero's journey, you can see how living your life as an everyday hero means that you have a daily experience of your creativity. The more challenges you have, the greater the likelihood that you will be able to refine your practical creative skills and develop the wisdom of the hero.

What is the nature of your own hero's journey? What are the challenges that you have met during your lifetime? What is your usual approach to dealing with challenges? People tend to be creatures of habit. We are in the stage of innocence, and are comfortable with the way things are.

For a while that is fine—we need a sense of stability. But inevitably the call to adventure beckons us, and we must choose whether to answer it. The call either comes in the form of a crisis that won't be resolved with our usual methods, or in the form a natural yearning for a more fulfilling and meaningful life.

The power of the everyday hero comes from paying attention to what has already happened in life. Heroes in myths allow themselves to be seized by their fortunes. Each new situation is a surprise to them. Of course, part of this path is being open to what confronts you. But you can gain strength by being aware of exactly where you are on the path and how you got there.

You can make an initial assessment by using the exercise we call "The Movie of Your Life." In a sense, this gives you a chance to make up your own myth or story. With it, you can see where you have been and how you have previously dealt with challenges. The value of such an exercise is that it taps your inner knowledge in a way that just answering questions about your life couldn't.

As with all exercises, remain open. Give it a try and see how it works for you. Review your strengths. Get a sense of who and where you are and where you've been.

Man is a rope stretched between the animal and the Superman—a rope over an abyss.

Friedrich Nietzsche

Getting Ready to Watch the Movie of Your Life

Slowly read through the exercise below, using all your senses to make your memories and feelings as real as you can. As you read, watch the movie scene by scene, allowing a few minutes for each part to unfold before you read the next part. Plan to take about fifteen minutes for this exercise, knowing that movietime is like dreamtime, in which years of experience can take place in a split second. You will have only fifteen minutes of real time, but it will be all the movietime you need to profoundly reexperience and get a sense of your path through your life.

You may find this experience to be more powerful and produce the most insight if you make an audiotape of the movie instructions or have someone read them to you so you don't have to keep interrupting your imaginative process to read the next scene.

Most of us have some happy and some painful events in our lives. The painful events are the challenges that call us to become our own hero. You may have some challenges that are not yet resolved. When you come to these places in the movie, you can either change the movie so that you resolve the challenges, or just observe them, and feel the sadness inside yourself. If you feel the sadness, you are probably ready to embark on a journey to grow past the pain of your local story. If you change the movie, notice how you change it, and use that as a clue for how to deal with current challenges.

Start by making sure you're sitting comfortably. Take a moment to close your eyes and breathe in and out a few times. Breathe naturally. Simply shift your attention from your thoughts to your breathing. Take a minute or two to collect yourself, here and now, feeling relaxed and ready to watch the movie that's about to be shown.

THE MOVIE OF YOUR LIFE

*Imagine you are in a movie theater, sitting in a comfortable plush seat.
You can feel the soft fabric of the seat, and the smooth wood of the
armrest. The smell of popcorn is in the air, and you hear the munching
and rustling of people in the row behind you. You are looking forward
to the film. The lights dim.*

*The music for the film starts playing, and on the screen, in ten-foot
letters, appears the title. It is "Your Name. . . . (The words scroll up
and the rest of the title appears.) . . . This is your life."*

*How interesting to see what the film director has chosen to in-
clude. You sit back in your chair, ready to be entertained by a moving
and profound story.*

*The first scene begins with your birth, but special effects have been
used so you see and experience it from the perspective of the baby. You
experience the contractions and the shift of environment. This is certainly different from anything you've ever felt. You are uncertain about
the strangeness, but curious, too.*

*In the next scene, some people are with you in a home. What do
they look like? Who are they? What are they doing? What room are you
in? One of them picks you up and talks to you. You feel safe and happy.*

*Then there follows a montage of what seem to be preschool scenes.
Various people and places appear on the screen. You are a main character in each of these scenes. You see people and events you'd forgotten
about. Allow yourself a few minutes to reexperience this part of your
life, with all your senses.*

*The next montage is of your childhood and early school years.
You watch in fascination, and are drawn into the action. Relive it fully,
with the experience of that young child who is you.*

*You are in high school now, and scenes from your adolescence
come tumbling back to you. School, weekends, vacations, important
people and events. Experience who you were, and the highs and lows of
this time in your life.*

*The movie rolls on to the prime of adult life. Friends, relatives,
events from work and play, intense joys and painful agonies all come
alive again.*

*The scene changes to you now. Where are you? What are you
doing? Who are you with? How do you feel? What is your work? Who
are you? Who are you, really? The camera lingers here, and the brilliant*

filmmaker has an uncanny way of communicating what is beneath the surface.

The scenes change to later adulthood. An older you is sitting in a chair with family or friends around. Who is there? Where are you? You are reflecting on what you have done with your life. What work did you do? Who did you love? Where have you been? What gives your life meaning? Did you do what you wanted to with your life? What was that? What is the great wisdom you have as a result of the challenges you have met?

Finally, the movie comes to a close. It is a profound film. It touches you deeply. As the music of the last scene fades away you find yourself with new insight and respect for the hero of the movie. The theater lights come on, and you walk out into the street, knowing you have witnessed something of great importance for you.

Commit random gestures of kindness, perform senseless acts of beauty.

Anonymous

This exercise activated your creative imagination and used your senses to review your journey in life and picture where you might go. You might feel almost overwhelmed now. Perhaps you remembered some key points in your journey: challenge and initiations on the path, feelings of falling into a bottomless pit, or celebrations when you transcended and transformed the struggles.

THE CHALLENGES IN YOUR LIFE

Use the chart we've supplied to record the most significant challenges and their outcomes at each stage of your life. Try to record those events that pushed you to call on your creativity. Record the outcomes, both positive and negative. You may remember no significant challenges in a particular stage, or you may remember several. For later adulthood, jot down what you anticipate your major challenges to be.

You may have begun to notice a pattern or trend in the sorts of challenges that are central for you. Review the list of challenges below.

- Pursuing your true purpose
- Bringing loving relationships into your life
- Living stress-free in the here and now
- Achieving personal and professional balance
- Finding your way to prosperity

Which of these five challenges are the most important to you? In the left-hand box for each stage of life jot down which challenges you encountered (or anticipate encountering) at that stage.

Throughout history, the most common debilitating human ailment has been cold feet.

Anonymous

Stage of Life	Challenges	Outcomes
Early Childhood Challenges?		
School Years Challenges?		
Young Adulthood Challenges?		
Now Challenges?		
Later Adulthood Challenges?		

What patterns, if any, do you notice about the way you resolved or didn't resolve those challenges? Do you have typical ways of responding to situations? This exercise may have given you some insights. You probably learned early how to survive in your family. Are there certain kinds of challenges you run from and others you rally to? Did you learn to make commitments and then find yourself trapped in them? Did you find it safe to avoid commitment at all cost? Do you find it hard to make decisions? Are you better in certain types of situations than in others? What sort of people do you shy away from and with whom are you at ease?

In the space provided, or in your journal, write down any habitual ways you handle the challenges that were in your movie. Your task as you work through this book is to call on those elements of your pattern that are your strengths, and to relinquish those that hold you back from truly being an everyday hero.

Remember, you are the hero on this path. Let this book be your ally as you embark on this creative journey to resolve your challenges and allow your inner hero to come out of hiding and shine in your life.

If you think there are no new frontiers, watch a boy ring the front doorbell on his first date.

Olin Miller

PART TWO

THE CHALLENGES

Discovering and Pursuing Your True Purpose

To follow your bliss is to live and work with passion and compassion. When you do this, you increase the meaning, satisfaction, peace, and purpose in your life. The trouble is that you often don't know what that bliss, that higher purpose, is. You might at first enjoy a certain freedom by allowing life to take you where it will, but sooner or later you find yourself asking the question, "Is that all there is?" You begin to experience a lack of meaning in life and yearn for a sense of direction and fulfillment.

This chapter assists you in perhaps the central adventure in life: the search for your ultimate purpose. Everyone has such a foundation of purpose at every point in his or her life—they just don't recognize it. Now you will not only recognize it, but you'll begin to take responsibility for living with it in every part of your life.

Fortunately, every moment and every situation presents an opportunity to experience your highest purpose. You need only open your eyes and your heart. When have you felt the joy of being alive? What are your most important values? How do they manifest themselves in your daily work and interactions with other people? In the last twenty-four hours, what has stirred your soul? If you answered "nothing" to this last question, what *would* stir your soul? Living

If you do follow your bliss, you put yourself on a kind of track that has been there all the while, waiting for you, and the life you ought to be living is the one you are living. When you can see that, you begin to meet people who are in the field of your bliss, and they open the doors to you. I say, follow your bliss and don't be afraid, and doors will open where you didn't know they were going to be.

Joseph Campbell

There is more to life than increasing its speed.

Mahatma Gandhi

with purpose is a matter of living with awareness of who you are and what you want. Of all the challenges you confront, this challenge is most fundamental. As Joseph Campbell says in the quotation on page 51, other challenges seem to have a way of working themselves out more easily when you see clearly on this core issue.

The exciting thing is that resolving this life challenge is not very difficult, even though it can sometimes seem almost impossible. Recall our discussion of the creative process and the hero's journey in earlier chapters. In both of these processes, the path to illumination or breakthrough takes you through the pit of the unknown on the road to your destination. While the creator does not at first feel very creative, nor the hero heroic, the very process of exploration itself naturally brings out one's creative or heroic nature—often in surprising ways.

In mythology, each story of a hero's journey is in some sense a quest for purpose. As such, it can give us inspiration for what we are going through every day. This chapter uses the legend of Perceval and the Holy Grail to take you on a creative journey.

The story of Perceval has been told for over eight hundred years in countless versions, for both children and adults, in poetry and prose, and even in operatic form in Wagner's *Parsifal*. Late twentieth-century psychologists have used the story as a metaphor to explain adult human development, and psychologists probably will continue to do so through the twenty-first century.

The story inspires us because it contains essential truths. As you read it, reflect on your own path through life. What god-given gifts and limitations were part of you at the beginning of life? What parental words of wisdom do you still hear in your head, even though they may be outdated? Who or what is your Red Knight? Who is your Gournemant? Who is your Blancheflor? What is your Grail? In what ways are you like Perceval? What is your vision for your life?

In this chapter, to **prepare** for this part of your journey, you read the story, identify elements of it in your life, and take on a guiding motto to live by. Your **journey** itself consists of exercises that challenge you to clarify your purpose. The chapter ends, as do all good hero's journeys, with the eternal **return**, a chance to recognize that you are your own hero and acknowledge what you have learned from your travels.

PREPARATION

Perceval and the Holy Grail

Perceval was the son of a woman named Heart Sorrow. Her husband and two older sons had met their deaths as brave knights, so she had raised Perceval in a distant place to prevent him from becoming a knight and meeting the same fate. Perceval himself was a total innocent. In the beginning, he lives and reacts only in response to others. One version of his name, *Parsifal,* means "innocent fool," another means "press on through the valley." In fact, he really doesn't learn his name and true identity until much later in the story.

One day, in the spring, Perceval rode out to throw his javelins—something he did very well—when suddenly, out of nowhere, five magnificent knights in full armor rode by on their huge war-horses. The youth was entranced. He thought they must have been gods or, at the very least, angels. He asked question after question about who they were, what they did with their lances, shields, and the like.

After they had left, he hurried home to tell his mother that he was going to join the knights. This was her worst nightmare, but she saw that there was nothing she could do to dissuade him. She agreed to let him go, but gave him three instructions: he must go to church every day, where he would receive adequate food and drink; he must be respectful of all fair maidens; and he should not ask questions. At that Perceval left, and his life's adventure began.

The next day, Perceval came to a glorious tent set in a meadow and topped by a gilt eagle. Having never actually seen a church, he assumed that this is what the beautiful structure was. Attempting to follow his mother's orders, he dismounted and entered. Indeed, food was set out, so Perceval took his fill of wine and venison.

A beautiful maiden was alone in the tent, asleep on a brocade bed. Her handmaidens had left to gather flowers in preparation for the arrival of her lover, a knight. The maiden awoke, and Perceval forced himself upon her, kissing her seven times and taking away her ring, believing that this would seal his lifelong relationship to the maiden in the chivalric ways of knighthood. She protested that her lover would soon return and would surely kill him for what he had done. But Perceval left before the return of the knight, who was indeed in a fury when he found out what had happened.

Perceval sought King Arthur because he had heard that the king could make one a knight. On the way, he passed a magnificent knight, attired completely in scarlet. This Red Knight had been terrorizing King Arthur and his

court, and none could better him. The Red Knight had threatened Arthur with the loss of his kingdom if no one could defeat him, and boldly took the king's golden goblet—still filled with wine—to seal the insult. No one was brave enough to take him on.

Knowing nothing of this, Perceval, the innocent fool, told the knight that he intended to take all of his armor, weapons, trappings, and horse. The Red Knight wryly replied that that sounded like a good idea and that Perceval should hurry back from being knighted to have a try.

Nearly everyone in Arthur's court scoffed when the youth announced that he wished to be knighted, even though the king himself was willing to knight Perceval. But then a maiden, who hadn't smiled for six years, approached Perceval and smiled beautifully. She told him that he would be the best and bravest of knights. This fulfilled a court fool's prophesy that only when she had seen he who would be the flower of chivalry would she smile again. Sir Kay, one of Arthur's knights most offended by Perceval, rushed over to the woman and knocked her down, asking her how she dared call such a bumpkin the best and bravest of knights. Perceval waited no longer. He left the court to challenge the Red Knight.

The Red Knight greeted him with incredulity. "Lad, can it be true/ King Arthur hasn't any knights/ who dare to come uphold his rights?/ If no one's coming, do be frank." Perceval responded defiantly, and sent his javelin through the knight's head. The knight fell to the ground, dead. One of Arthur's squires who had followed Perceval to the encounter helped him put on the Red Knight's armour over his rough country clothing. Perceval then mounted the Red Knight's horse and told the squire to take his old horse to the king, return Arthur's goblet, and issue a warning to Sir Kay that his treatment of the maiden would be avenged.

Perceval rode off, intending to go back home to his mother, but he came upon the castle of a nobleman, Gournemant of Gohort, who persuaded him to stay and trained him in the skills of knighthood. Perceval was so eager for the knowledge that he confided to Gournemant, "I've never laid eyes on or seen/ a thing that I have felt so keen/ a wish to learn. I wish I knew/ as much about the arms as you." So keen was he to learn, that he practiced until he was exhausted.

Gournemant taught Perceval everything he knew, and gave him a new set of armor, convincing him to finally relinquish the homespun outfit from his mother. By putting a spur on Perceval's right foot himself, Gournemant in fact granted him knighthood. The seasoned knight ordered the young man to stop referring to all of his actions as something his mother told him to do. But he did echo Perceval's mother by counseling him to always give help to maidens in distress. And while he didn't tell Perceval not to ask questions, he did tell him to speak less. This last instruction Perceval would follow blindly, almost to his detriment.

Perceval left Gournemant, still determined to return home, but then came upon another castle, this time the castle of the maiden Blancheflor. As he sat with this woman, who was to become the love of his life, he was so quiet—remembering Gournemant's warning to not talk too much—that the courtesans began to whisper that he was dumb.

All the lands around the castle were barren. Of the original three hundred ten knights who guarded it, only fifty remained. That night Blancheflor came to Perceval's bedroom to explain why and to tell him of the plight of her kingdom. He agreed to avenge her against the knight who caused this problem. They slept together, very romantically, that night, but Perceval, true to his mother's admonition, remained completely chaste.

Perceval defeated the knight who had been terrorizing Blancheflor's kingdom, and, as he was to do many times in his adventures, sent the vanquished knight to King Arthur. Blancheflor's kingdom was restored to its former glory, and all the kingdom, especially Blancheflor, wanted Perceval to rule it with her as his own. But he left once again, to return to his mother.

His next encounter was with a strange fisherman and his servant who were fishing from a boat in a river. This fisherman sent Perceval to his castle, which seemed to rise out of the valley as the knight approached it. Meeting the fisherman and going to his castle were probably the most critical events of Perceval's life. The fisherman was really a king and his castle held the Holy Grail, the chalice used in the Last Supper.

Perceval could see, however, that the Fisher King's kingdom was desolated. Many years earlier, when he was guarding the Grail, the king had looked as a woman's robe opened in a revealing way. For this he had been punished, and had a wound in his thigh that would not heal.

Now, the Fisher King had to be carried around on a litter. His kingdom was totally barren. Even though the Grail resided there, he was not able to be healed by it. His only time of happiness was when he was fishing. A court jester had prophesized that he would only be cured when a true innocent came to his court. Moreover, this innocent had to ask the questions, "What aileth thee?" and "Whom does the Grail serve?"

Even though Perceval was that true innocent, he didn't ask the questions. He saw the king in his malaise. A spear with a bleeding tip and the Grail itself were carried by a procession that passed both the king and Perceval and

into a room. Perceval had three chances to ask about the Grail and whom they were serving in the other room but, because his mother had told him not to ask questions and Gournemant had told him not to talk too much, he didn't. The Fisher King was carried off to bed, and Perceval drifted off to sleep thinking that he would ask in the morning.

But in the morning the castle was empty. As soon as Perceval and his horse stepped off the drawbridge, it closed and the castle disappeared. No matter how much the distraught Perceval shouted, no one answered him. His opportunity had been lost.

However, living up to the meaning of his name, 'Press on through the valley,' Perceval set off in a gallop in a vain search for the inhabitants of the castle. He came upon a maiden sitting under a tree who held the dead body of her knight and lover. She asked him his name, and for the first time in his life, he uttered his name, "Perceval."

The maiden asked Perceval where he had been. He told her and she was aghast that he hadn't asked the correct questions in the Grail Castle and she rebuked him. Because he had failed to ask the questions that could have saved the king and the kingdom, he had brought untold misery to many.

The maiden said he should be called Perceval the Wretch, or Unlucky Perceval. She also told him that she was his cousin, and that his mother had died of a broken heart when he left her. He left the maiden to avenge the death of her lover knight and, in fact, press on through the valley in his search for the Grail Castle.

Perceval then had a series of adventures in which he vanquished several knights and sent them to King Arthur to be in his service. In time, Arthur realized that Perceval was one of his greatest allies and set out with the knights of the Round Table to find him. Three of the knights reached Perceval just as he was studying three drops of blood on the snow from a wounded goose. This image had sent Perceval into a reverie about his Blancheflor; he saw the red drops as the red of her lips and rosy cheeks and the snow as her white complexion. The three knights tried to rouse him from his thoughts so that they might bring him to Arthur.

One by one, the first two knights broke into his reverie and rudely ordered him to return with them to Arthur. He struck both down automatically, without thinking. The second knight turned out to be Sir Kay and thus Perceval avenged the smiling maiden in Arthur's court. The third knight, Sir Gawain, approached Perceval courteously, with respect for his thoughts of Blancheflor and so was able to lead Perceval back to Arthur.

Perceval was treated with great honor on his arrival in Arthur's court.

But then the maiden from the Grail Castle appeared and told everyone of the pain Perceval had caused so many by not asking the critical questions about the ailing king and the Holy Grail. Perceval was defamed in front of everyone, and his moment of triumph was turned into a moment of shame.

Perceval vowed that, until he learned the answers to the two questions he failed to ask, he would not sleep two nights in the same bed, would follow any passage, no matter how strange, and would accept any fight, no matter the odds. Despite his utter failure at the Grail Castle, he was now ready to accept its challenge again; he was ready to ask the questions.

Perceval did indeed go through many more adventures—five years of them—in his quest to meet this challenge. Then, one Good Friday, he was stopped by three knights, one of whom accosted him for bearing arms on a holy day. Perceval seemed to come out of a dream. He had forgotten everything about his life, and now, as the knight was telling him about Good Friday, something awakened him. He asked where they came from and they directed him to a hermit who was holding a religious service.

Perceval approached the hermit after the service, hoping to get answers to his questions. The hermit (who turned out to be Perceval's uncle) reviewed all of Perceval's mistakes, particularly those in the Grail Castle. He told Perceval that his mistakes came from not treating his mother properly and yet also from following her advice too slavishly. He absolved Perceval and told him to return to the Grail Castle.

Many endings to this tale have been written by different authors. The most satisfying has Perceval return to the castle, ask the right questions, and heal the Fisher King, whose land begins to thrive. Some versions of this legend don't tell the answer to the question, Whom does the Grail serve? Some say that the Grail served the Fisher King, although that doesn't seem possible because he was so afflicted. The most meaningful answer is that the Grail serves the Grail King who lives deep within the castle. Some say that the castle, its land, and its king are metaphors for the body, life, and soul of Perceval and all of us.

THE MANY MEANINGS OF PERCEVAL AND THE HOLY GRAIL

At one level, Perceval's tale is simply one of many medieval adventures of knighthood. Yet this legend, naive and fanciful as it may seem to a modern reader, is truly a reflection of our life today. In our early years, we are like Perceval in his youth—unsure of our identity and able only to listen blindly to the advice of parents and teachers. We do not yet understand our call to adventure. We travel through the peaks and valleys of life, sometimes reaching the heights of success, and sometimes experiencing failures that shake us to the core. We think we know our purpose, but we usually don't really know our *true* purpose and vision. We confuse our purpose with our abilities and with our early successes for which we are rewarded. We ignore the presence of grace in our lives. Like Perceval, we often don't know where we are going on our path, or how to ask the right questions that can shed light on our journey.

There are battles everyone must fight. Some are major initiations, in which you must battle for your very identity, like Perceval's conquest of the Red Knight. Some are minor but essential challenges, such as the absent-minded fight with Sir Kay, when an annoying but significant obstacle to finding your purpose has to be eliminated. And in your battles you may see the equivalent of Perceval's allies, Blancheflor and Gournemant. You might even have a breakthrough experience in which you discover what your Grail is, and celebrate knowing your purpose in life.

You can also see Perceval's use or neglect of the four hero's tools throughout his story. He exhibits the first tool, *faith in his own creativity*, when he decides to become a knight and, with overwhelming confidence, tells the Red Knight that he is going to take everything from him. In his adventure, Perceval repeatedly succeeds beyond expectations, simply by assuming that he is going to succeed. You have probably experienced some moments like this. It is possible to make them more frequent and enlarge them so that you live from your creative resources and according to your unique purpose more of the time.

In Perceval's case, even though he exhibits a certain faith in his own creativity in many situations, he often submits to the voice of judgment, represented by the admonishments of his mother and Gournemant, the criticisms of his maiden cousin, and the maiden at King Arthur's court. In fact, his lack of action in the Grail Castle might largely be credited to his own internalized voice of judgment, just as we can trace many of our fears and failures to voices of judgment we have internalized from people in our own lives. However, Perceval does exhibit the second tool, *absence of judgment*, when he ignores the ridicule of Arthur's court, particularly from Sir Kay. And we can see a beautiful combination of faith in his creativity and absence of judgment when he turns immediately from the shame of the maiden's attack to renew his question with confidence.

Perceval uses the third tool, *precise observation*, several times. He exhibits it when he sees the five knights riding by his home at the beginning of the story. Note that when Perceval is younger, his precise observation is colored by his mother's voice of judgment: he thought the tent to be a church because his mother had described churches to him. It is not until he is older and wiser that his skills of precise observation have the quality of deep personal knowledge that is part of acting creatively.

A key to precise observation when we are older is to see both with the open curiosity of childhood, and with scientific objectivity. When we do, we can sense a certain resonance, a feeling even in the act of perception itself, that tells us when we are being true to our own unique purpose, such as Perceval has when he receives training from Gournemant. When Perceval is so enthusiastic about Gournemant's training, he makes the transformation from youth to man.

Like Perceval, we often fool ourselves into thinking that those moments of excitement are the ultimate truth of our lives and feel we are living truly only when we are carried away with this kind of enthusiasm. In fact, it is only through experience that we begin to know our overall higher purpose. We must pay attention to what we enjoy doing and do well, and yet we have to go beyond that, to something higher and more profound. We must keep asking questions and meeting the challenge of discovering and living within our own purpose.

By asking *penetrating questions*, the fourth tool, Perceval begins to move quickly toward finding his purpose. At the beginning of his quest, he asks one of the five knights many questions about his lance, his armor, his shield, and so on. But then, just as for most of us, his inner voice of blame and criticism intervenes to stop him from asking questions at the most critical time. Because of this, he has to go through a great deal of pain and a much longer search. In one sense, he does not at first answer the call to adventure to find his true purpose. Once he asks the key questions, and begins to react and respond based on his higher purpose in life, not only is there great benefit to him, but to everyone around him.

This process recurs not only in legends but in the lives of truly successful people. Once you meet the challenge of discovering your true purpose, the benefits affect everyone around you. You can make your unique contribution every day.

There must be more to life than having everything.

Maurice Sendak

YOUR PATH TO PURPOSE

Take a moment now and review the tale as a story that says something quite profound about your path. Put yourself in the role of Perceval, but see that role enacted in the legend of your life. Answer the following questions in the space provided below or in your journal. Make sure you write something for each one.

My strength is as the strength of ten because my heart is pure.

Alfred, Lord Tennyson

1. *What part of the Perceval legend made you think, "Yes, I've experienced something like that myself."? What particular event does it relate to, and how did you experience that event in terms of discovering or not discovering your life's purpose?*

2. *What are the most important ups and downs you have experienced in your life, as Perceval did in his adventure?*

3. *Have you ever been motivated by the glitter or external aspects of a profession, job, person, or purpose in the same way that Perceval was by the knights at the beginning of the story? What was that, and what was its appeal for you? What did you do in your life to follow such external motivations?*

4. *Have you ever felt deterred from finding or fulfilling your purpose in life by admonitions from your parents or others—just as Perceval was held back? What were some of these admonitions?*

5. *Have you ever refrained from asking questions in a situation where you thought later that you should have? Describe one significant situation.*

6. *Have you ever had, if only momentarily, the feeling that you were doing something exceedingly well, almost effortlessly, in the way that Perceval was able to defeat his opponents? What were you doing? Where does that gift of ability come from? Do you have a sense of gratitude for it? To whom or what? And how has that gift helped or hindered you in finding purpose in your life?*

The inner king is the one in us who knows what we want to do for the rest of our lives, or the rest of the month, or the rest of the day. . . . The inner king is connected with our fire of purpose and passion.

Robert Bly

7. *Can you identify with the definition of our hero's name that means "innocent fool?" Have you ever felt that way? What was that like?*

8. *Can you identify with the definition of Perceval's name that means "press on through the valley?" How does that apply or not apply to your experiences and way of life?*

9. *Is there something that you are searching for, something healing and inspiring to you, that calls you on with purpose? What is your Grail?*

By seeing the archetypal truths embodied in a story such as Perceval's, you begin to see how the same types of experiences occur in your life. Much of the time you don't realize your real purpose. Like Perceval, you do what others tell you until circumstances seem to force a realization of your purpose. What can you do about this? First of all, you can identify with and learn from the hero in the story. You don't have to go into all the blind alleys, or through all the turmoil that

Perceval did. You can pay attention without judging. You can ask the appropriate questions that teach you to have faith in your creativity. Then, when difficulties come, you can deal with them with the strength of knowing your purpose.

MAPPING YOUR PATH TO PURPOSE

On the next few pages you will map your current position on your path towards a life of meaning and purpose. You may wish to repeat it after you have completed all the exercises in the chapter—you will then have a record of your everyday hero's journey.

This self-assessment exercise has two parts. First, you will draw a visual log, an intuitive pictorial record of yourself on your path towards finding your life's purpose. Then you will write a verbal log, in which you record some brief statements about your quest for true purpose.

Visual Log

Before you do your own visual log of your path to purpose, take a look at an example drawn by a woman named Melissa, which may give you some ideas. Melissa is a college student who had held a number of jobs and been in several relationships, though, when she drew these pictures, she was recently happily married and held a job that she enjoyed. She told us that she found the hero's journey to be an excellent metaphor for inspiring her when her life was not going well, adding that "the process of drawing me on my path *always* shows me things that I didn't realize before. They're like a mirror." See Melissa's visual log in the margin.

Melissa drew herself leaping from the call to breakthrough, with a faint ghost of herself waiting to welcome her to celebration. "I feel pretty clear about my purpose," she said, "but it's not been easy. That's why I drew all those other little journeys going up and down to get me to where I am now. The shackles of my confusion are still wrapped around my ankles, and if I forget to be mindful of my purpose, they'll drag me into the roaring sea of unknowing at the bottom. I just have to know that part of me is wise; part of me always knows my purpose. I have to let that part guide me."

Melissa drew figures to show where she is on her quest for purpose. You might not draw any figures at all. Instead, you may draw colored shapes or a doodle or scribble to represent how you feel.

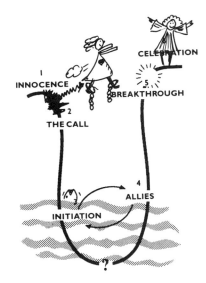

So may a thousand actions,
    once afoot,
End in one purpose and be all
    well borne
Without defeat.

William Shakespeare

Use the basic outline of the path we've provided to create your own visual log. Use colored markers or paints and let yourself play. Draw a stick figure at the point on the path that intuitively feels right to you, to represent how you feel about where you are in dealing with this challenge. Use color, or show this symbolically. You might like to draw other symbols for the aspects of the journey that relate to the challenge of living your life with purpose and meaning. If you feel as if you're in several places at once, draw several figures or symbols. There is no right or wrong way to draw your visual log. It is simply a means to represent yourself and what you are encountering on your path. It

The greatest formal talent is worthless if it does not serve a creativity which is capable of shaping the cosmos.

Albert Einstein

A Visual Travel Log

Where I am at the start of this journey

Date: _____

6
CELEBRATION

5
BREAKTHROUGH

1
INNOCENCE

2
THE CALL

4
ALLIES

3
INITIATION

should be intuitive. Don't think about what you draw. Do it spontaneously, and have fun with this record of your quest. Don't worry if it's not accurate in a factual sense. Chances are that it's highly accurate in a creative sense. Take enough time so that you feel you really do express, visually, your position on your path of identifying and pursuing your highest purpose.

You don't have to interpret what you draw. Remember that your intuition often speaks in symbols that your rational mind does not, at first, understand. That's OK. Later, you can review your drawing and see what meaning you find in it. In this way, reviewing your visual log is like interpreting a dream whose symbols came from the depths of your subconscious without you intentionally designing them or understanding them.

This log may be a new way of expressing yourself. Don't be uneasy about it. This is your workbook and no one but you will see your pictures (unless you want to show them), so it's safe to experiment with a more intuitive and creative way of understanding and expressing yourself.

Verbal Log

Now you are ready to write about where you are in the six phases of the hero's journey.

The verbal log lists the phases, and you are to jot down a synopsis of what you have done, are doing, or think you might do for each one. You might simply list important events or people, or you may record your insights, reflections, and what you think are your next steps.

Melissa wrote a variety of things in her verbal log.

INNOCENCE (Feeling comfortable with my situation)

> My life is about living with purpose.
> In my work. And in my relationship with Arthur.
> Being loving. In both.

THE CALL TO ADVENTURE (Identifying and recognizing my challenge)

> To break free of my workaholic rut and remember that I work best when I'm emotionally nourished.
> I keep getting it and then losing it. Getting off track or bogged down.
> Too much work. I keep forgetting my true purpose.

INITIATION (Really being tested)

> Getting caught up in details pulls me away from my higher self.
> Work pressure with Tim is forcing me to remember to make time for me.
> Sometimes feel like I'm drowning.
> I am learning to practice what I preach.

ALLIES (Finding strength and help)

> Arthur Tim Heather

BREAKTHROUGH (Reaching new awareness or resolution)

> My purpose is not to be miserable!!!!!
> I can accomplish my goals by being in top emotional and physical shape.
> My deep purpose is to inspire people, *including me.* (Mustn't forget this part.)

CELEBRATION (Returning home and being different)

> Not quite there yet. Got to trust.
> Finishing the LLN project.

The slogan "press on" has solved and always will solve the problems of the human race.

Calvin Coolidge

Melissa starts the breakthrough section by saying, "My purpose is not to be miserable." You may not find this very exciting or meaningful, but she thought it critical at the time. Notice that similarly she writes only about people when she lists allies. It is possible to have allies that are organizations, seasons, animals, weather, plants, even objects.

Sometimes Melissa's writing shows a relationship to her drawing and sometimes it doesn't. For example, the trust that she will live consistently with her higher purpose was evident in both, and the waves in her picture suggest the drowning she described verbally. But in completing her visual log, Melissa identified an inner guide that seems to represent an intuitive approach to living with true purpose that is not found in her verbal log. There, she identifies that both people and work are important on her journey of realizing her true purpose of being loving. When you complete both logs for your self-assessment, you might, like Melissa, have slightly different insights in each. The value is in looking at your *composite* description of yourself.

Before doing your verbal log, consider your life as your own personal hero's journey that perhaps, like Perceval's, is made up of many smaller adventures that constitute phases of the journey. Sit somewhere quiet and take time to contemplate each of the steps of your path toward living with true purpose, starting with the phase of innocence. In your log, jot down what comes to mind for each of the phases. If you do not have anything to say for a particular phase, leave that section blank. As is the case with the visual log, there is no right or wrong way to do this exercise. Do it in the way that is useful for you.

Here's a test to find whether your mission on earth is finished: If you're alive, it isn't.

Richard Bach

If one advances confidently in the direction of his dreams . . . he will meet with a success unexpected in common hours.

Henry David Thoreau

A Verbal Travel Log

Where I am at the start of this journey

Date: _____

INNOCENCE (Feeling comfortable with my situation)

THE CALL TO ADVENTURE (Identifying and recognizing my challenge)

INITIATION (Really being tested)

ALLIES (Finding strength and help)

BREAKTHROUGH (Reaching new awareness or resolution)

CELEBRATION (Returning home and being different)

DO WHAT YOU LOVE, LOVE WHAT YOU DO

In spite of all of his wanderings, Perceval was able to keep moving towards his purpose; at first it was an imagined purpose, including joining what he thought were angels, and going into the tent he mistook for a church, but later it was his true and higher purpose—his quest for the Grail. He could do this because almost all the time he did what he loved to do. And even when he had to do things that were difficult, he did them with passion.

If you consider your life, you'll probably find that, like Perceval, you felt most fulfilled when you were either doing what you loved or when you somehow saw the higher purpose in your life and were able to love even the drudgery connected with it. If your experiences don't appear to confirm this, you will be interested to know that psychological studies indicate that the most important factor in success—in terms of self-fullfillment and satisfaction—is whether people love what they are doing.

In our observations of everyday heroes—men and women like you, who succeed in this way—we find that they don't play by rigid rules. Instead, they work with nondirective credos known as *heuristics*—rough guidelines or general rules of thumb one has for learning or discovery. The word *heuristic* comes from the Greek *heuriskein,* meaning "to discover." In our work we've tried many different heuristics on thousands of people and have seen how each individual can create a way for dealing with life challenges by living by them. Just by living by a heuristic, each person makes profound discoveries.

All available evidence says that it is in living with creative spirit or doing what you love that you will find your purpose. There is a mystical connection between what we feel deeply about in our soul and our highest purpose in life. Make that a focus while you complete this chapter. Live by the motto Do What You Love, Love What You Do. Follow this suggestion for at least a week. Keep it alive in the back of your mind. You may want to write it on a piece of paper and carry it with you. Write it on your calendar so you can keep reminding yourself to do only what you love and love all that you do.

As you live your week with this motto, you will be in a prime position to discover more clearly what your purpose is, and how you do or do not live your life according to your purpose. Experiment. See what happens. In our creativity courses, people have found that living

I would like to learn, or remember, how to live.

Annie Dillard

with mottos is one of the most important vehicles for developing their practical creativity.

Below are some things you might do this week.

When you work, you fulfill a part of earth's fondest dream assigned to you when that dream is born.

Kahlil Gibran

- Be conscious as you do things. If you find that you are not loving a certain activity, just stop and see how that feels.
- Increase the amount of time you spend (to as close to 100 percent as possible) in activities that are intrinsically interesting, personally rewarding, and feel natural to do.
- If you encounter a required task that does not meet these criteria, figure out a way to transform it, or your attitudes about it, so that you love doing it.

Do What You Love, Love What You Do

We've found that our students don't get the benefit of living with the motto unless they stop to observe their actions. Take some regular time every day (most people find that the evening is best) to reflect on your last twenty-four hours. Make notes in your journal or in the margins of this book about your experiences. Remember that heroes increase their probability for creativity and strength in dealing with challenges by paying attention to their actions. Don't let the voice of judgment get in your way. See what happens when you live with the motto Do What You Love, Love What You Do.

THE JOURNEY

You are now prepared for this journey to your true purpose. You've reflected on the parallels between the story of your life and the story of Perceval's quest for the Grail; you've constructed visual and verbal logs of where you are on this path right now; you've begun to live with this chapter's motto. Like Perceval, you can ease your travels by doing what you love and loving what you do.

In the journey section you'll start by discovering what it is you love to do and by making commitments to doing those things as much of the time as possible. As you do, you will be encouraged to see how these activities could move you closer toward your life's work.

Your journey will take you even a bit farther as you intellectually and physically examine the interaction between your work (as in your job) and your Work (as in your reason for living or your highest purpose). Even though at this point on the path toward purpose you may have a limited idea of your purpose, as Perceval first did, you will soon see what really matters to you.

At that point, you'll be ready to travel to the only place you can discover your basic values—inside yourself. You will do this with a meditation that allows you to know what your own Grail might be and how it can affect you. With this knowledge, you'll be able to review how your life has led to this point and what the adventure is going to be like in the future.

Your work is to discover your work and then with all your heart to give yourself to it.

Buddha

FIGURING OUT WHAT YOU LOVE

What do you love? What do you do? Are they the same, or do you find yourself filling your days with things you do but don't love? On the following chart, make a list of your twenty favorite things to do— those things that truly make your life feel worthwhile. They might be small, like having a morning cup of coffee, or more major, like volunteering in a soup kitchen.

You're probably familiar with the old To Do list—an ever-growing list of responsibilities you have to get done whether you want to or not. You write them down and cross them off when they're out of the way. And if you wait long enough, some of the items become obsolete and disappear by themselves. Such a list is very common, but it isn't usually a Love To Do list. The difference with this list is that each item on it is there because it is a reward in itself, not because it is a responsibility. Here's your chance to construct your own Love To Do list. Start right now, using the spaces below. If you have more than twenty things you love to do, write them in the margin or on another page and insert them here. Have fun. Work quickly. No one else needs to see this list. Don't worry about the columns marked A, B, and C. We'll get to that later.

A	B	THINGS I LOVE TO DO	C
		1.	
		2.	
		3.	
		4.	
		5.	
		6.	
		7.	
		8.	
		9.	
		10.	
		11.	
		12.	
		13.	
		14.	
		15.	
		16.	
		17.	
		18.	
		19.	
		20.	

Look at your list and consider it from the perspective of someone who doesn't know you, but who is trying to figure out what kind of person you are. In the margin or in your journal, jot down any insights you have. This may stimulate you to think of more things you love to do or to eliminate or change some that you have on your list. Then, while still in that contemplative state, do the following.

1. Write Last Year above column A. Then go back and put a check in the far left-hand box next to each item to indicate those things you have done at least once in the last year.
2. Then check those things you have done in the last week in the box in column B. Write Last Week above that column. What do you notice? How many things, and what sort of things, do you do? Why don't you do the other things on your list? Writing about your reflections or drawing something now can help in your explorations.
3. Write To Do above column C. Put a check in that column for each thing you love to do but don't normally do (and didn't check in column B) that you will commit to doing this week. This is your To Do list. Make sure you check at least seven things, so you can do at least one per day.

When you have done something on your list during this week, circle it. Plan to do and circle as many of these as you can. As you go through your week, notice what you do and don't do. Notice the reasons you tell yourself why you do not do certain things. Notice what happens when you do things you love.

GETTING BEYOND THE CONQUESTS AND THE OBSTACLES

As you work on this chapter's challenge and live with the motto of doing what you love, you'll go through two kinds of experiences, sometimes almost simultaneously. First, like Perceval, you'll enjoy the satisfaction of doing precisely what is right for you. You'll begin to get a glimmer of the Grail of your life—of what it would be like if you did less of what you don't love and more of what you do. You can even begin to see what it might be like to have every part of your life in accord with your true purpose for living.

At the same time, however, even when you just consider the possibility of doing only what you love, some common judgments begin to come up. You can torment yourself with mental blocks or arguments that hold you back from seeing doing what you love as an acceptable way to live. What are some of these reasons you might have for not always doing what you love? Jot down three of them.

Notice your negative reasons or excuses. Ask yourself where you got them. Just as Perceval got his judgments that "You shouldn't ask questions" and "You shouldn't talk too much" from two of the most influential people in his young life, so we take on the judgments of our parents and teachers, often without realizing that we are hurting ourselves with our slavish interpretation of them.

In our creativity seminars, we find that the most common inner judgments people encounter when they start to live by the motto of this chapter are those in the margin.

If you notice yourself holding such judgments about the motto, you are in good company. Many people truly believe that a life of purpose is measured by how hard they work or how little they take care of themselves. They believe that personal enjoyment is not a relevant factor in a life of true purpose.

Perhaps for them it isn't. But we find that living and working with joy and passion—doing what you love and loving what you do—is not antithetical to making money or to helping other people. In fact, you often find that when you're living consistently with your purpose in life you're making money and benefiting people at the same time.

Now review your list of twenty items again. It may not be feasible for you to incorporate all those things into your life all the time, but think how you might include more of them, particularly the seven you committed to doing this week.

There are probably an infinite number of ways you could move toward alignment with your true purpose. As a hero, you have to find your path without being a slave to what others insist is the right way to go. To find and travel your path you have to be willing to be open to different experiences, routes, and tests.

Think of it in terms of a trip. Each route to a destination is different. The key is not that one of the routes is best, in absolute terms; it is that the adventure is different on each. The trick is to not get stuck thinking that any particular route is your true destination. This is similar to Perceval thinking that joining the angels, as he thought the knights were, was his true purpose. This was *part* of his journey to purpose, but it was not his ultimate purpose.

If you believe that there is only one route to fulfillment and purpose, you may set yourself up for a difficult journey with a strong probability of disappointment. But if you hold a *sense of purpose* as your destination and know that there are several routes to get there, you will appreciate the journey regardless of the route you choose—including relishing and learning from the detours. When you enjoy your journey, you will be living with true purpose on the way to your destination.

Begin to develop some useful responses to the judgments from inside yourself and from others that may be keeping you from your true path. Before you go any further, take some time to consider the following questions. Write your answers here or in your journal.

What things could you do more often than you do now, even if not all the time? How could you work that out?

What things could you do in such a way that they benefit other people as well as yourself?

What things that you love could you do for money? Really think about this. How could you incorporate them into making a living?

Work can provide the opportunity for spiritual and personal, as well as financial, growth. If it doesn't, then we're wasting far too much of our lives on it.

James Autry

How could you live your life in such a way that your true purpose in being alive becomes clear?

Keeping these questions in mind, what path do you see for your life? Don't try to be particularly sensible, logical, or responsible. Simply reflect on the questions above and let your creative imagination loose on what this might be. Don't think about this as some kind of final answer. Live with the motto for this week and then come back to these questions to see if your answers have changed.

HOW TO LOVE WHAT YOU DO

Even if you could answer all of the questions above so that you made a life in which you loved everything you did and also made money and benefited people, you would still have to carry out necessary activities that might not be very pleasant. How can you live with the second half of the motto for this challenge: the Love What You Do part?

The more you examine this question, the more you will realize that living with the second part of the motto is just as involved with your ultimate purpose as the first part. Remember how Perceval continued his training with Gournemant even beyond fatigue, and that the most important part of his life, in terms of the challenge, was after he made the vow not to rest until he was able to return to the Grail Castle.

Logan Pearsall Smith said that the true test of whether one has found his or her purpose in life is a love of the drugery it involves. The key to doing what you love is to live your life in such a way that you experience joy and purpose. Doing what you love doesn't mean living in sloth or selfishness. It doesn't necessarily mean that all you do is bestow goodness on suffering souls and then meditate in a flower garden. It *does* mean that you feel fulfilled in whatever you do. It also means that you figure out a way to love doing whatever you *have* to do.

When you live with purpose, even drudgery can incorporate a sense of purpose and fulfillment. For example, you might be bothered that you have to clean the kitchen when you cook, stay up late when you are studying, or make a long commute to your job. But if these tasks are necessary to express your essential self, you can see them in a larger context. Instead of gritting your teeth, you can begin to see ways that such tasks can be done with grace, give you a break, allow you to think, or even be made into a game.

The everyday hero accepts even the small challenges and faces them with courage and creativity. He makes considerable self-effort and also accepts and has faith in the grace that comes his way. Your challenge here is to think of one task you absolutely have to do this week that you do not love to do. How can you perform this task so that you love it?

Identify one thing that you must do this week. Then jot down three ideas for ways to do it so that you can love doing it.

I never thought of achievement. I just did what came along for me to do—the thing that gave me the most pleasure.

Eleanor Roosevelt

SOMETHING UNPLEASANT I HAVE TO DO

THREE IDEAS FOR ENJOYING IT

Now go about your business for the week, and make use of at least one of the ideas you just wrote. When you have actually done the unpleasant task, write a brief evaluation, here or in your journal, of what happened in your attempt to love doing it.

EVALUATION

You just took on the challenge of transforming something un-pleasant into something with meaning and purpose in your life. How did you do?

Of course, this task was probably something relatively minor in terms of your entire life. In a sense, this experience represents one act of heroism in your lifetime hero's journey—the taming of one dragon or the completion of one seemingly impossible task. But just as Perceval's development into a true knight consists of his inner evolution that comes from his successful completion of his various adventures, so this one instance of loving the unlovable represents one step toward your own knighthood. Many of these small journeys can lead to your finding and continually living in alignment with your highest purpose.

WHAT IS YOUR *WORK*?

You have come a long way from the innocence from which you began this journey. You passed through an initiation by facing the challenge to live congruently with your purpose. You're beginning to form some essential truths about what you must do with your life. Until now, though, you've been exploring activities as a way to get a clearer idea of your purpose. But what drives your love or hate of those activities is your underlying value system. Now it is time to examine those values themselves.

In a sense, you could say that your Grail is epitomized by your values, and that your life's work is your search for your Grail. In order to answer the question What is my Grail?, you need to answer the question, What is my life's Work?

We use two forms of the word *work* to differentiate between our everyday professional work and our essential life's work. Our work is what we do every day, our job or profession. It is what we put on tax forms and what we tell people when we are asked about our occupation. It's who we are on the everyday level of existence, without being heroic.

Our Work, with a capital W, refers to our reason for being in the world. It embodies our highest purpose and transcends our everyday work. It is what we might tell people we do in front of a roaring fire when we're sharing intimacies about what is and isn't meaningful. For example, you could be attempting to live a loving life and inspire others to care about themselves and the planet. In fact, you already do this through your work by attempting to make their lives more effective in tangible ways. You may see your Work as being a *lover*, in the broadest definition of the word.

In his inaugural address George Bush said, "We, as a people, have such a purpose today. It is to make kinder the face of the nation and gentler the face of the world." Whether or not you agree with him, his assertion described a higher purpose motivating specific actions. It described the Work of the American people.

All of us have both our Work and our work, whether we have articulated this or not. It is our Work that gives us meaning, and very often is set aside in order for us to do our work to pay the bills. Do the two have to be separate? How can you have both going at once? Make some notes on these questions about your work and your Work before continuing.

What is your work, and what is your Work? Can you identify both?

How does the work you do tie into your Work, or true purpose for being?

Psychologist Jean Houston thinks of our work as being in the horizontal plane. It is visible and on the level. Our Work is on the vertical plane—it comes from our depths and connects us to our heights and ideals. She devised this exercise to help you make this distinction.

Physically Experiencing the Intersection of work and Work

Stand up with your arms stretched out horizontally. Imagine your arms represent your work—the way you reach out and make your mark on the world. Imagine your body represents your Work, a vertical axis between solid ground and the heavens. Close your eyes for a few moments and see what images or words come to you for your work and your Work.

Keep standing like this and physically feel the intersection of both of these within you. Notice that they intersect somewhere in the region of your heart and shoulders. Do you do your work with heart? Or do you feel the weight of the world on your shoulders? Does your Work enter into your work through your heart? What metaphors and images come to mind about this?

Visually Mapping the Relationship
of work and Work

The blank graph provided shows the horizontal axis of your work and
the vertical axis of your Work. Draw images and write words around
the axes to describe your work and your Work. Use colored pens and
pencils. When you have finished, plot yourself on a graph, using lines
or dots or any other form of graphic representation. For example, do
you feel that your work and Work are well integrated, and that you do
indeed live with heart? Then you might draw a heart at the intersection of the two lines. Are you very clear about your Work and purpose
in life, but unsure about what work you might do? Then you might
draw a heavy line on the vertical Work axis to show that this is your
current location in terms of the two axes. Or, perhaps you have a job
you love but you haven't really given much thought to your higher purpose until now. You might draw a dot over on the left-hand side of the
horizontal work axis to represent you on this graph. Use your imagination and intuition, and see what happens.

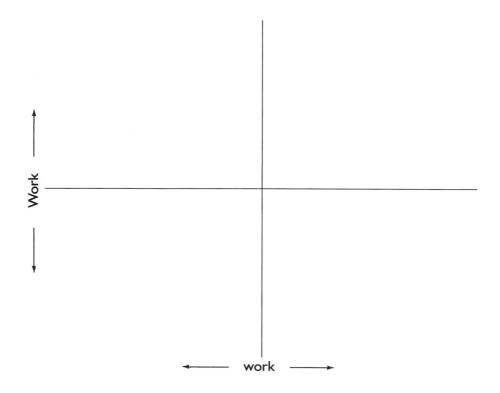

WHO ARE YOU? WHAT ARE YOUR VALUES?

True purpose is not just about *doing*; it's also about *being*. It's about who you are. It's about living a life of value, a life with integrity in which you act in consistency with your deepest principles.

Often, we are so concerned with doing things on the daily level that we operate on automatic pilot. We deal with people and events without being particularly aware of how our interaction reflects or does not reflect our inner values and true purpose. We act habitually rather than consciously. Perceval did this with the maiden in the tent at the start of his adventures. He might have thought he was aware of his own inner values and true purpose, but if he had been, he would not have pushed himself upon the maiden despite her protests.

Similarly, when Perceval was on the quest for the Grail and had a chance to ask the questions but didn't, he was not acting with full awareness. He was not consistent with his inner value of being a knight who found the Grail. His actions were based on his rather narrow interpretation of other people's descriptions of his purpose.

One way to remember your core values is by relaxing, and turning your attention inward instead of outward. When you temporarily take the time to stop *doing*, and simply *be*, you allow yourself to slow down enough to hear your inner voice.

You can practice *being* by meditating. Some use meditation purely for relaxation. Some use it to clear their heads. Others see meditation as part of their spiritual practice.

Sometimes it is difficult to meditate: we are part of a culture that emphasizes action and material phenomena and discourages inner experiences that are considered mystical. However, meditation is simply the experience of relaxation and inner contemplation. You can do it for whatever reason feels appropriate. Try the following meditation.

As in other exercises, try to either make a tape of this activity (reading the instructions aloud and allowing enough time for you to experience it fully), or have someone read it to you. If you can't, read the exercise until you are quite familiar with it, and then do it in its entirety.

PRACTICE BEING YOURSELF

Sit comfortably in a chair. It is important that your spine be straight, that your arms and legs be uncrossed, and that your feet are flat on the floor. This helps reduce tension, and allows for both a literal and metaphorical flow of energy in your body. Make sure your back is supported, or you might feel some strain as the meditation progresses, which could distract you from its goal.

Close your eyes and take a long, slow, deep breath, so that your belly rises and your lungs fill, and then exhale, easily and effortlessly. Take another breath, this time holding it for a moment after you have breathed in, to mark the turning from inflowing to outflowing breath, and then let it go. Take a few more breaths like that, feeling comfortable as you sit, just noticing the inflow and outflow and paying attention to nothing but your breathing. You have nothing to do right now but to be here, be still, and breathe with awareness. Don't try to change or force your breathing, just take deep breaths and notice them. Do this for a few minutes.

If you are reading this aloud, pause here to allow enough time to do this breathing. In the future, when you need to pause more than a few seconds in an exercise, you will see four periods inside parentheses (....) to show you that you need to wait for a while before continuing with the instructions.

Now, still keeping your eyes closed, notice how your body feels when the breath comes into it. Notice how it fills up and expands when you breathe in, and that it sinks down a little when you breathe out. (....) Notice how you feel inside. Can you feel yourself relaxing in your body and in your head? Keep noticing your breathing, and how you feel. (....) Notice whatever thoughts may come up, but don't really pay attention to them. Let them be like birds that fly into your consciousness or vision, alight for a moment, and then fly off. Watch them as they do this. Watch them as you would birds. Don't try to catch them. Notice the silence in between your thoughts. Just sit and be for five minutes. Appreciate just being here and alive and being you. (....)

Slowly open your eyes and look around you with the same sort of awareness, without focusing on any one thing. Practice being aware of the world around you and of your inner world, without holding onto thoughts. (....) Notice what it feels like to really see without selecting one object to be the center of your attention. Notice how your vision is different when you look and see in this manner. In the martial art of aikido, this is referred to as seeing with soft eyes. When you see with soft eyes you see with a clear fresh vision. You notice things you hadn't been aware of before. Practice simultaneously seeing with soft eyes and thinking with soft thoughts. Don't let one thought come along and grab your attention. Remember the image you had of thoughts like birds. (....) Keeping the same awareness, consider what values are important to you. Let your thoughts drift, with this as the theme. What values are most important to you? Watch the images or feelings or words that come floating into your consciousness. (....)

Maintaining that awareness, become even more conscious in conventional terms, and write a list of your important values. Don't simply reel off a list like love, honesty, virtue, on automatic pilot. Really *ask* yourself what values are important and see what comes into your consciousness. In the margin, or on another piece of paper write down words or phrases that describe you and what is important to you.

Now, still keeping a sense of your essence—of your quiet, still place—reread your list and rank your human values. Write a 1 next to the most important one, a 2 next to the second one, and so on. Contemplate your set of values. Tinker with them if you wish. Reflect on these questions, and answer them below, using very specific examples.

- How do you live (or not live) by these values? What are you doing to ensure that you do things and are surrounded by people and situations that embody these values?
- How do you encourage these values in others? What do you do to attract others with these values into your life?
- How do you handle situations in which these values aren't present?

How do I live by these values?

How do I encourage them in others?

What do I do when these values are not present?

WHAT IS YOUR GRAIL?

The original Grail was a chalice used at the Last Supper; it represents a container of that which gives life higher purpose and meaning. Perceval's quest for the Grail represents the universal quest for meaning in our lives. If the chalice illustrated here were your Grail, what would be in it? Review all the exercises to this point and consider your experiences in living with this chapter's motto. Contemplate your cherished actions in life and the values underlying them. Then fill the Grail we've provided with the colors and shapes of your life's Work—that which gives your life meaning, your purpose as you sense it now. Do not use words, just use symbols of your higher purpose. Experience them appearing from both within and without you.

It is your work in life that is the ultimate seduction.

Pablo Picasso

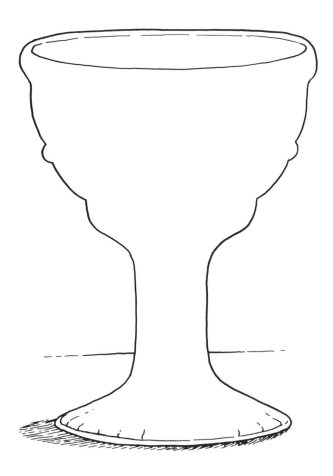

TAKING RESPONSIBILITY FOR YOUR ADVENTURE

Now that you have developed some sense of your Grail, you can begin to look at your whole life—until now and in the future—as a hero's journey story. When you know what you love to do, as well as your values and overall vision, you can see what might happen to you in the future. And you can adjust and deal with the events in your story, just as Perceval did in his adventures.

Someone once asked author Archibald MacLeish what life would be like in the year 2010. He said, "Whatever we make it to be." In the same way, everyday heroes know—with a faith that goes beyond reason—that their future is going to be what they make it to be. You know that you have the power to see where you have been, where you are now, and where you are going in your adventure toward purpose. You also know that you need only take responsibility for the future, and your own inner creativity will align that future with your purpose.

The following exercise has you imagine how your journey will come out, so that you can enter the return section of this chapter with an awareness of the larger context of your path. Write a brief Who's Who description of yourself for each decade of your life, up to the age of ninety-nine, making sure you include things you enjoyed and were good at, as well as major challenges you had. Your entries may be simple, like John's entry for 0–9 years.

Born in Chicago.
Left at home a lot with babysitters.
Pretty good runner until he got overweight.

If you need more space for a more detailed description, use the margins or your journal. Push yourself to fill in something for all the decades through 90–99 years. Often, people find it difficult to go more than a couple of decades into the future, but the most interesting answers really come from those later decades. Work quickly and be relaxed. There are no right answers, and you'll see more interesting results if you put things down almost without thinking, particularly for the decades in the future. Keep toying with this until you are satisfied. You might want to adjust things in your future, but stop at some point and make an overall assessment.

WHO'S WHO LISTING FOR: _____

0–9 Years

10–19 Years

20–29 Years

30–39 Years

40–49 Years

50–59 Years

60–69 Years

70–79 Years

80–89 Years

90–99 Years

Once you are satisfied with your *Who's Who* listings for all ten-year periods, look at them and make an assessment. Notice that you may have had experiences that were similar to those of Perceval. Notice if there were times when you really began to sense your purpose. See if there have been times when you stayed too long with something that really wasn't right for you.

Notice any difficulty you had in extending your imagination to the future. We don't mean setting specific goals for where you should be at a particular age. Instead, this exercise can tell you what kind of overriding vision you have for your life at this moment. Examine what you have written, looking for a pattern that might be forming for your future. This will give you some idea of the stage you're in now regarding the challenge of finding your life purpose. Make a commitment to take responsibility for the future.

———— THE RETURN ————

TO LIVE WITH PURPOSE

You have come a significant distance on this quest. You have met the challenge to identify those things that give you a sense of purpose in your personal and professional life, and to describe ways to live that are more aligned with your true purpose. You are like Perceval at the very end of his story. You have identified your Grail and are asking questions.

The last phase of the hero's journey is the return. At the end of the journey, the hero returns home wiser, internally richer, and ready to share with others. Similarly, you return to your same work and personal life, but things are different because you are renewed. Now you celebrate the difference you have made in your life.

As you have probably recognized over the course of this path, there are three possible types of changes you might make in your life to allow you to experience your purpose more readily.

1. Make some minor changes about what you do—for example, bringing in more of what you love, or redirecting your path with small steps.
2. Make a major change, like going into a new line of work, changing aspects of your primary relationship, or taking up a hobby that you always wanted to do.
3. Change your attitude or rethink your values. For example, is your work really so low in meaning, or are you just not noticing the meaningful aspects of it?

Below you will restate and sum up your purpose in life as part of your personal hero's declaration. You might be fulfilling your purpose right now. Or perhaps your life isn't currently fulfilling it. What action can you take to reach the pinnacle of living a life that is totally meaningful and aligned with your purpose? Write down a few things you might do in each category.

———— HERO'S DECLARATION————

My purpose in life

These things give me meaning in life

Actions to increase purpose and meaning in my life

Small Steps	Major Changes	Attitude Shifts

ONE DAY AT A TIME

Now that you have written down your purpose and some specific actions to make sure you will live consistently with your vision for your life, your challenge is to live with purpose on a daily basis. The original Chretien de Troyes legend of Perceval's search for the Grail ended with Perceval reviewing the mistakes and glories of his travels, and then setting forth for the Grail Castle for his ultimate discovery of whom the Grail serves. The result of his knightly adventures was that he was now able to be different and to ask the right questions.

Your day-to-day life gives you your opportunity to be different in the way you live with purpose: living each day, one day at a time, being fully aware of your purpose in all that you do and appreciating the meaning of your life.

Start the next exercise when you have a fairly normal day ahead of you, and you know you will be able to get back to this book in twenty-four hours.

Under the heading below, describe your purpose in life. This sounds like a simple instruction. You just did this on the preceding page, didn't you? This time, however, approach the challenge in a qualitatively different manner. Don't intellectually think of your purpose. Let a feeling or knowing about your purpose emerge intuitively. Then write it down or draw a symbol for it.

It may help you to take a few moments to close your eyes and remember the still, quiet place inside you.

My Purpose in Life

Now do whatever you ordinarily would do for the next twenty-four hours, without forgetting your purpose. At this time tomorrow, open your workbook to this page again, and take a few minutes to again remember the still, quiet place inside you. Reflect on how you lived the last twenty-four hours.

What Happened?

What things did you do and what attitudes did you have that were aligned with your purpose in life? How much did you consciously pay attention to joy and meaning in these twenty-four hours? How much were you on automatic pilot? Jot down your observations. Be sure to include any notes to yourself about significant differences you noticed, and situations that caused you to forget your purpose.

Observations on Living One Day with Purpose

FOLLOW-UP: MAPPING YOUR PATH
FOR PURPOSE

The last part of this chapter, as with each of the challenges, is to complete another visual log and verbal log of your travels. How are you different in terms of where you are on your own everyday hero's path toward having a life that is 100 percent aligned with your true purpose? These final logs can be valuable in three ways.

1. You have time to reflect on where you have been, and summarizing your journey intuitively and rationally allows you to remember its most important parts.
2. Comparing these logs to the first ones you did in this chapter provides an instantaneous picture of where you were then and where you are now.
3. After you have completed all of the challenge chapters, it will be rewarding to review your logs for a composite picture of your inner journey. Most people notice new details and connections every time they do this.

Don't look back yet to the logs you first made when you started this chapter. Recall that the visual log is an intuitive mapping of where you are on your path of pursuing your true purpose. The verbal log is a chance to characterize this challenge in your life now in terms of a hero's journey.

First, draw the outline of the hero's journey visual log on a sheet of paper or in your journal. (Before you start to fill in the visual log, add the labels for innocence, the call, initiation, allies, breakthrough, and celebration in their appropriate places.) Prepare yourself by taking a few moments to breathe and be still. Allow the memory of your journey over the last week to come into focus. Use colors to draw a figure or other symbols to represent yourself on your path.

For the verbal log, note where you are on this path using each of the same six labels, innocence through celebration.

Compare your new visual and verbal logs with each other, and then make comparisons with your logs at the start of the journey in this chapter for even further insights. If you are not keeping a journal, insert your current logs in this book so that they will be handy to review and contrast with your other logs at a later date.

REFLECTIONS ON YOUR PATH

Now that you've completed this chapter and have worked on the purpose challenge for a week or so, write about your experiences of this path. This Week in Review can consolidate and legitimize your experience so far. Write it as a letter to yourself (or to us or some friend or relative) so that you can get into the informal, reporting format that characterizes a letter.

Keep this letter or statement as tangible evidence of your journey. Then, if you feel the need to do some more work on this challenge in the future, or just want a boost regarding your true purpose, you can go back to this review of what you just accomplished.

CELEBRATE!

How are you celebrating your completion of this path? What are you doing to reward yourself for your successful journey? How are you making a public statement of your private changes? Make sure that in the days ahead you continue to acknowledge and celebrate your journey and the higher purpose in your life.

6

Bringing Love Into Your Life

*This is love: to fly toward a
    secret sky,*

*to cause a hundred veils to fall
    each moment.*

First to let go of life.

*Finally to take a step without
    feet. . .*

*Heart, I said, what a gift it has
    been*

to enter this circle of lovers,

to see beyond seeing itself. . .

Jalaludin Rumi

In modern society, while we may feel lonely at times, a real problem is that we are surrounded by relationships. The very tangle of these relationships can cause many troubles. It is one thing to find purpose in your life, but your happiness is also connected to your interaction with other people—not only love relationships but friendships and, in general, how you relate to everyone you encounter in life.

Somewhere inside, you know that the world is creative and that the coming together of two or more people, however negative it may seem, has the potential for positive synergy and love. The whole seems to equal more than the sum of its parts, and there may be moments when you seem to experience the divine in your interactions with others. The trouble may be that these are only moments amidst the chaotic churning of our interactions with most other people.

The paradox about love is that when you stop expecting a perfect relationship, and simply start caring about both yourself and others, you actually begin to experience nurturing relationships and thrive in them. In fact, once you can love *yourself* and, in a sense, find your beloved within yourself, you can then meet a beloved outside you. Just as in fairy tales and myths, in which the breakthrough and celebration often involve a marriage, on a deeper level the story is almost always about finding love inside oneself. When the self is whole and compassionate, life will be fulfilling.

When you understand this, you realize that whatever you feel when relating to others is really a reflection of your own inner state.

When you are angry with someone, that anger reflects a need you have within yourself. The quality and quantity of your criticism of others is really a reflection of the quality and quantity of your own self-blame and criticism from your inner voice of judgment. Equally, the loving compassion you feel for others mirrors the love and compassion you have for yourself.

It takes your heroic nature to deal with the challenge of bringing love into your life. You have to develop your essential quality of compassion—loving kindess first for yourself and then for others. Once you have the strength to recognize love within yourself, you can begin to recognize it within others. Just as a rose doesn't chase us, but draws us to it by its beauty and scent, you will attract and nurture others by grounding yourself in your essential creative nature; you will be able to give to each individual without getting involved in a destructive way. Many find that when they treat others with love and respect, they are treated that way in return. As the late meditation master Swami Muktananda said, "When you and I experience that we are the same, then love arises between us."

Another way of understanding this is to see love—the core of rewarding relationships—not as a commodity that you give or get, but as a state of being that you can *choose* to be in. Then, if you are in love, you are in a state of being that others around you might share. Something like that can't run out. It just is.

The power of true love is catalytic, synergistic, and creative, like what you experience in the beginning of a new love affair. Tasks that seemed impossible before become possible. You see people you thought of as difficult as, instead, eminently easy to deal with. If this effect can come from a love affair, just imagine what can be achieved by opening to the true internal love of a compassionate heart that can "see beyond seeing itself," as the poet Rumi says.

Ultimately, the love within you becomes a love of the infinite and a profound gratitude for the gifts of life. The love of an everyday hero comes from an inner creative spirit, and relates to an ever greater creative spirit to which we give thanks. As one great sage said, "Our thankfulness is itself a blessing, in addition to the blessing for which we are offering our thanks." In this way, the frustrations and highs of our daily interactions with people turn into a path that brings out our essential love.

Your path in this chapter starts with the story of Beauty and

Without any intentional fancy way of adjusting yourself, to express yourself as you are is the most important thing.

Shunryu Suzuki

Beast—on the surface a romantic tale, but underneath a message about compassion that can lead to extraordinary relationships with others. As you read the story, imagine all the characters as aspects of you at different times. When have you had the compassion of Beauty? The devotion of her father? When have you been stuck, like the Beast, yearning for someone to see the goodness inside you?

——— PREPARATION ———

Beauty and the Beast

Once upon a time there lived a very rich merchant with his six sons and six daughters. Oh, they lived well!

But then hard times came to the merchant and his family. He received news that all his ships, with their cargoes of gold, silver, exotic herbs, and priceless china, had sunk in a series of freak storms. Soon thereafter, he discovered that the clerks who managed his trade in far lands had pocketed all his profits and disappeared. To make matters worse, his home caught fire one night. The merchant and his children were able to escape, but all their expensive clothes, furniture, and other belongings were destroyed.

The family moved into a small, simple cottage, nothing like the mansion in which they had been living. Almost all the children moaned and complained that they didn't have pretty clothes, priceless jewelry, and expensive toys anymore; only the youngest and most beautiful of his daughters, who was also the only one who saw her father's sadness, tried to cheer everyone by reminding them that at least they had each other to love.

"Fat lot of good that is," whined her brothers. "We want golden building blocks and exotic hand-carved ivory toys."

"And we hate our home-spun clothes. We want velvet and lace and gold brocade. We don't care if you love us," pouted her sisters.

The years went by, and one day the merchant heard that one of his ships had not sunk after all, but had reached a distant port with a huge and precious cargo. He left immediately to meet the ship, first asking his children what they wished to have. Of course, they demanded the richest and fanciest things you could imagine. But Beauty, for that was his youngest's name, asked for nothing. The merchant, confused, again asked her what she desired.

"Just for you to come safely home, Father," she said. "But if you'd like to bring me something, I'd love a rose. It's been so long since I've seen or smelled one."

The merchant then set out on his long journey. After six months of traveling, which used up the little money he had, he arrived at the port. Meanwhile, however, the crew, who had heard about the fire but heard nothing from the merchant, supposed him to be dead, divided the cargo amongst themselves, and scattered to the four corners of the earth.

A dreadful blizzard swirled about the downhearted merchant as he turned from the port and started his long trip home. He trudged through the snow for hours, with no food and only a ragged jacket for warmth. Finally, when night fell, he climbed into a hollow log for shelter.

The next morning, the snow was so thick that he couldn't find the path. Freezing and weak, he set out, slipping and stumbling through the woods, and soon found himself in a very strange place. An avenue of orange trees led to a beautiful palace. Oddly, there was no snow on the avenue, the trees, or the palace. The merchant was tired, cold, and hungry, so he went into the palace to ask for help.

All the candles were ablaze in this sumptuous, warm place, but no one was to be found. After looking into twenty or thirty rooms, the merchant, exhausted, fell asleep in a chair. He woke to find soft music playing, a fire burning in the hearth, and a wonderful, freshly made meal spread out on a table next to him.

"Well," he thought, "someone knows I'm here. I'll eat some food and wait here for the host or guest to join me."

After many hours no one had shown up, so the merchant had another nap, finished the meal, and went walking in the garden to see if he could find anyone. He walked with a heavy heart, wondering how he could return to his children empty-handed.

The gardens were wondrous. There were seven hundred seventy rose bushes, all blooming with perfect roses, each more beautiful than the last.

"At least I can take Beauty her rose," said the merchant to himself. And he picked the most beautiful one.

Suddenly there was a noise behind him. He spun around and found himself face to face with the ugliest Beast imaginable. The Beast roared at him, "I saved your life! I fed you and made you warm! And you repay me by stealing my roses! You must die for this!"

Despairing, the merchant pleaded for his life. He told the Beast of his misfortune, and his unsuccessful journey to recover his wealth and procure gifts for his children. "At least the one thing I can take is this rose for my youngest one, Beauty. You have so many and they are so lovely. Please forgive me."

The Beast thought for a while and said, "I will spare your life if you will promise to bring me one of your daughters to marry. I am so lonely here, all alone. But your daughter must come willingly, in full knowledge of what she'll find. You may have one month to see if one of your daughters will come. If not, you must return yourself. And don't try to escape your destiny! I'll search everywhere for you if you don't keep your promise."

The merchant agreed, and asked permission to leave immediately. "No," replied the Beast. "You are not strong enough, and it is getting dark. In the morning I will have a horse ready for you, and a good breakfast. You may leave then. Don't forget your rose."

The next day, true to his word, the Beast provided the merchant first with a marvelous breakfast and then with a horse that seemed to fly back to the little cottage in the woods. The merchant was overjoyed to see his children after his six-month absence, but brokenhearted that he had no gifts for them. "Except for you, Beauty," he said. "Here is your rose. You have no idea what it cost!"

The kindhearted merchant could not bring himself to burden his children, and he told them nothing of his agreement with the Beast. When the month was over, however, and he prepared to return to the Beast himself, his children were bewildered. Why was their father leaving? At last, he told them the whole story of his journey, of the rose, and of the Beast's command.

"I must return to the Beast, now, to keep my promise. Remember that I love you." His heart was heavy and sad.

"Wait," cried Beauty. "I caused the problem with the Beast. He probably was mean because he is very, very lonely. I'll go to him with you, father."

At first the merchant protested, but Beauty was insistent, so they climbed onto the horse and returned to the strange palace. Beauty didn't feel afraid, although her father was deathly afraid that he was delivering her to her doom.

When they arrived, again, there was no one to be seen, and the palace was ablaze with light. After exploring many rooms, the merchant and Beauty found a table laden with a delicious supper, which they eagerly ate as the ride had made them very hungry. As they were finishing, the Beast walked in and said in his terrible voice, "Good evening, and welcome."

The merchant was too frightened to speak, but Beauty hid her fear and said, "Good evening, Beast."

At this, the Beast seemed pleased. He said to the merchant, "You lived up to your word. Tomorrow you may leave." In the morning, after a refreshing night's sleep and a scrumptious breakfast, the Beast took Beauty and the merchant into a room filled up with treasures of all sorts.

"Before you go, you must fill these two trunks with everything in here that you wish to take back to your children," the Beast instructed. And even though Beauty and the merchant piled jewels and clothes and toys and foodstuffs high into the trunks, they noticed that the more they put in, the larger the trunks became, and that there was always room for more.

"I don't know how I'm going to carry this back home," the merchant gasped, trying to lift one of the trunks. "The Beast has played a cruel trick on us. He knows they're too heavy."

"Don't doubt him so," replied Beauty. "Leave the trunks and let's go down to the courtyard."

In the courtyard were two horses, one already loaded with the two trunks, and the other saddled and ready for the merchant to ride. The merchant mounted the horse, sadly and somewhat apprehensively bade his daughter farewell, and, quick as a flash, was gone.

Beauty felt very sad and had no desire to explore the palace or talk to the Beast, so she went back to her room and fell asleep. She had a dream in which she was walking by a stream as a handsome Prince appeared. In a soft voice the Prince said, "Oh Beauty, things are better than you think. Don't be deceived by appearances. Try to see through my disguise and learn who I am. I love you deeply. Don't leave me till you have rescued me. Be as loving as you are beautiful. When you make me happy, you will be happy." The dream continued, and a lovely lady appeared. She said to Beauty, "Remember, see beyond appearances. See with your heart, not your eyes."

In the morning, Beauty thought about her dream. The Prince was wonderful, but what did he mean about rescuing him? And why did both characters tell her not to trust appearances? Beauty did not know. So she put the dream aside and spent the day exploring the palace. She found room after room of interesting things to do, look at, and play with, so that the time flew by until supper. After she had eaten the delicious meal that had mysteriously appeared, the Beast came into the room.

"Good evening, Beauty," he said, in his terrible voice. Beauty responded warmly to him, hiding her fear. How could he be terrible if he were treating her so well? They talked for hours about the things Beauty had discovered in the rooms, when suddenly the Beast asked, "Beauty, do you love me? Will you marry me?"

Beauty, frightened, did not want to anger the Beast by saying no. "What should I do?" she wondered aloud.

"Speak your truth from your heart," said the Beast.

"No, no, no!" cried Beauty. "I don't, and I won't."

"Then goodnight," responded the Beast, sadly. And he left.

Beauty went to bed and again began to dream. The Prince came to her and said, "Beauty, why are you so unkind to me?" That dream led to another and another and another, and the Prince was in all of them.

The next day, as Beauty amused herself by walking by the stream in the palace garden, she realized that it was the stream from her first dream of the Prince.

"Who is this Prince?" she wondered. "He must be a captive of the Beast."

Many weeks passed. During the day Beauty amused herself around the palace and ate the delicious meals that appeared whenever she was hungry. In the evenings, the Beast would come to her and, each time after they had talked, ask her to marry him. Beauty was no longer afraid of him; in fact, by now she was quite fond of him. But she could never say "Yes." She was not in love with him at all. She was almost more fond of the Prince who came to her in her dreams every night. The adventures were always different, but every night the Prince and the lovely lady told her not to trust appearances, and to see with her heart. She still did not know what they meant.

One day, when the Beast came to talk to her, Beauty was sad. "I miss my family so much. I want to see them."

"Oh Beauty, will you desert your Beast now? Do you hate me? Is that why you want to go away?"

"No, sweet Beast. I long to see my father and brothers and sisters again. Let me go for a month, and then I promise to return and live with you forever."

"I cannot say no. Go with my blessing, and take four trunks of treasures to them. But keep your promise and come back in a month, or it will be the death of me. To go and return you don't need horses." He gave her a ring. "Wear my ring on your finger, and simply turn it around one time to find yourself there or here. Please be true to your word, or I will surely die of grief."

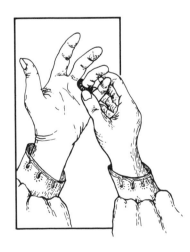

Beauty filled the four trunks and went to bed. She dreamed of the Prince lying sadly by a stream. "Why are you leaving me so that I might die?" he asked. "I'll be back," replied Beauty. "I'm just going to see my family. I promised the Beast I'd return to him." "Ah," retorted the Prince, "but will you really come back to someone so ugly?" Beauty faced the Prince squarely. "I care for the Beast. I'd never want to cause him pain. He is loving and wonderful. He can't help it if you think he's ugly. Without thinking, she twisted the ring around her finger as she dreamt.

Suddenly, she found herself waking up in her father's cottage. Her brothers and sisters were there, too, although they had become so accustomed to her absence that they did not seem pleased to have her back. During this month, Beauty never once dreamt of the Prince. Then, late in the month, she had one dream in which she was walking in the palace garden and came upon the Beast lying on the ground groaning. The lovely lady from her other dreams appeared and said, "You haven't kept your promise. Your Beast is dying."

Beauty woke in a panic, and knew she must return immediately. She hugged everyone goodbye and turned the ring on her finger.

In an instant she was back at the palace. Somehow, she found no pleasure in all the interesting rooms, and could hardly wait for her time with the Beast after dinner. But the hour for dinner came and went, and still no Beast. Beauty waited until, propelled by a sense of urgency, she found herself drawn to a remote part of the garden she had not yet explored. She realized she was by the river she had seen in her dream, and suddenly, there was the Beast, lying on the ground, groaning.

Beauty was terrified. "Oh no, dear Beast! Don't die! I never knew how much I loved you till just now." She stroked him tenderly.

The Beast spoke in barely audible tones, "Do you really love *me*, a Beast? I thought you had forgotten your promise."

"I do love you, Beast," whispered Beauty. She kissed his lips. "And I am ready to marry you."

Suddenly there was a flash of light, and it was not the Beast but the Prince who was lying by the river in Beauty's arms. Beauty jumped up in shock. She looked up and saw the lovely lady from her dreams walking toward her.

The lady smiled at Beauty and said, "The Beast was really a Prince who had been put under a spell by a wicked fairy who was jealous of his mother, the Queen. The only way the spell could be broken was if a maiden should willingly come to see beyond his appearance and consent to marry him."

So Beauty knew the meaning of her dreams. She and the Beast were married the next day, and all her family came to dance at the wedding. They lived happily ever after.

THE MANY MEANINGS OF BEAUTY AND THE BEAST

We recognize in Beauty and the Beast that almost all types of personal relationships are touched upon—male and female, parent and child, sibling, male only, female only, love, friendship, and, perhaps most importantly, one's relationship to one's true self.

If you reflect on the story as if it were a dream that you had, you can probably recognize aspects of yourself and your life. Whether you're a man or a woman, you can see in this adventure your journey toward creating truthful and rewarding relationships.

Consider Beauty, for example. Despite a destructive family situation, Beauty continues to love. The pattern of our relationships in later life is often set early by those within our family. And often, just as in Beauty's situation, there can be negative messages given to us about relationships early in our family experience. Beauty doesn't have a mother, and her brothers and sisters make many comments that could destroy her natural instinct to love and respect others. Even though her father is away much of the time, Beauty tries to fill in for her absent mother by her relationship with him.

When love speaks, the voice of all the gods—
Makes heaven drowsy with the harmony.

William Shakespeare

- We see her *faith in her own creativity* as she keeps putting her love forward in all kinds of situations, and a certain grace continues to protect her.
- Beauty's *absence of judgment* is put to a great test when she meets the Beast, but she penetrates the Beast's ugliness to see his inner beauty.
- This is true *precise observation*, because she ultimately sees beyond appearances, just as the mysterious lady (who probably represents her maternal influence as well as her divine aspect) and the Prince of her dreams keep urging her to do.
- And both Beauty and her father, too, *ask penetrating questions* about the nature of the castle, about the Beast, and about their own inner experiences.

Whether you are a man or a woman, you can also fully experience the Beast's plight. Who has not felt that his or her true nature is hidden within? Perhaps it is hidden by negative tendencies and the voice of judgment rather than by physical appearance, but it is hidden nonetheless. And this can be no less painful and frustrating than it was for the Beast. Yet, you can also see how the challenge of relationships can be overcome, even in a case such as the Beast's, by heroic application of the four tools.

YOUR PATH TO LOVE

Reread the story of Beauty and the Beast. As you do, think about how the story may indicate something about your challenge of finding relationships and love.

When you are ready, answer the following questions. Try to respond to every question, even if your answer is brief. Quickly write whatever comes to mind. Don't think about what you write, or worry about what others might think. Don't let your voice of judgment get in the way. Do this for yourself to begin to understand your challenge of relationship.

Love sought is good, but giv'n unsought is better.

William Shakespeare

1. Beauty's way of relating to people is influenced by her early experience in her family. What was the nature of your early experiences in life that affects your relationships with others now?

2. Beauty's father is important to her because he foreshadows her love relationship with Beast. The absence of Beauty's mother is important, and also her presence as the inner guide of Beauty's dreams. In your relationships, who is your main influence, your mother or your father? What is the nature of that influence? What pattern in relationships did you learn from your parents?

3. Beauty seems to be especially good at resisting outside influences, such as the gibes and criticisms of her siblings and the general social distaste for ugliness. To what extent do social pressures affect your relationships and how you care about yourself?

4. Beauty becomes lonely for her family and almost destroys the Beast and her love for him because of it. How much does loneliness affect your ability to love. Can you think of a time when your loneliness caused you to do something inappropriate about a relationship that may have had negative effects? What was that situation?

A joyful heart is the inevitable result of a heart burning with love.

Mother Teresa

5. To other people, the Beast's positive attributes and inner potential are masked by his ugliness. What is it that is masking your inner potential from the world and preventing you from revealing it?

6. Beauty's father seems to define his relationship with all his children, except Beauty, on the basis of what he can give to them. Do you ever feel that your role in your relationships is defined by your ability to give to others? What is the nature of those relationships, and what is it you are giving?

7. Beauty's inner guidance comes to her through repetitive dreams. Have you ever had messages come to you through repeated or singular dreams that helped you with love or relationships? Reflect on one of those dreams.

8. Do you think you are getting a repeated message in some way or another that you are ignoring? What is that possible message, and how can you be more attentive to it?

9. *The Prince inside the Beast was dying. He represents a treasure that we all have within us that has the potential of dying if we neglect it. What is a possible neglected treasure within you? What evidence do you have that you are neglecting it, and what can you do about it?*

A spring of love gushed from my heart
And I blessed them unaware.

Samuel Taylor Coleridge

10. *Beauty alone is able to see the inner goodness of the Beast. Is there anyone whose inner goodness you are not perceiving or appreciating? Who is that? What are the qualities you are not perceiving? How can you increase your ability to perceive those qualities?*

MAPPING YOUR PATH TO LOVE

Let's look now at your experience of the love and relationship challenge as a hero's journey. You will begin this assessment using visual and verbal logs like those in the last chapter. Illustrating and writing logs allow you to have a clearer sense of where you are. Then, months afterward, reviewing the logs can bring back an awareness and understanding of your journey that you may not have had at the time.

Visual Log

Before you begin, look at the example of our student, Melissa. Her visual log shows the call to adventure as a picture of a time bomb exploding her heart. "The first of many," she wryly told us. "In every relationship, there it was, just waiting to go off, and break my heart in two." Her initiation and pit section of her log symbolically showed a car accident that actually happened during a despondent period following a broken engagement. When it came to allies, she symbolically showed books and friends who supported her as a jumble of tiny hearts. And six months later, she met a man she eventually married. On her log she drew a large and vibrant heart representing herself and the quality of her marriage at the start of her everyday hero's journey.

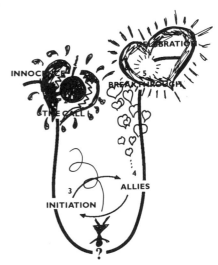

Now, draw your journey on the blank log provided. Your picture will look very different from Melissa's. It would not be unusual if you didn't have the sense of breakthrough that she seemed to have with her marriage. Just look at the shape of the path, and allow your hand to pick up whatever colored markers it is drawn toward, and to draw whatever sorts of doodles it wants. Enjoy yourself.

There is a passion for hunting something deeply planted in the human breast.

Charles Dickens

A Visual Travel Log

Where I am at the start of this journey

Date: _____

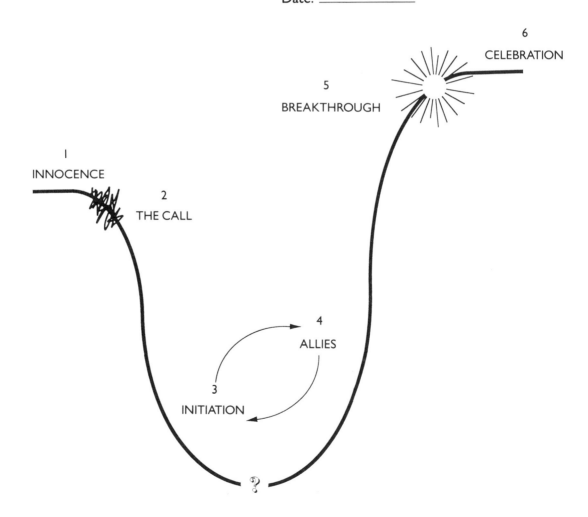

Verbal Log

Once you have completed your visual log, fill in the verbal log, using your visual log and whatever thoughts come to mind as you worked with the log. Then, after you have finished both of them, contemplate what the issue of love means for you now and where you are headed as you move toward the journey section.

Melissa's verbal log reflected this journey with different details. It implied the beginning of her realization of the call to deepen her relationship with her husband and carry that and her inner awakening of love out to all her relationships. Her assessment was that there was still much to be done as this chapter began for her. And it suggested the type of work she needed to do, and her strengths.

INNOCENCE (Feeling comfortable with my situation)

> Childhood—pretty mindless. Best friend, Susan.
> Lots of rejection from parents, but I didn't know any better.

THE CALL TO ADVENTURE (Identifying and recognizing my challenge)

> Moving. Lost touch with Susan.
> New relationship with Rusty in high school—first boyfriend. It exploded when he dumped me at graduation. ON MY OWN!!!

INITIATION (Really being tested)

> HA! Rusty was first of many. I had a monopoly on broken hearts.
> Why me? I gave a lot. It's not fair. Bottomed out.

ALLIES (Finding my strength and help)

> Women friends—commiserating. Where are the men?
> My "teachers"—learning I need to love *me* to have a solid, loving core.
> Nature—fills me with strength, calmness, hope.

BREAKTHROUGH (Reaching new awareness or resolution)

> Tied up with really trusting myself. Basically I really like *ME*.
> Tied in with my purpose: loving deeply on many levels. Love life, people in general, food (!), special people, me, my work. . . .

CELEBRATION (Returning home and being different)

> It's taken over 1/4 of a century, but I'm happy. Healthy relationship.
> My work is with people. Their response to me nourishes me.

A Verbal Travel Log

Where I am at the start of this journey

Date: _____

INNOCENCE (Feeling comfortable with my situation)

THE CALL TO ADVENTURE (Identifying and recognizing my challenge)

INITIATION (Really being tested)

ALLIES (Finding strength and help)

BREAKTHROUGH (Reaching new awareness or resolution)

CELEBRATION (Returning home and being different)

SEE WITH YOUR HEART

The last step of the preparation for your journey is to adopt a motto that will guide all your actions. This time, live with the advice of the lady in Beauty's dream and see beyond appearances as you *See with Your Heart*. If you can adopt this as your motto, you will find reward instead of difficulty in all of your relationships. People will become not only the most enjoyable but also the most valuable part of your life.

When you See with Your Heart, your vision goes beyond what your eyes can know. Your vision is not clouded by your voice of judgment. You see the good intentions of people; you understand their fears and yearnings. When you See with Your Heart, you can see the best in people, because you can see *their* hearts. You see love.

M. Scott Peck tells a story called "The Rabbi's Gift," which illustrates what your life can be like when you See with Your Heart.

An abbot of a dying Christian order with only five monks left, all over seventy years old, went to seek advice from an old rabbi visiting in the forest near the order's decaying house. They commiserate on the lack of spiritual awareness left in the world. They embrace, and as the abbot is about to leave, the rabbi says, "I have no advice to give. The only thing I can tell you is that the Messiah is one of you."

This was the rabbi's gift. Once the abbot reported this to the other four aged monks, each wondered who the Messiah was. "Is it brother Patrick? Is it perhaps brother Juniper? Could it be me?" They began to treat themselves and each other as if each were potentially divine. And people who happened to be hiking near the monastery were attracted by the extraordinary love and respect there. More and more people came to play and pray. Some began to talk to the monks. A steady stream of them asked to join the order. And it began to flourish once again.

To See with Your Heart means to treat others and yourself as if they or you were the Messiah in hiding. If you can disregard the outer messages that others seem to give to you (which come from the voice of judgment), as Beauty did with the Beast, then you will experience the joy of loving relationships.

When you see the best in people, they tend to behave the way you see them. As a speaker told one of our classes, "When I relate to the best part of a person and ignore all the other parts of that person, he starts presenting more and more of the best part of himself to me and any problem usually goes away." In fact, loving relationships are never without some kind of conflict, even in the best of circumstances. But when you See with Your Heart, there can be valuable conflict. It isn't against the person, but comes from compassion, from everybody being confident of their creativity and seeing it in others. People may have a disagreement, but when they are communicating from their hearts, the aim becomes to care and to truly see the other, not to win or have power over the other. As the poet Rumi says, there is a true gift in being able to see, with the heart, "beyond seeing itself."

Of course it does take courage, especially at first, to See with Your Heart. But remember that the Latin word for heart, *cor*, is the very basis of the word courage. We saw it in Beauty. If she didn't have courage, she wouldn't have accompanied her father back to the Beast's palace, nor would she have fared so well once she was there. Have the courage to take a tip from Beauty, who saw the best in the Beast, even though it was very difficult for her to do so.

Try seeing with your heart in all aspects, small or large, of your life for a week, and write about at least one of your experiences.

Often just paying attention to your experiences can help you on your journey immeasurably. Make a habit of taking time at the end of each day to make some notes in your journal or in the margins of this book. In this case, write something about what happens when you live by the motto See with Your Heart. Don't let your voice of judgment get in the way. Sometimes people feel they haven't really had any experiences and don't have anything to write, but the act of writing itself can almost always lead to insight. See what happens when you live with the motto See with Your Heart.

> *See*
> *With*
> *Your*
> *Heart*

―――――― THE JOURNEY ――――――

You have prepared for your journey to bring love into your life by reflecting on the parallels between your personal story and that of Beauty and the Beast. You have a visual and verbal log of your position on this path, and you've begun to live with the motto See with Your Heart. Now you are ready to continue the journey of introspection that can bring you to a new attitude and view of love.

SEEING WITH YOUR EYES, MIND, AND HEART

How do you see others? If you are like many people, you probably don't simply see with your eyes, but also with your heart and mind. The activity below helps you discriminate between these three ways of seeing: with your eyes—the observable facts about a person or relationship; your mind—assumptions, expectations, and judgments; and your heart—compassion for their experience as a human soul.

Think of someone for whom you care deeply. Write his or her name in the space provided. Recall a recent interaction you had with this person. Picture this person very clearly in your mind's eye. Notice what you think about the person. Observe how you feel about him or her in your heart. Now write down these impressions in the appropriate spaces. See someone you work with in these same three ways, and make notes of your experience in the second column. Do the same for yourself in the third column.

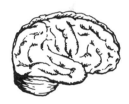

	Care About:	Work With:	Self:
My eyes see...			
My mind sees...			
My heart sees...			

What do you notice about these different ways of seeing? How does your impression of each person (including yourself) change according to the way you see?

As you interact with people, pay attention to the way you see them. If you seem to be only seeing with your eyes, or if you are bringing in your mind as a filter, consciously pay attention to your heart and try to see them through it. Seeing with your heart means that you need to check in with your caring and feeling center as you go about your daily business. Note your observations.

Love is the natural state when the choice for fear, guilt and grievances is unmade.

Willis Harman and
Howard Rheingold

HEALING YOUR HEART

If your heart feels full and rich, you are in luck. It should be fairly easy for you to be in touch with your loving center and to be "in love" as you go through your day. Remember, we are using this phrase "in love" to mean in a loving state of being that just *is*, and that other people will feel when they interact with you.

However, you may be like Melissa, whose visual log we discussed earlier. Until recently, she did not feel good about the state of her heart. Or you may be like Beauty, who had an unrewarding early family experience, or like the Beast, who was unable (until the very end) to get Beauty to see him for who he really was in his heart. Sometimes we are not loved back by another person, and we need to find ways to heal the overwhelming ache. We also need to find ways to be loving of ourselves.

If your heart feels heavy, sad, or wounded, you may find it difficult to see clearly with it, or to find a nourishing relationship. While this book can't change the facts of your past or your external situation, it can help you review how you see your past and change internally how you feel about your situation.

First of all, you can create the experience of having a heart that is alive and nourished. If you can do that even once, you will later find it easier to remember that feeling. A simple way to do this is to go to a place that feels good to you. Many people like to be in nature—in a backyard, in a quiet park, by a lake, under a tree, or wherever they can feel in touch with the pulse of life. If you cannot go outside, sit by a window and open it slightly so that you can feel the air. Close your eyes and imagine that you are outdoors in a place that you love. Use all your senses as you imagine or remember this special outdoor place.

Now do the following:

1. *Start by sitting or lying on the ground (in your imagination, if need be) and feel the energy of the earth underneath you. Let your body relax into the ground. Imagine that mother earth is supporting you and infusing you with life energy. Take a few minutes to do this. Feel the energy seeping into you.*

2. *Close your eyes and breathe deeply and slowly. As you breathe in, imagine that you are breathing in all the energies from the elements of nature that are in this place that you love. It may be the warmth of the sunlight, the cleansing power of the rain, or the rustling of the wind in the leaves that fills your consciousness and eases away any pain. It may be the unending pounding of the waves, or the smell of damp dirt. Close your eyes and spend about five minutes breathing it in, filling up your lungs with it, filling up your heart with it, filling up your head with it, filling your whole body with the healing energies of nature.*

3. *As you breathe in, think to yourself, "My heart is healed." At each point between your inhale and your exhale, take a moment to acknowledge that the healing is happening and you are becoming attuned with the eternal life-giving forces of nature. As you breathe out, feel yourself breathing out darkness and pain to make room for incoming light and joy.*

4. *After you have done this for a few minutes, open your eyes and look around. Do things seem softer or brighter or sharper or calmer or more alive? Most people find not only a sense of relief, but a slight difference in perception immediately after doing this exercise. Notice how your heart feels. Does it feel slightly, even if temporarily, better?*

This activity is a type of meditation, and is most effective if you do it once or twice daily. Each time it will be easier to stop paying attention to the pain in your heart, and to pay attention to the ways you can feel united with nature.

SAYING WHAT NEEDS TO BE SAID

Sometimes when there has been a problem in a relationship, you might be left with a lot of things to say to that person, or wish that they would say certain things to you. If you don't feel ready to say them, or

Only our love hath no decay;
This no tomorrow hath, nor
*   yesterday,*
Running it never runs from us
*   away*
But truly keeps his first, last,
*   everlasting day.*

John Donne

if it is not possible to have a conversation, it may be helpful to say them in private. This way, you are not left holding onto them, stuck like the Beast, under a spell preventing him from having a loving relationship.

The two figures in the illustration below have empty thought bubbles, waiting for words. Whom do you want to talk to? What do you want to say to that person? What do you wish they would say to you? Write a sentence in each bubble that captures the unsaid words that each of you has.

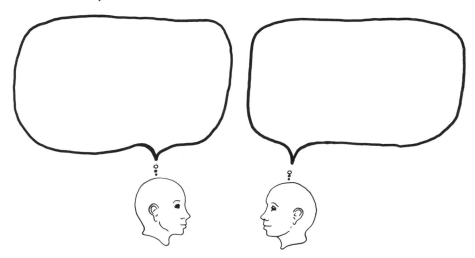

THE UNSENT LETTER

Is there anything else you want to say to this person? Take some stationery and write a letter to the person, saying everything you feel. Write the letter intending to communicate your true and deep feelings, not blaming, criticizing, or hurting.

Now decide whether you want to send the letter, send a revised version of it, tell the person some of it, or simply keep it as a secret expression of your heart.

SEE LOVE IN YOURSELF

Sometimes difficulties in relationships arise because we assume that our feelings for someone are somehow generated by them. We do not recognize that we create our own feelings. If you love someone, it is *you* doing the loving, not them. If you are angry at someone, *you* are the one with the anger.

An important step that you can take to See with Your Heart is to acknowledge that the love you feel for others comes from you, not from them. Beauty was a very loving person, as we saw by her care for her father, so her love for the Beast was very much part of who she was. You can begin to take responsibility for those feelings and for your actions, instead of assuming that the other person is somehow making you feel that way. This is the beginning of taking control of your relationships.

The concentration technique below helps you understand how you create your experience of the world. Its effect is greatest if you can close your eyes and have somebody else read it to you. Or you can read just a paragraph at a time, and then close your eyes and take some time after each paragraph to experience it.

Close your eyes and picture somebody you love very much. It could be somebody you have been away from for quite a while. It could even be somebody who has died and whom you are yearning for. Or it could be somebody you saw earlier today. Just seeing that person in your mind's eye as you experience deep feelings of love. See and experience this person in your mind and feel the full, rich feeling of love that you have. When you have done this to your heart's content, open your eyes and read the next paragraph.

Imagine that this person is about to arrive at the airport. You are waiting to meet them. They come out of the jetway and you throw your arms around each other. Feel and experience the love fully. When you are ready, open your eyes and go on to the last paragraph.

Keep reveling in the love that you feel, but now concentrate on the feeling and experience of love itself and drop the picture of the person from your mind. Continue to revel in the love and begin to recognize that this love is emanating from you, not coming from the other person. Feel the love welling up from your heart and filling you. Feel it spilling out of you and into the air all around you. What you are experiencing now is your own compassion in the form of loving kindness for yourself. Close your eyes and experience this for as long as you wish.

Seeing Yourself with Heart

Now that you have had some direct experience of the love within you and the power of your inner attitude, you can begin to see yourself with heart. Do this by simply sitting in front of a mirror so that you

As you allow the beloved to grow within you, you will discover a steadfastness to the spiritual journey.

Jean Houston

can gaze into your own eyes. Be comfortable as you do this. It's all right if you blink. If any thoughts arise, just let them go too as you continue to look beyond the surface level of your face and deep into your own eyes in the mirror. Keep gazing like this for as long as you wish. Try to push yourself as far as fifteen minutes to see what happens.

As you look through your eyes into yourself, notice who and what you see. You might want to do this mirror exercise immediately after the concentration exercise above so that you're experiencing your inner love, then open your eyes to gaze into yourself from your heart. You can also create a strong effect by placing a lit candle between your face and the mirror.

SEE OTHERS WITH YOUR HEART

Of course, it is not enough to see the love, creativity, and loving kindness only within yourself. You need to be able to see it in others, too. Experience this connection with others by really looking at another human being the same way you looked at yourself in the last exercise—from the heart to the heart through open eyes. You might prefer to do this exercise with someone with whom you feel comfortable—a spouse or a close friend.

In this concentration technique, you focus intensely on another person by looking into their eyes for about two minutes. You may initially find it very difficult to maintain eye contact for more than a few seconds. Remember that you're on a creative quest. You're a hero. Against all odds, push on calmly to make a remarkable connection.

The point is not to stare the other person down—it is to see them fully, to see all that they are behind their eyes. The eyes have been called the window to the soul. Look into this window and see what you find. Try not to have expectations. Whatever you find, keep looking at the person. Tiny observations can be important. (At the very least, you will develop your ability to make eye contact during conversations, and that will make you a better observer and a better listener.) Before you start, set a timer for two or three minutes.

Sit, facing the other person, with your feet flat on the floor and your hands comfortably in your lap. Take a few deep breaths together, slowly breathing in and out, so that your breathing is coordinated. For about the first minute, take ten slow breaths so that you begin to feel that you are resonating together. For the next couple of minutes, look into each other's eyes. Relax. The point is simply to be open to each other and allow the other person to look into your eyes while you look into theirs.

When the timer sounds, close your eyes briefly and savor your experience. What did you see? Did you have any experience of unity or diversity? Did you have any special feeling toward or impression of the other person? What thoughts went through your mind? Did your thoughts stop?

When the two of you open your eyes, tell each other what happened.

What do you think Beauty would have seen if she did this exercise with the Beast? Do you think she would have seen the Prince?

In fact, if there is a Beast in your life—someone you have mixed feelings about, or someone you love but also have negative feelings about right now—it might be helpful to do this exercise with that person. Then each of you can tell the other what you experienced.

Seeing Thou or Seeing It

Martin Buber, in his book *I and Thou*, describes two ways of reacting to other people. In I-It relationships, we see the other person as an object, as someone who meets our needs. In an I-Thou relationship, we see the great humanness in the other to such an extent that we recognize how sacred that other human being is. Of course, the latter sort of relationship is much more fulfilling.

Most of us can appreciate the *Thou-ness* of our intimate loved ones, but do we see it in people we don't know as well? Do you see the person working at the gas station as a Thou or an It? The bagger at the grocery store? Your boss? Your co-workers? Your subordinates?

Now that you've experienced your inner heart and have also been able to see into others with it, you can try approaching every relationship, however insignificant, with an attitude of I-Thou. Every time you interact with another person this week, silently acknowledge that you and they are honoring each other as divine human souls. So what if the waitress is rude? Silently love her and recognize her beautiful and fragile humanness. Notice what happens inside and in your interaction with her and others when you see them in that way.

Don't forget to have an I-Thou relationship with yourself! During this week, do not treat yourself as an object or an it. Love and appreciate your divine essence, however awkward or egocentric it might appear.

Notice what happens to you as you experience an I-Thou relationship with others and yourself for a week. Write down your observations below or in your journal.

Who Is My Teacher? What Did I Learn?

Everyone can be a teacher if you let them. In fact, when you relate to the world this way, those lessons in life come flooding in and you find yourself graduating from real-life Kindergarten to real-life University faster than you could have imagined.

You'll also find that the quality of your interactions changes, and, more importantly, the quality of your experience inside yourself changes. You find yourself almost automatically feeling more peaceful, compassionate, and loving. The inner experience of love seems to exist in its own terms. You are closer to being in love—in a state of being that is loving and, like Beauty's rose, draws other people toward it.

To get into a receptive frame of mind, write down a list of names (or description if you don't know someone's name) of half a dozen people you have interacted with in the last couple of days. Then, next to each name or description, write down what you learned from that person.

During this week, then, try to see everyone as a potential teacher. Be open to the lessons that might come your way as a result of being with this person. At the end of the day, reflect on your last twenty-four hours and note in the space provided or in your journal of those people who came into your life and what you learned from them. You may have learned something significant, or just had a small and subtle reminder. In any case, you will come away enriched from your contact with each human being in your life.

THREE STEPS TOWARD NOURISHING COMMUNICATION

Once you have experienced inner love and can see it in yourself and others, it is important to begin to communicate those experiences to others, although sometimes this can be difficult. Often in our communication we do not express our feelings, but instead talk about things, or what the other person should or should not do. Sometimes we don't really listen to the person who is talking to us. Sometimes we simply feel that we would be too vulnerable if we were to expose our feelings.

When this happens, true communication doesn't occur. In any relationship, real communication consists of two people listening to and *hearing* each other, and speaking their own truth when they respond. If we are rehearsing what we will say, or assuming we already know what we are being told, we are not really listening. If we say what we have prepared, or avoid our feelings and simply judge the other, we are not really making a connection with them.

Over the next several days, there are three things you can do to practice seeing with your heart in relationships. Make a point of doing each of these at least once every day, and notice what happens in your relationships.

To See Beyond Seeing Itself

We all know that we communicate nonverbally, but how often do we really pay attention to the body language or voice tone of the person with whom we are talking? How often do we pay attention to the way someone phrases what they are saying, or listen for what is *not* said, as well as to what is said? How often do we look into someone's eyes and see into their soul?

This week, take special care to see beyond seeing itself, the way Beauty saw beyond the appearance of the Beast. Try this first with yourself. Observe your own communication and way of relating with others. If you are alone, set your watch to beep every hour, and take stock of how you are dressed, how you are moving or sitting, the sorts of thoughts and feelings you're having. Notice how you interact in conversations and with others. Look in the mirror or catch your reflection in windows as you walk by. Who is that person there? What are you (seen as another person) saying about your relationship to yourself and others by the way you are?

Also, no matter whom you are with, observe *what* they are communicating in addition to the words they may speak. Honor and respect others and try to see what is behind everything they do. If they ask a question, for instance, see if you can determine what is behind that question. Try to put yourself in the other person's place as you observe them; see if you experience what it might be like to be in their body, dealing with the things in their life. Practice observing someone on the bus or walking in front of you down the street. Notice how much richer your experience of yourself or the other person seems when you fully see them.

Reflect Like a Mirror

A nourishing relationship is one in which we feel recognized and responded to, and in which we acknowledge the significance of what the other person contributes to the relationship. One way to encourage others to respond meaningfully to us is by letting them know that we truly see and understand them. You can do this by practicing what is called *reflective listening*.

In reflective listening, you don't just simply sit quietly while someone is talking to you. For all they know, you could be tuning them out, daydreaming, or preparing your next response when you do this. Instead, you let them know your impressions of what they are trying to communicate. (And, of course, if you are seeing with your heart, you are picking up much, much more than the words alone!) This way, they are assured that you are with them, and they can correct any misunderstanding as it happens. This is also helpful to the other person, because you can help them clarify their thoughts and feelings as they hear you reflecting back your impression of what they are communicating.

Do this by being like a mirror, which reflects back all the details without interpreting or changing them. Remember that this mirror reflects back unsaid feelings, as well as the words. Every so often (at the end of a thought, or every minute or two) gently rephrase what you are hearing—with your ears and heart—perhaps leading in with something like: "Let me see if I'm following. I think you're saying . . . ," or "It sounds to me like you're feeling . . . ," or "Ah, so you're. . . ."

When you're doing this, let your reflections come out naturally, as a fluid part of the conversation. It will hone your ability to see with your heart as well as enrich that relationship.

Speak from Your Own Heart

The third thing you can do in communication is to focus on expressing your own feelings. Recall that when the Beast caught Beauty's father stealing a rose, his first response was to roar that he would kill him. Her father did not become defensive, which would have further provoked the Beast. He simply told the Beast about his own situation and apologized for picking the rose. The Beast then rethought his initial response and confided that he felt very lonely. The two were able to eventually reach a resolution that worked out for both of them.

If a relationship is going smoothly, it is easier to speak from your heart. In a disagreement, the tendency is to become defensive, justify one's actions, blame the other person, or reiterate one's point rather than risk the vulnerability of speaking one's own truth. Yet when you think about it, you see that attempting to win at all costs often destroys the relationship. What a cost! Being able to stay centered in one's heart and communicate in a way that may seem vulnerable actually has the most potential for a win-win situation in which the goal is accomplished *and* the personal or professional relationship thrives.

The way to do this is to replace statements like, "You never . . . ," "You make me so . . . ," "You should . . . ," with statements like, "Right now I feel . . . ," "I need _____ from you. What do you need from me?" When you do this, you are entering into an honest dialogue with the other; you are inviting them to be an ally on this particular journey to resolve the current issue together. In the first examples above, you are trying to achieve power over them—which they will in all likelihood resist, and react by trying to achieve power over you. But when you speak from your heart, you make a connection with another in which you work together instead of trying to compete.

Try all three ways of improving communication—seeing beyond seeing itself, reflecting like a mirror, and speaking from your heart—and make notes for yourself about what happens. In any relationship in which we can do these three things, we feel safe to be who we really are and we can thrive.

SEEING LIKE A CAMERA

This last exercise of the journey section is an activity you can do with a friend that will let you both play a bit in the relationship and find out how well you are seeing with your hearts. You heart sees without interpretations, assumptions, and judgments. Your heart sees the hearts of those people it observes. This little game asks you to practice pure seeing, the way a camera sees.

Decide who will be the camera, and who will be the photographer. If you are the camera, your friend, as the photographer, will stand behind you. Your eyes are the camera lens and your right shoulder is the shutter button. Keep your eyes (the lens) shut until the photographer takes a photograph by tapping you on the right shoulder (pressing the shutter). You will then open and close your eyes, just as a camera lens does.

The task of the photographer is to walk you around by holding onto your shoulders; "set up the picture" so that different colors, textures, and shapes will be in your line of vision; and then take the picture by depressing the shutter button (your right shoulder). The photographer should take care not to bump or break the camera, of course. Assume there are twelve to twenty-four frames on this roll of film.

Your task, as the camera, is to be the perfect tool to record every detail of the picture exactly as it is, with no distortion. Trust that the photographer knows what he or she is doing. When the shutter button is pressed, the lens (your eyes) opens for less than a second, and the image in view is recorded forever on the film (your memory). All you

Chung-Kung asked about perfect virtue. The Master said, "It is when you behave to everyone as if you were receiving a great guest, employ people as if you were assisting at a sacrifice, avoid doing to others as you would not wish done to yourself; and have no murmuring against you from the public, and none in the family."

Confucius

have to do is to see what is in front of you, without any preconceived notions. Just notice what you see in each of the twelve to twenty-four pictures that you take. This is fun if you each take a turn to be the camera and the photographer, and then discuss the photographs you set up and took.

How does your seeing change when you see what *is,* without filtering your perception through your expectations? What sorts of details do you notice? Do the photographer and camera see the same thing in each picture? Did you catch yourself anticipating that you would see particular things? What sorts of things do you expect to see in relationships? In your relationship with this friend?

How do you become a better wife? By not trying to make him a better husband.

Gurumayi Chidvilasananda

This activity also lets you play with your friend, almost in the manner that children play. Children aren't afraid to touch each other, to play make believe, to trust each other, and to see with their hearts. Talk with your friend about these things, and about what it was like to play together. What elements of this play can you bring into your everyday relationships?

You can play this as a party game, too, with a number of pairs involved. Have fun with it, but at the same time don't forget to reflect on your experiences, especially in terms of what they tell you about seeing with your heart, the way you perceive yourself and others, and the way you are communicating.

——— THE RETURN ———

TO BRING LOVE INTO YOUR LIFE

As you follow your path, you, an everyday hero, have for your protection not a sword or a magic potion, but your very own heart. Beauty, her father, the Prince/Beast, and the woman in Beauty's dreams are all inside you, guiding you. In fact, they are also outside you, in the form of the people with whom you interact every day. Realize this, and listen to what these allies can tell you.

They have told you or reminded you of many things: that a loving relationship with yourself is fundamental to having loving relationships with others; that you have the power to heal your own heart; and that you have the ability to see with your heart and feel the difference.

Now you are returning with greater wisdom and compassion to the relationships in your life. How have you changed? How are they different? As an affirmation of the increased nourishment in your relationships, make your hero's declaration now. Complete the statements below and use colors and drawings to illustrate your heart.

Choose Love, Love!
Without the sweet life of Love,
living is a burden—as you
have seen.

Jalaludin Rumi

——— HERO'S DECLARATION———

My heart sees

This is my heart, in the center of me and all my relationships

I am

ONE DAY AT A TIME

Now that you have described your heart and your self, your challenge is to see with your heart in all your relationships, even with yourself, on a daily basis. Whether you are with a loved one, a colleague, a stranger, or simply by yourself, recall your path through these pages, and the wisdom of the characters from the story of Beauty and the Beast.

The test of your travels is to be different in the quality of all your relationships—to be in love all the time, and invite others in to join you there. This starts with your living just one day being fully aware of the love within you, becoming a being of compassion as you go about your daily life.

Start the next exercise when you have a fairly normal day ahead of you, and you know you will be able to get back to this in twenty-four hours.

Under the heading below, describe what you now know about your self in relationships. This sounds like a simple instruction. You just did this on the preceding page, didn't you? This time, however, approach the challenge in a qualitatively different manner. Don't intellectually think of love. Let a sense of feeling or knowing about the wisdom of your heart emerge intuitively. Then write it down or draw a symbol for it.

It may help you to take a few moments to close your eyes and remember the still, quiet place inside you.

Good management is largely a matter of love. Or if you're uncomfortable with that word, call it caring, because proper management involves caring for people, not manipulating them.

James Autry

My Heart Knows

Now do whatever you ordinarily would do for the next twenty-four hours, remembering to See with Your Heart. At this time tomorrow, open your workbook to this page again, and take a few minutes to again remember the still, quiet place inside you. Reflect on how you lived the last twenty-four hours.

What Happened?

What things did you do and what attitudes did you have that made your heart feel nourished? How much did you consciously pay attention to all your relationships in these twenty-four hours? How much were you on automatic pilot?

You are your own friend and you are your own enemy.

Bhagavad Gita

Jot down your observations of your day below. Be sure to include any notes to yourself about significant differences you noticed, and situations that caused you to forget about seeing with your heart.

Observations on Seeing with My Heart for One Day

FOLLOW-UP: MAPPING YOUR PATH FOR LOVING RELATIONSHIPS

Now you are ready to complete new visual and verbal logs of your travels. How are you different now? How are you different in terms of where you are on your own everyday hero's path toward bringing love into the relationship in your life?

Don't look back yet to the logs you first made when you started this chapter. Recall that the visual log is an intuitive mapping of where you are on your path of bringing loving relationships into your life. The verbal log is a chance to characterize this challenge in your life right now in terms of the six stages of the hero's journey: innocence, the call, initiation, allies, breakthrough, and celebration.

You can prepare the outline of the visual log and the six headings for the verbal log yourself on a sheet of paper or in your journal. Once your logs are ready, your task is to depict your current situation regarding relationships (including the events of the past week), first visually and then verbally. What happened for you? How did real events and people reflect the quality of love in your life this week?

Prepare yourself by taking a few moments to breathe and be still. Allow the memory of your journey over the last week to come into focus. Use colors to draw a figure or other symbols to represent yourself on your path in the expressive pictorial log.

After you have completed the visual log, take some time to contemplate it. What are your drawings and colors telling you about your search for love now? What does it remind you of about your journey on this challenge? When you are ready, make notes about where you are regarding the six stages of the hero's journey in your written log.

Once you are satisfied with your new visual and verbal logs and how they relate to each other, you can compare them to the ones you did earlier in this chapter and see what insights you gain about how you have met this challenge and what still needs to be done.

REFLECTIONS ON YOUR PATH

Now that you've completed this chapter and have worked on the loving relationship challenge for a week or so, write a letter to yourself about your experiences of this quest. This Week in Review can consolidate and legitimize your experience so far.

Keep this letter or statement as tangible evidence of your journey to this point. Then, if you feel the need to do some more work on this challenge in the future, or just want a boost regarding your bringing loving relationships into your life, you can go back to this review of what you just accomplished.

CELEBRATE!

How are you celebrating your completion of this journey? What are you doing to reward yourself for your successful journey? How are you making a public statement of your private changes? Make sure that in the days ahead you continue to acknowledge and celebrate your loving relationships.

7

Living Stress-free in the Here and Now

Trust no future, howe'er
pleasant
Let the dead past bury its
dead!
Act,—act in the living present!
Heart within and god
o'erhead.

H. W. Longfellow

You, as hero, must be ready to face challenge after challenge. Once one dragon is slain, another appears to test your mettle. You may have already experienced this in dealing with the challenges of the last two chapters. Once you have a sense of your purpose in life and begin to expand that to include your relationships, other challenges begin to appear. You find yourself filling up all your available time, deadlines appear, worry increases, and sometimes the stress becomes so great that even if you have found your purpose, you can't enjoy it because of the worry, frustration, and demands on your time.

Time is almost universally seen as overwhelming. Father Time, with his scythe, makes his annual appearance on December 31st to remind us of our mortality and the goals we haven't accomplished. The Roman god Janus, with his two faces looking toward the past and the future, certainly represents our culture's de-emphasis of the present.

In India, Kali, the goddess of time, is depicted as laughing at us. Even more, she holds a bloody sword and a severed head in her left hand, to remind us of the ultimate end of time for us in this life. Her other hand, however, makes a gesture of blessing that says, Do not fear. Time can be your refuge, if you live within it. You can make it your ally in your hero's journey. It can help you to conquer stress, fears, and worry.

But we are a culture obsessed with time. Our vehicles move faster and faster, to minimize what we think of as wasted time. Our science explores to the beginnings of time itself. And we have made the measurement of time one of our major industries. We can measure time down to the nanosecond or million millionth of a second! All around us digital watches beep on the hour, bells ring on the hour and quarter hour, huge digital signs flash the exact time at us from buildings as we rush along. Devices that save us time abound.

We add to this hurrying our own concept and experience of time in this culture. We tend to see the past as a huge receptacle of all the things that have gone wrong for us, the background that will never leave us, the times that were better than the present, and the security that we no longer have. The future, on the other hand, is seen as an enormous, forboding void in which all sorts of tragic and wonderful things can happen, full of deadlines and expectations—all of which take away our experience of the present.

In fact, the most dysfunctional aspect of our culture's view of time is that we are either dwelling on the past or worrying about the future; the present doesn't really seem to exist at all. The challenge of time and stress seems to come from this lack of the present in our lives. Procrastination, being too busy, never having enough time for ourselves, worry about deadlines, fatigue, inability to concentrate, frustration with a lack of efficiency, and fear about the future all arise from our inability to live in the present.

The more you expand the present moment, the more you experience the past and the future as being quite minor. By becoming absorbed in whatever you're doing (including, by the way, making assessments of past experiences and planning for the future), you'll be better able to meet the challenge of living stress-free in the here and now. When you live in the present, you are without stress, because the worries of the past and the future cannot touch you. And the more you live in the present, the more efficient and joyful your life becomes, so that the worries that can lead to stress disappear.

Consider your relationship to time. How often during the day do you check your watch? Are you the tortoise or the hare? Do worries or fears enter your mind while you are supposed to be doing something else? Do you feel overburdened? Do you ever feel that you have reached your limit, that you can't go on anymore, or that you are just too busy?

Take a moment right now to be in the present and consider how the challenge of time and stress comes into your life. Keep this in mind as you go through this chapter. See if your relationship to time and stress is altered as you become more absorbed in this challenge.

You gain strength, courage and confidence by every experience in which you really stop to look fear in the face . . . You must do the thing you cannot do.

Eleanor Roosevelt

The story we have chosen to begin your adventure is an old one of uncertain origin. It has appeared most recently as a Russian folktale, but like all profound myths and stories, it has been told in many forms and cultures throughout the centuries. It tells a truth beyond time and place. And that is why this tale is so appropriate as you start this path.

——— PREPARATION ———

The Peasant Who Married a Goddess

Once there lived, in the Kirghiz Steppes a peasant farmer named Ivor. While Ivor was warm and friendly to everyone he chanced to encounter, he was thought to be something of a simpleton by the people of the nearby village, for he spent virtually all of his time tending his field and was occasionally seen staring blankly across the plains into the distance. The villagers were sure that Ivor, even though he was lovable, would never amount to anything, and they chuckled good-naturedly whenever his name came up in conversation.

One day, after working hard on his land, Ivor sat in a meditative way (for meditating is what he was doing when villagers saw him staring over the steppes) at the edge of his field. Suddenly, he heard a barely perceptible sound, felt a warm presence, and smelled a scent of nectar that seemed to come from somewhere behind him. He turned and saw an enchanting being. When he glanced into her eyes he felt that he was experiencing a timeless dream. Her beauty and presence were more than he could cope with in his normal, waking mind.

"Good afternoon, Ivor," said the woman, breaking the spell and allowing Ivor to come back to consciousness. "My name is Kalisha," she continued, in a musical voice. "I am here to be your wife."

Ivor felt very confused; he had never considered getting married. He didn't think he had time for it. Keeping his little farm going was all he could do, wasn't it? And how could he cope with this woman who was so beautiful and pure that she could make time stand still? Even the most worldly and successful man in the village wouldn't be fit for her. Besides, where would they live? He had only a manger where he slept with his animals. And why was such a striking woman asking him to marry her? Was this some kind of trick? Was somebody trying to make him look foolish?

Ivor's mind raced with worries, reservations, and fears. His heart pounded with the possibility of the moment and he heard himself say, as he felt himself becoming lost in Kalisha's eyes, "Of course we will become husband and wife. Our wedding will be tomorrow morning at eleven, followed by a feast and celebration."

His words were made final by Kalisha's smile and the kiss she gave him. Sensing his confusion, she sweetly murmured that everything would be all right. And in that moment he knew that it would be.

And so they were married precisely at eleven the next morning. Their life together was idyllic. Ivor discovered that his land had a richness that hadn't been there before. All his concerns about what would happen if they got married were unfounded. He was able to build a house without neglecting the fields. In fact, everything seemed to thrive. His actions always seemed appropriate and he did everything at the right time. The villagers' opinion of him changed to one of admiration and respect, and they saw even more clearly his lovable nature.

For his part, Ivor could never get over his good fortune. He attributed everything that happened to fate, not to anything that he had done. He thanked God for this new purpose in his life and for his union with Kalisha.

Then one day certain prominent villagers, including Ivor and Kalisha, were invited to a banquet at the hunting palace of the nearby Prince. Little did they suspect how this dinner would drastically alter their lives.

The Prince was immediately drawn to Kalisha. He couldn't take his eyes off her. This soon became awkward for everyone. When he found out that she was married to Ivor, he was in agony. He had to have her for his own, but she was already married. What could he do? After the villagers left, the Prince called his ministers to him and old them of his dilemma.

One of his ministers had a plan. They would have a lottery among the villagers for the chance to do some tasks which, if completed in the allotted time, would give the winner the hunting palace, all of the palace's treasures, and its surrounding land. Of course, if the lottery winner did not complete the challenges in time, there would be an alternative reward, but neither the challenges nor the alternative prize was specified in the announcement. Naturally, the minister was scheming to fix the lottery so that Ivor would be the winner, the challenges would be impossible to complete, and the alternative prize would be a trip to the land of never-ending snow where Ivor would certainly die. This would free the Prince to marry Kalisha.

Ivor was too happy with his life to be interested in the contest, even though the whole village was thrilled by it. Kalisha loved Ivor with all her heart and knew that the Prince and his minister had evil designs. But she encouraged Ivor to enter his name in the lottery. So Ivor, who was completely unaware of the Prince's interest in his wife, entered the lottery, not with any interest in the riches that might come from it, but simply out of love for Kalisha.

On the day of the lottery drawing, Ivor was, of course, declared the winner. His first challenge was to separate by hand the chaff in a veritable mountain of wheat. He was to do this in one night. The villagers were stunned. They hadn't realized until now how much the Prince's infatuation with Kalisha had obliterated his humanity. To accomplish this task would have taken *all* of the village at least a week! And if Ivor was not successful, the villagers were told, then he would be sent to the land of never-ending snow.

For the first time in the years of their marriage Ivor began to worry, even though he did have faith that his wife would not have urged him to enter this contest if it would have brought him harm. As sundown of the appointed night approached, however, all sorts of frightening possibilities went through his head. He knew he wasn't very good at separating wheat from chaff in the first place. This was something his wife always did. And how could he possibly complete a task that would take many others a much longer time to do? And if he didn't complete the challenge, would he ever see Kalisha again? His hands literally began to shake in fearful anticipation. And if his hands were shaking now, what chance would he have of completing a challenge that needed such steady, sure work?

Just as he was burrowing deeper and deeper in such thoughts, Kalisha kissed him gently on the head and said, "My dear Ivor, everything will be fine if you'll just concentrate on the task at hand. Become absorbed in every grain of wheat, every hull, every speck of dirt, every moment as you do your task, and all will be perfect."

She spoke the truth. Ivor dutifully reported to the palace, where he was shown to the enormous vault that contained the mountain of wheat. They locked him in, and Ivor, remembering the words of his wife, set to his task. At the break of dawn, when the Prince's guards opened the vault again, they found Ivor with two piles—one of gleaming golden wheat and the other of chaff. In fact, Ivor had so much time that he was able to make for himself a bowl of wheat before the guards came in.

The Prince and his minister were infuriated. But they had another challenge in store for Ivor. In one night he was to clean and process a huge pile of raw cotton and then make it into uniforms for the palace guard.

Again Ivor had doubts and fears. Maybe a whole team of workers could accomplish this, but he didn't even know how to sew! And again Kalisha kissed him on the head and told him that everything would be all right if he could just put everything out of his mind and concentrate solely on his task.

He followed her instructions this second time, and when the guards came to get him in the morning, all of the uniforms were hanging along the length of the wall of the huge inner vault of the palace.

There was still another challenge for Ivor, but this was to be the last one. What was it that the Prince and his minister could devise that could put Ivor into jeopardy? Since he had completed the first two challenges with such skill, the villagers reasoned, the final challenge would have to be very difficult indeed to prevent him from winning the hunting palace, its treasures, and the surrounding countryside.

The challenge for Ivor was beyond anything anyone had imagined. He was to build an entirely new hunting palace overnight on a remote plain using materials that had taken the Prince's forces weeks to assemble. He would have no equipment, only his own hands and wit.

Despite his success in the first two challenges, Ivor felt this was too much. His mind raced with possibilities, all of them dire. The strain was too much for him; he felt that he would have to give up even before trying, and hope for the best in his voyage to the land of never-ending snow.

Once again, Kalisha kissed Ivor on the head and urged him to go ahead, saying, "You've done so well. So much time has passed. There is just one more challenge and, although it seems enormous, if you just concentrate again on exactly what you are doing, if you stay absorbed in the moment and don't let any thought of any other thing enter your mind, everything will turn out for the best."

Late in the afternoon before the night in which Ivor was to meet his third challenge, he was brought to the far plain where he saw all of the materials ready for building. There were stones of all shapes and sizes, finishing pieces for the turrets, enormous piles of gravel and cement, huge slabs of marble, tall stacks of lumber, paints and dyes for murals, cloth for tapestries, metal in various shapes and sizes, and many objects, whose purpose he didn't know, laid out in the vast array before him.

He began to have a glimmer of doubt as the shadows of the evening began to lengthen and the guards left him to his challenge. How could he do everything in front of him in the allotted time? Even if he had time, would he have all the skills needed to build a palace? Why had this wife, whom he trusted so much, put him in this position?

"We had such a good life," he thought. "Why did she urge me to do this?" And then he had a thought that had never occurred to him before: "Maybe she's trying to get rid of me. Maybe she'd prefer to be married to the Prince. He already has a palace and a whole lot more land than I do."

The instant he had that thought he remembered his wife kissing him

on his head and telling him to concentrate only on the task at hand. The memory of her kiss and words were so vivid that he seemed to reexperience them with all his senses and to the depths of his soul.

Then he fell into a trance. He was completely aware of everything that was going on, but it was as if he were an observer of his own actions. The full moon became much brighter, and he could see with tremendous clarity. With greater concentration, speed, and power than he ever thought he possessed, he started digging a hole for the palace foundation. He was so focused on what he was doing that for the rest of his life he would be able to describe in great detail every handful of dirt and every rock and root he came across that night.

He continued with godlike precision, appropriateness, power, and blinding speed throughout the night. All the while he observed himself working with detachment, joy, unity, and a kind of energy that were totally new to him. Somehow, it seemed that he was in union with his wife, Kalisha, in a way that he had never known. It seemed that during that time he established a connection with everything and everybody in the universe. He was participating in a flow that involved giving and taking energy from everything and everybody around him.

It became clear to Ivor that it didn't really matter whether he finished the palace in the allotted time or not—what *was* important was the process of building it. His trivial ideas about his and Kalisha's life together, about his wife being interested in the Prince, about the difficulties of building this palace in one night (much less those of meeting everyday challenges) were meaningless to him now.

And, of course, he did build the palace on time. The Prince and his ministers, who had exposed their cruel natures to the villagers, were forced to leave. He and Kalisha became rulers of the province. The kiss of Kalisha, who actually was a goddess, resulted in his transcending the limitations set up by the Prince, and also allowed his own divinity to shine through. And no matter what he did, he lived in the awareness that every moment is eternity and that eternity, with all its bliss, could be found in each moment.

THE MANY MEANINGS OF
THE PEASANT WHO MARRIED A GODDESS

This story has survived for so long because it says that, no matter in which age of history you are living, you have a powerful grace strengthening you when you put forth your full effort in whatever you do.

The story is a model of the hero's journey. At the beginning, Ivor is in a fairly stable period of his life. He tills his fields, stares out over the plains and, even though he is regarded as a simpleton by the villagers, is also loved by them. The appearance of Kalisha sets him on a path that pulls him into the pit of the challenges. His ally, Kalisha, then sees to it that he eventually comes to a new relationship with time, without stress; he becomes godlike in his relationship with the universe. Notice, too, that many small hero's journey events—such as his first meeting with Kalisha and each of the three tasks—occur throughout the story. Both Ivor and Kalisha use all four of the everyday hero's tools. They demonstrate *faith in their own creativity* when they come together and are married, and as they meet each new challenge. This is particularly so each time Kalisha assures Ivor that everything will be all right, and when Ivor reexperiences this in a flash of recognition before the final and most difficult challenge of building the palace.

Ivor uses the second tool for creativity, *absence of judgment*, when he makes a breakthrough, as when he abandons his confusion and decides to marry Kalisha, and in the calm attitude he adopts for each of the tasks, undertaking them without judgment, and in a state of grace.

Ivor and Kalisha use *precise observation* as the primary tool to meet the challenge of living stress-free in the here and now. It is only by total concentration and focus on each challenge that Ivor is able to move into that higher state that allows him to succeed and also see a higher purpose for his life. His precise observation starts with a broad view of the situation, such as his assessment of all the materials for the palace. From there, he moves into more focused activity.

At many points in the story Ivor asks *penetrating questions.* These are only the tip of the iceberg for him. Often his questions seem to come from his inner voice of judgment. But the questions follow his fears or worries to their source and then there is an explosion of truth. You can see how dramatically the questions serve him in his challenge of building the palace—his breakthrough comes when he asks the most painful of all questions for him: Is Kalisha untrue? Clearly, it is important to use observation and questions to go to the source of whatever strong experiences you have, even those of anger or fear. When you use questions to probe those experiences, you break through them to discover your own power and compassion at their base. However, if those dragons aren't faced, if those challenges aren't met, your life is indeed without meaning.

To dare is to lose one's footing momentarily. To not dare is to lose oneself.

Soren Kiekegaard

YOUR PATH TO LIVE
STRESS-FREE IN THE HERE AND NOW

When you do something, you should burn yourself completely, like a good bonfire, leaving no trace of yourself.

Shunryu Suzuki

Answer each of the questions below. Work quickly and easily, getting into the flow of creativity just as Ivor got into it when he was building the palace. Write something for each question whether or not it initially seems relevant to you. Don't worry about it; just do it. You can always go back and add answers or edit what you have written later on. Remember, no one needs to see what you have done here; it is just for you.

1. Ivor stops working to sit quietly and meditate. Do you take enough relaxing breaks from your work? If so, what is their effect? If not, describe a work situation coming up for you soon and write down exactly what you might do to take a meditative break and what effect it could have.

2. Ivor is faced with seemingly impossible tasks to be completed by impossible deadlines. What are the seemingly impossible challenges and deadlines in your life right now?

3. Have you ever had an experience like Ivor's when he surveys the overwhelming collection of materials and considers his challenge of building the palace? What is one recent experience when you felt overburdened? How did you feel? What did you think? What happened?

4. If you consider the story as a dream, can you see the Prince as an aspect of yourself that sabotages you with a desire for having or being what it is not? What might be the Prince within you? Describe the part of you that causes stress in this way in your own life.

5. *In dealing with the challenge of time and stress, do you have an ally such as Kalisha? Is there an aspect of yourself that pushes you toward who you are rather than toward who the world thinks you should be? What is this aspect like, and when has it surfaced? Consider whether you have any friends or relations like this—completely supportive of you and on your side. Or do you also experience some higher power as your ally? Write about these various forms of Kalisha in your life.*

6. *What keeps you from being in the state you wrote about in the last question more often?*

7. *Ivor was not very concerned by other's opinions, except when he made comparisons. He compared himself with others when he was confused about marrying Kalisha and when he confronted each challenge. To what extent does comparing yourself with others cause stress? Think of a particular incident when you were bothered by a deadline or stressful situation. Do you recognize now that it had to do with thinking about your own feeling of inadequacy in comparison with someone else? Describe it.*

8. *Ivor became confused and worried when Kalisha appeared to him, even though this was the most positive event that had occurred in his life. Do you find yourself worrying when opportunity presents itself? Look back at an incident in your life that was like this. What happened? How did the situation work out? What could you do to decrease fear and worry if a similar situation occurs?*

9. *It is said that "God helps those who help themselves." Kalisha blessed Ivor and instructed him to concentrate. He therefore worked with a blessing but also with his own effort, absorption, and skill. Have you ever felt similarly blessed and absorbed in meeting a challenge and had success beyond what you could have imagined? Describe this. To what do you attribute that extra energy?*

10. *Ivor is transformed from a peasant to a god in the challenge of time and stress. In what sense can you see yourself as both a peasant and god in this challenge? Describe these peasant-like and god-like qualities.*

Now that you've answered these questions, consider your own path towards living stress-free in the here and now. Have faith that you can, like Ivor, transcend the seeming limits of time and stress, and don't forget to pay attention to the story that is playing out in your life. Get rid of your judgments and expectations that the story has to have a particular ending, and see how a better ending unfolds.

MAPPING YOUR PATH TO LIVING STRESS-FREE

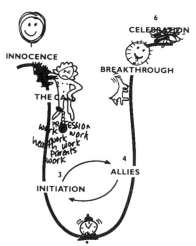

Now assess your life experience with visual and verbal logs. First, look at Melissa's visual log. When she looked at her drawing she gasped, "Oh, I get it! I'm the one that's holding me back by holding on to the call! I really need to let go of that." She had drawn herself holding tightly to the symbol for the call to adventure, which she described as her work responsibilities. In the drawing she looks as if she's holding on for dear life and almost refusing to let go. Her main source of relaxation was to play with her dog, and you can see how important that was to her because she placed the dog at the breakthrough. The smiling faces, she explained, represented freedom from stress, a condition she could only remember and look forward to again. Interestingly, while Melissa thought she knew what and why she was drawing, it wasn't until after that its significance jumped out at her.

Visual Log

Now, draw where you are in your journey. Your picture might look very different from Melissa's. You may be further along the path with this challenge. Totally different images may come for you. Just look at the shape of the path, and allow your hand to pick up whatever colored markers it is drawn to, and draw whatever sorts of doodles or pictures it wants. Be in the present moment as you draw, and enjoy yourself as you chart where you are now on your path to meeting your challenges of time and stress.

Time is but the stream I go a-fishing in.

Henry David Thoreau

A Visual Travel Log

Where I am at the start of this journey

Date: _____

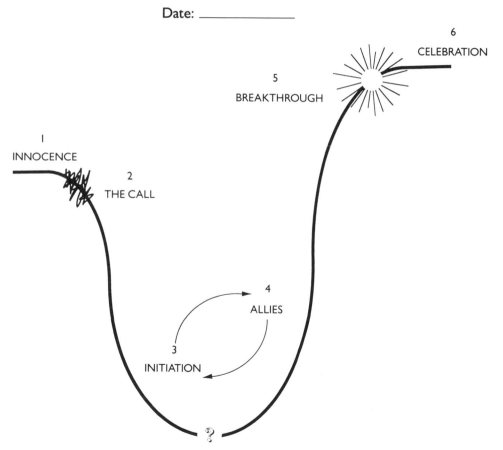

1
INNOCENCE

2
THE CALL

3
INITIATION

4
ALLIES

5
BREAKTHROUGH

6
CELEBRATION

Verbal Log

Now you are ready to write down where you are in the six phases of the hero's journey.

Melissa's verbal log clarifies the images she portrayed in her visual log.

As if you could kill time without injuring eternity.

Henry David Thoreau

INNOCENCE (Feeling comfortable with my situation)

Can't remember. When I first started working. Or when I was a kid, maybe.

THE CALL TO ADVENTURE (Identifying and recognizing my challenge)

Professional track.
Feeling I need to earn my living.
People offering me more work.

INITIATION (Really being tested)

Aaaaak!!!!! I'm in it!
Weighted down by all my work and other responsibilities.

ALLIES (Finding strength and help)

My dog. I relax and play with her.
Walking in the woods.
Meditating, when I remember to.

BREAKTHROUGH (Reaching new awareness or resolution)

When I don't feel so *compelled* to do so much!
A rich sugar daddy.
Actually—it's about simply trusting that things will work out and I don't need to be such a workaholic.

CELEBRATION (Returning home and being different)

Leading a balanced life.
Knowing how to slow down.
Meditating with more regularity.

Melissa already knows that she would do well to take more time to meditate, as Ivor did at the start of his story. Your challenge may be similar, or you may see completely different things. Remember that there really isn't any one particular way of filling in this log. Use it as an opportunity to jot down what's true for you about time and stress in your life. The words you use might expand on your pictures in the visual log, as Melissa's did, or they may be quite separate. This is something you do for yourself, so use it in a way that is useful for you.

Do diddle di do
Poor Jim jay
Got stuck fast
in yesterday.

Walter de la Mare

A Verbal Travel Log

Where I am at the start of this journey

Date: _____

INNOCENCE (Feeling comfortable with my situation)

THE CALL TO ADVENTURE (Identifying and recognizing my challenge)

INITIATION (Really being tested)

ALLIES (Finding strength and help)

BREAKTHROUGH (Reaching new awareness or resolution)

CELEBRATION (Returning home and being different)

JUST DO IT!

For the next week, while you work on the challenge of living stress-free in the here and now, remember the motto, Just Do It! As Ivor was able to clear his mind and trust that his actions would be right, you can act from faith in your own creativity, destroy judgment, and live with total clarity and awareness of the present moment. As Kalisha told Ivor, concentrate on whatever is in front of you to do. Live in the present. Forget about the past and have no worries for the future.

To do this, clear your mind by taking several deep breaths, all the way into your belly. Fill up your rib cage, your chest, all the way up into your shoulders. Pause between inhalation and exhalation, and then easily let each breath go, starting from the bottom of your belly, all the way up to the top of your shoulders.

Or stretch, meditate, take a walk, exercise. Take a nap, or flip a coin. Whatever you do, Just Do It! Begin with small things, such as getting out of bed, writing a letter, or starting work on a project. Get in the flow of what you do. Don't be concerned with success or failure. Just act in each situation with your best ability.

Empty your mind of worry over what might go wrong, is going wrong, has gone wrong, or will go wrong. Remember, as Shunryu Suzuki said in *Zen Mind, Beginner's Mind*, "If your mind is empty, it is always ready for anything; it is open to everything."

If you find that you can't free yourself from worry, be disciplined about it. Set aside some time each day to really and truly worry. During the rest of the day, when worries come up, simply say to them: "Go away. You may come back and really bother me later." Quit worrying until then. Once you empty your mind you can practice the Zen art of being here now, with a still mind, without chatter.

Below write your challenge of time and stress in the form of a question. Understand that the answer is hidden within your question. Write a paragraph about it—just let your hand pick up a pen and write, as if somehow doing it by itself. What seeds for an answer do you see in what you wrote? Write your question and your response right now. Just Do It!, without thinking of all the reasons why you can't.

To remind yourself of this challenge, make a copy of the motto Just Do It! and put it where you are likely to see it. Write a few notes every day in your journal about what your experiences were with this motto. Apply it to your quest to meet the challenge of living stress-free in the here and now, as you work with the exercises in the journey section. Remember, if any of the exercises don't quite fit, change them so they are valuable for you, and Just Do It!

Just
Do
It!

——— THE JOURNEY ———

As the story of Ivor begins with him living his daily life, you will start by looking at your daily life. What are the things that fill your waking consciousness? What people, projects, activities, responsibilities, and situations have been taking your energy and attention in the last week or two?

People

Projects

Activities

Responsibilities

Situations

To what extent do you feel that you have been fully focused on each of these? To what extent have you felt like a juggler with too many balls in the air, so that you were not able to address all of these with the kind of care and attention you might like?

Take two colored pens, one in a color you like, the other in a color you don't like. With your favorite color, circle the items on your list that you had enough time for and have not felt stressed about. With the other color, circle those items that you have not had enough time for, or that have caused you stress in some way.

What do you notice as you look at your list? Don't judge yourself if there aren't enough circles of one color or are too many of another color. Simply observe how you've represented your current state of affairs.

STAND AND STARE

At the start of the story, Ivor takes a break from his work and stares off across the plains in a meditative frame of mind. Taking this time to detach from his work to stop *doing*, and simply *be* for a few moments, was essential to Ivor's happiness. Poet William Henry Davies puts it this way:

> What is this life, if, full of care
> We have no time to stand and stare,
> No time to stand beneath the boughs
> And stare as long as sheep or cows.

What is our life if we, too, do not find time to do this? We have all found ourselves so caught up in the things we have to do that—even though we know better—we forget to let ourselves *be*. When this happens, we find that instead of becoming more efficient or getting more work done, we actually become less efficient and more stressed. We find that when we don't take time for ourselves, to rest our inner resources and "stand and stare," we are quickly depleted of our energy and clear-headedness.

In recent years, Western society has become aware of the wisdom (long appreciated in the East) of taking time out to experience our connection to the eternal qualities of the world. Transcendental meditation has entered our culture as a tool for stress reduction, and benefits many people who don't consider themselves particularly spiritual.

You don't need to know how to practice a complex system of meditation to reap the benefits that Ivor and modern-day meditators have. You simply need to remember to take some quiet time to replenish your reservoir of calm.

For the next week, commit yourself to taking at least fifteen minutes a day to empty your mind of its chatter, judgments, thoughts and oughts, and simply stand and stare. You might do this out in nature, like Ivor. If thoughts come into your mind, simply observe them as an interested witness and watch them pass on through. Just *be* for fifteen minutes. How long is it since you took time just to be; to pay attention to subtle nuances like your breathing or the sound of silence; noticing your thoughts without trying to follow them? It's easier to do this if you fill your mind with something that leaves no room for your thoughts.

Try focusing on your breath, perhaps breathing in for a count of seven, holding your breath for a rapid count of three to feel that point between breaths, and breathing out for a count of seven, holding again, and breathing in again. Let the monotonous numbers and the sound and feel of your breath fill your consciousness. It's also often easier to stop thinking if you close your eyes; this cuts off visual stimulation and makes it easier to bring breathing to the front of your consciousness.

If thoughts and worries still flutter around your mind, imagine that as you breathe in, the air coming in is tiny dots of golden light. Imagine these particles of bright light filling your lung cavity and spilling over, filling the area inside your skin. With every inhalation, imagine the dots of light coming in through your mouth or nose, filling you up inside, and flowing out through your fingers and toes and the top of your head. Keep breathing this way. If you notice tension or a negative thought, imagine that it is made of a cluster of tiny black dots. As the breath comes in, the golden dots of light wash over the black clusters of dots, disintegrating and dispersing them. Keep doing this; breathing in the golden dots of light, letting them fill you up, flowing out with the debris from the black blocks leaving you a being of light and energy. Once you feel yourself full of golden light, continue to breathe like that for a few minutes, feeling the vibration and energy of the light nourishing you on deep levels, beyond words. When you feel it's time to open your eyes, do it slowly, bringing yourself back into the here and now, but changed. Bring yourself back as a radiant being of

light who is energized but calm, one who finds it effortless to transmute anything that interferes with this light into tiny dots of black dross that wash away as the light pours through you.

A variation of this is to lie on the floor while music plays loudly. This works best if you play harmonious or classical music with no words, and roll up your sleeves or bare your feet so that your skin is exposed. Listen to the music with your whole body, allowing it to filter into you through your skin, and to fill up your body. Feel it as if it is inside you, and you are the music. Feel the music physically overcoming any thoughts or aches and pains. When the music stops, feel the calmness and energy that are in you. Keep that awareness as you bring yourself back to your daily life.

The Elasticity of Time

There is a paradox here. You won't experience it fully until you have given this experiment a trial of several consecutive days. You will notice that even though you are taking time out from your hectic day to practice stillness, your increased energy and clearheadedness will allow you to have time to accomplish more things and have more rewarding interactions with people. What you are experiencing when this happens is the elasticity of time.

It may sound funny to think of time as elastic, but you have probably already experienced it in your life. There are times when minutes seem to take hours because nothing is happening or whatever is happening seems to dull. Then there are other times when you become so absorbed in what you are doing that hours seem to go by in minutes. Both of those cases demonstrate the elasticity of time. You experience *timeless time,* in which you control the boundaries that are put upon it.

This phenomenon occurs when you take time to "stand and stare"—to recharge your batteries—and later find that you can accomplish a great deal more in a given period of time than you thought possible. In one workplace, for instance, employees were asked to spend a short time each day doing nothing—their productivity went up eighty percent.

A key for living without stress is to know about timeless time, and to have faith that you can indeed have the experience of more hours in a day by taking time out. You need to Just Do It, however; don't just read about it or think about it.

CLARIFYING YOUR STRESS

Once you have established a way to tap your own creative resources and find your inner place of peace, you can clarify the challenge of time and stress for yourself and consider the types of action you might take.

Ivor was able to experience his creative source in the present moment to complete three types of tasks. Sorting the wheat was painstaking, detailed work he needed to do simply to survive, much like our own routines, which can feel like drudgery. Making the uniforms involved doing something for others—sewing the clothes that would identify the palace guard as a social unit. Building the hunting palace was an immense, open-ended project with no set rules or formula for how to succeed—a project of such overwhelming scope that it would seem daunting to anyone.

When you think of the things you have to do in your life, what aspects of these three types of tasks cause you stress? Write, in the table below, a few words to describe the current tasks in these three categories that cause you stress.

Routine Work	Doing Things for Others	Huge Projects

For each item, there are also (as Rochelle Myers suggests) three possible ways to reduce the stress. You can handle some stressors by meeting them head-on. You can simply live by the motto Just Do It! Ivor took action on his tasks without knowing whether he would succeed. His realization was that worrying about the outcome didn't help, so he might as well do what he could and give it his full attention so as to experience it fully. You can learn to resolve some stress-provoking aspects—such as getting your car fixed or cleaning your room—by Just Doing It in this way. To make it easier to meet them head-on, you might identify small steps to take, or make a public commitment to someone, telling them that you will deal directly with this challenge.

Some items on your lists may require more information or greater insight before you can resolve them. Usually these involve interactions with other people, such as co-workers or family members. Or they can have to do with seemingly large life decisions, such as career or relationships. What do you need to know in order to Just Do It and meet these challenges? Remember the tools of precise observation and penetrating questions. Find out what's really going on, and question, question, question until you find a way to Just Do It!

You may not be able to resolve all your challenges by direct confrontation or greater insight. Some may require you to change your

JUST DO IT!

ISSUE	Meet head on	Gain greater insight	Change perspective

perspective. For instance, if you are in what appears to be a no-win situation, try to revise your perspective, and figure out how to win from it after all, just as Ivor was able to change how he viewed his three tasks and thereby succeed.

Select the most pressing issues from your lists. On the chart, write down what you need to do to meet the challenge of living stress-free in the here and now by confronting each issue head-on, gaining greater insight, or changing your perspective.

Play around with your lists. You may find that each issue is best dealt with by just one of the three types of action steps. On the other hand, a combination of approaches may seem reasonable. Keep this in mind as you do the exercises for each of the three approaches.

Meeting Head-On

Experiencing the elasticity of time by taking time out to "stand and stare" is one way to live in the present, without stress. There are other ways, too. When Ivor approached his three tasks, he did so with grace—with the ability to be fully involved in each challenge as he was meeting it. He was so engrossed that nothing else mattered. And he Just Did It! Have you ever been so involved in doing something that it became the only thing that was important for that moment? Have you ever approached a challenge with such passion that you felt at one with it, as if you were in timeless eternity? How can you recreate that experience with your current situation?

Take one of the issues you wrote about earlier that could be dealt with by meeting it head on—by just doing something about it. Rewrite this issue below or draw a picture of it.

If you feel overwhelmed by a mountain of obligations, as Ivor was when faced with the mountain of wheat, one simple way to get back on track is to sort out what you need to do. You can think of this as identifying all the separate small pieces of wheat that constitute the mountain. Then you can literally move this mountain one small piece at a time. It's much less daunting this way. Once Ivor approached the task piece by piece, he was able to separate each grain from the chaff. In fact, what had once been intimidating became so engrossing that he was carried away and went further than the task at hand, even making himself a bowl of wheat—all in the time-frame that earlier had seemed too short for the job.

What are the individual components of the issue you wrote or drew above? If you were to break this issue into very small, discrete steps, what would they be? You might think of this challenge as a mini hero's journey. The preparation involves assessing the situation now, identifying where you want to go with it, and committing to answer the call to adventure. The journey itself consists of your initiation and the challenges to stay on the path, with the help of your allies in the form of other people and higher powers, as well as your own inner strengths and abilities. Your breakthrough will be your resolution, and the celebration, of course, will be the return at the end of the journey, to a place where you feel once again calm, knowing that you have accomplished your mission.

Break this stressful situation down into smaller parts now, identifying specifically what constitutes each phase of your journey.

INNOCENCE (What is the initial situation?)

CALL TO ADVENTURE (What needs to be resolved?)

INITIATION (What is the sequence of *specific*, small steps to meet this challenge?)

ALLIES (What and who are your inner strengths and supportive people?)

BREAKTHROUGH (What is your goal or resolution?)

CELEBRATION (What will it be like after you've succeeded?)

Once you have recognized your situation, and until it's resolved, you are in the initiation phase. The way to pass your initiation is to take each of those small steps, one at a time.

The steps you just identified are concrete actions you can actually take to confront a real challenge that causes you stress. Sometimes you might plan particular actions, even quite plausible, small steps like the ones you wrote down, and yet still feel too stressed to carry them through. When this happens, the path to success may consist of examining and altering the feelings and attitudes you are holding inside yourself.

To see how this works, think again of the situation that is causing you stress. Imagine three scenarios in which you confront the issue in three different ways. It is important to first read the instructions for the first scenario, then close your eyes to visualize it for two to three minutes, and then write down your experience, *before* reading the instructions for the next scenario.

Scenario One: The First Path. Think of a stressful situation coming up in the next week. Imagine yourself in that situation, failing miserably! Everything that could go wrong does go wrong. You are more incompetent and inept than you ever dreamed possible, worse than your worst fear. You make an idiot of yourself in every conceivable way. Let all your senses come into play as you visualize this awful situation vividly in your mind's eye. When you have finished, let that image fade. Notice how you feel, and write it down.

Scenario Two: The Second Path. Now imagine yourself confronting the same challenge. This time, however, remember all the similar situations you have been in before, and remember ones that worked out well. You do a good job; you are the best you know how to be. You do everything right and you are successful. Bring all your senses into play as you imagine the scenario working out just as you hope it will. When you have finished, let that image fade, and notice how you feel. Write down how you feel.

*Come out of
the circle of time,
and into the
circle of love.*

Jalaludin Rumi

147

Scenario Three: The Third Path. As you envision this third scenario, hold your thumb and index finger of each hand together in a circle. Keep each hand like that during this visualization. We'll explain later.

Picture yourself facing your challenge once more. This time see yourself being incredibly, undeniably brilliant in your approach. No holds barred—stand on the table, swing from the chandelier, speak poetry on bended knee, give a stunning, extemporaneous speech that moves everyone to tears. All the amazing, outrageous talent that ever was and ever will be pours through you as you rise to heights never thought possible. You are *more* than successful! And all in just three minutes of everyday time, though it may be hours of imaginary time.

When you have finished, let that image fade and notice and write down how you feel.

What do you notice about the three scenarios? What did you observe about your emotional and physical feelings during and after each one?

Many people, when they are stressed about something, replay in their mind their worst fear. Then, when they are in the actual situation, since this is the scenario they have primed themselves for, this is the path that they follow. Can you see how dwelling on the worst can be a self-fulfilling prophecy?

Many people know this, so they try to imagine a more positive way of dealing with the challenge. However, their mistake is to tie themselves to things that have worked well for them before. These normal, satisfactory approaches may still work, but the outcome is not particularly wonderful, even though it may be adequate.

In the third scenario we asked you to push yourself beyond your wildest dreams to imagine being the sort of hero that only exists in fantasy land. True, you may not do all that you did *here* in the real situation. But recall how you felt when you were on top of the world. Recall how that feeling carried you through. Jot down the ideas you have now for ways to bring your feelings from the third scenario into your real-life situation.

We asked you to put your fingers together so that you would associate that position with the feeling of the utmost self-confidence, joy, flow, and success. Do this a few times when you are in different situations, and this finger position will serve as a physical reminder to anchor you to your best feelings and possibilities. Then when you are in a real situation when you want to recall your most heroic nature, simply touch your fingers in this way: it will serve as a trigger mechanism to call up those feelings. It really works! You can even do it as you write, and simply hold the pencil in the middle of your anchor. No one even notices that you're doing it!

Take a moment to consider what is the *one* key quality that made your third scenario work.

Then take your brightest, most vibrantly colored markers and a card you can carry with you this week. In large letters, write on it the word or phrase that sums up this quality. Take time with this. Draw letters with the same care that the ancient monks took on their illuminated manuscripts. Surely the illumination that you have from your third scenario is worth this care.

Through the week, remember the word or phrase that characterizes your brilliant success in the third scenario. Repeat it to yourself when you are falling asleep, walking to the store, driving your car, or meditating, and, of course, say it silently, holding your fingers in your anchor, when you are meeting stressful challenges on your path.

Gaining Greater Insight

Now select another issue that you listed earlier as one that caused you stress. But this time make it one that you feel requires greater insight; something more than meeting it head on or changing your perspective on it. Write or draw a symbol for this in the space below.

Now try precise observation, and ask penetrating questions about this stressful challenge in your life. Gaining greater insight should help you deal with it.

Test an action question. First, see how an action question works for you on this issue. Ask what you should do. You may find that you can

come up with something valuable; at the least you'll be able to compare this usually limiting question with the results of the more open-ended exercises to follow.

Ask a series of insight questions. Ask yourself about the stressful situation using the following questions, which will tap your multiple capacities.

> Intellectual: What else do I need to find out? (data, facts)
> Emotional: What do my feelings tell me? (feelings)
> Physical: What can I try out to see more? (senses, hands-on)
> Spiritual: What does my intuitive wisdom say? (meditate, dream, pray)

As you ask yourself each one, let it lead to other questions or a series of questions and answers. See whether the clarity you obtain leads to any resolution of your stressful situation.

Ask Why? repeatedly. Start by asking Why? about a small part of your issue. Ask the question, get an answer, ask Why? using the original answer as a base. Continue asking Why? with the curiosity of a child for at least three rounds or until you get into deeper and deeper levels of understanding.

Use the power of your other hand. This exercise (adapted from Lucia Cappachione and her book *The Power of Your Other Hand*) helps you to get in touch with your childlike capacity of wonder by allowing yourself to regress. Simply write a question related to your issue and then, with your eyes closed, contemplate the question for a few moments. Open your eyes and write your answer with your least dominant hand. (If you are right-handed, write this answer with your left hand, and if you are left-handed, write this answer with your right hand). Often the answers are quite surprising. They seem to be accessing some very deep place within us that we have forgotten.

Dream about it. For three nights in a row, write down a question before you go to sleep. Mull it over as you drift off. See if your creative essence provides answers in the form of a dream or thought upon awakening. Write them down.

Find an oracle. There are many ways that you can get hints about your key question or issue from outside yourself. For instance, in *Lateral Thinking,* Edward DeBono suggests that you put a question or issue into your mind, open a dictionary without looking, put your index finger on a page, and then use the closest word to your finger as a stimulus to your thought about the issue.

You can use much more mysterious and intriguing ways to accomplish the same thing. Tarot cards, the I Ching, or runes, for instance, provide rich imagery that is a bit like an instant dream for you to analyze. Angeles Arrien's *The Tarot Handbook* provides a fine guide to the use and interpretation of the Tarot, although you can do the following exercise with nothing else except a deck of the cards. If you're interested in the I Ching see R. L. Wing's *I Ching Workbook* or the computer program *Synchronicity*, and for runes see Ralph Blum's *The Book of Runes.* All three are excellent tools to use in the following exercise. Experiment with what works best for you.

Now, put yourself in a relaxed, creative, open state of mind. Play some of your favorite, relaxing music. Sit with your question or issue, feel the music and, without pre-choosing select a word (or pick a Tarot card, throw the I Ching, select a rune). Look at what you have and then start writing a response or interpretation to it. Write for fifteen minutes without lifting your pen from the paper. Imagine that automatic writing is propelling your hand. Watch what comes out and analyze it later.

Changing Your Perspective

Once again, pick an issue in your life that causes you stress, but this time look at one that primarily requires that you change your perspective. Most stressors that fit into this category are those that you can't do anything about, such as acts of nature, although some are because you've had bad experiences with them in the past. Fear and the voice of judgment tell you that you should be afraid.

Write one of these types of stressful issues below, or draw a visual representation of it.

The most important change of perspective you can have on this issue is to live more in the present. Ivor was able to transcend the stress of meeting his three tasks because he was in a state of flow. He was so thoroughly in the present moment with each one that there was no time spent worrying. His creativity just came pouring through. And you have to admit, his tasks were forbiddingly difficult. Have you ever been so absorbed in the present moment with a task that you felt one with it?

The following exercise allows you to expand your perception of time by focussing on each second of it. It is based on the idea that the universe is created, maintained, and destroyed by the breath of the Creator, and it allows you to have the experience of synchronizing your breath with that first creative breath.

To do this, sit comfortably with your back straight but not rigid and your hands in your lap. Hold your thumbs and index fingers together to make your anchor. If you are in a chair, let the back support you, and place your feet flat on the floor. You may want to read through the rest of these instructions so that you can then do this with your eyes closed. Or you might ask a friend to read them to you, or make a tape of yourself reading them aloud, allowing enough time for each part.

EXPERIENCING PRESENT TIME

Once you close your eyes, you can center yourself to prepare for this journey into present time with what is called the Full Yogic Breath. *Breathe deeply all the way in so that your belly rises, your ribcage and chest expand, and you breathe all the way up to your shoulders and neck. Hold the breath for a few moments, whatever is comfortable, and then exhale easily, starting with the air in your belly, and expelling it all the way up. Do this about three times and feel your mind shutting down. Feel your body beginning to settle in. Allow your jaw and tongue to go slack so that no subvocal muscle movements take place. Be at peace.*

Allow your breath to go back to its normal pattern. Don't try to control it at all. Just notice it. Notice how long it takes to flow in and out. Imagine how many seconds it takes. Realize that your breath does this about twenty-six thousand times every day.

Now imagine that it takes a full minute *for you to inhale and exhale each time. Continue to allow the breath to flow at its own rate, but imagine that it takes a full minute for its inhalation and exhalation cycle. Breathe six or seven cycles with this in mind. Experience what a minute is like.*

Now imagine that it takes your breath an hour *to inhale and exhale each time. Allow it to flow at any rate it wants while you experience each breath cycle as an hour.*

Do that for a few cycles, and then imagine that each inhalation and exhalation takes a day *to complete. Experience the fullness of a day with every breath.*

When you're ready, shift your consciousness to each inhalation and exhalation being a week *long. As you do this, you may notice your breath slowing down or even stopping, from time to time. Let it do whatever it's going to do. Don't worry. It will continue as appropriate.*

After a few rounds of imagining your breath cycle to be a week, imagine it as a month *in length. Experience one full cycle of the moon in your breath.*

After some experience with that, imagine that it takes a year *for you to breathe in and out each time. Remember, let your breath do whatever it is going to do, but experience a year each time it goes in and out.*

Now imagine that it takes a decade *for each breath cycle. Ten years exist each time you breathe. Notice what this is like.*

After some breaths, assume they take a century *each. Do that for a while, and know a full century.*

Now experience that each breath takes a millennium *to complete the path from the beginning of inhalation to the end of exhalation. Just notice what happens in each thousand years of breathing.*

Finally, allowing your breath to flow at its own rate, experience your breath as the Creator, with the beginning of inhalation starting the universe and being the beginning of time, to the end of the exhalation, which would be the end of time. Your breath marks off all time the universe has ever known. Experience eternity *in your breath. Continue this for as long as you like, experiencing yourself within time, noticing your mind-chatter dropping away. If thoughts intrude, go back to paying attention to your breath as it creates, maintains, and destroys the universe and time itself.*

When you have finished, come back to the present, maintaining the quality of consciousness you have just felt. Use this awareness and your quiet mind to apply the motto Just Do It! to the issue you're working on now and for all the decisions and activities you will face this week. Don't forget the creative source that is your breath.

Reframing Failure

Very often, an issue that needs a change in perspective is one with which you've failed in the past or one that is related to some fear that comes from your voice of judgment. The first perspective shift needed is to be reminded that failure, or falling into the pit, is a crucial part of the creative process and the hero's journey. If everything always works out, you may be leading a charmed life, but you will never need to call on your hidden gifts to recover from your fall. You will never rise to the heights of a true everyday hero if you never confront the possibility of failure. It was in confronting the impossible challenges that Ivor came to a state of grace (through the blessing of Kalisha, a symbolic part of self in this story) and was able to become godly himself.

You need to acknowledge failures as tests—as signposts telling you what doesn't work—and, perhaps indirectly, pointing you in a direction that will work. The creativity tools come in useful here. Observe precisely what happens in a situation that feels like a failure, without judging yourself for it. Question whether the so-called failure really is the final sort of situation it seems. Have faith that, if you keep following your path, the value of the so-called failure will come clear. Failures come in many guises.

Other people may say your idea isn't good enough. This is what a recording company told the Beatles in the early 1960s, and what Alexander Graham Bell was told when he first proposed his "telephone."

You may try something that simply doesn't work out. It is said that Thomas Edison tried over two thousand possible filaments for the electric light before he had a success. When someone pointed out that he'd failed so many times, he replied, "Nonsense, I now know two thousand materials that don't work! Think of how much closer I am to my goal!"

You may fail by acting in a way that is not consistent with your self-image. Carl Jung describes all of us as having a shadow to our person-

Jewel-like, the immortal
does not boast of its length of
years
but of the scintillating point of
its moment.

Rabindrath Tagore

alities. The shadow is the part of ourselves that we do not like, and which we keep hidden most of the time. If you think of the story of the peasant who married a goddess as a dream of yours, then the Prince is a shadow figure in this dream. The Prince is an antihero whose selfishness tries to do away with the real hero.

The voice of judgment has a field day with all of these, primarily because of the last one: that we deny our shadow side. We fear that we will do something that is seen as wrong or doesn't work because it will expose a part of us that we don't want others to see. But it is human to have a shadow side. As long as you deny your shadow and try to be the ideal, perfect person, you are under stress. You are in constant fear that your shadow might pop out in an awkward situation. The shadow then has control over you.

The amazing truth is, however, that if you can acknowledge your shadow, it can become a powerful, positive force in your life, beyond the mere relief you have of not having to hide it anymore.

The challenge is to turn the tables so you have control over your shadow, and you can do this by recognizing and acknowledging it. It's as simple as that. Once it has been seen and named, it is no longer a terrifying mystery. In fact, once you recognize it, you can see that dealing with it can also be part of your path to becoming a hero. By dealing with the demands of the Prince, Ivor was tested to find a way to live within time and without stress. If it weren't for the Prince, he would have continued to live a simple life with Kalisha, and would never have experienced the grace that transfigured him into a god. If you stand up to your shadow, it disappears, your stress is reduced, and you are transformed.

What is your shadow? Is it greed? A temper? Vanity? Dishonesty? Insecurity? Sloth? Take a moment to consider the part of you that you have hidden—that has unreasonable fear connected to it. Then use the most awful colors to draw an image of your shadow in the margin of this book or in your journal.

Your shadow may not want to lose its control easily even though, in reality, the two of you can peacefully coexist. Your shadow may feel that you have things to learn from it, as Ivor did from the Prince. It may want you to know exactly what it is. What does your shadow have to say to you? And what do you want to tell it? What have you learned from it? Why don't you need it anymore? What do you want from it, and what does it want from you? How can the two of you agree to peacefully coexist?

Act out a dialogue with your shadow, as if in a play for two actors whose characters are called Self and Shadow. You act both parts, perhaps shifting between two chairs, or standing up for shadow and sitting down for self. Allow your intuition to ask and answer the questions in the previous paragraph. Don't force the lines. Open your mouth and let the words come out with the feeling of flow that Ivor had when he had been endowed with grace by Kalisha. You may want to practice making your anchor as you talk, so that a brilliantly insightful dialogue emerges.

Have your self say, "Who are you, shadow, and what do you want?" Allow your shadow to answer. Just go on from there until you have come into a completely new perspective about your shadow. See how this new perspective affects the stress issue that you are highlighting. And notice how this new relationship to your shadow mitigates worry in your life and allows you to live with increasingly less stress.

THE BODY BEAUTIFUL

To meet the challenge of living stress-free in the here and now, you can tone your body as well as your mind, emotions, and spirit. Let your physical body be an ally to you on this path.

Resting the Body

Most of us get by on a less-than-optimum amount of sleep. Sure, we can make it on four or six hours a night, but we're probably not up to snuff in our alertness or our ability to deal with everyday stresses until we have closer to eight or ten hours of nightly slumber.

While it may be impractical to increase your sleep to ten hours, remember that there is a difference between operating at a peak-performance level and squeaking by with a bare minimum of sleep. Just as meditation relaxes and recharges your body and mind, so too does sleep. If you are not sleeping as much as you might, try giving yourself thirty extra minutes and experience the elasticity of time as you discover that your day seems to be lengthened, not shortened.

Perhaps it is not quantity but *quality* of sleep that concerns you. Commit to yourself that if you wake up during the night for more than fifteen minutes, you'll get up and do something enjoyable or productive. Many people find that either they actually accomplish something in the dark hours, or they end up falling back to sleep before the fifteen minutes are up. In either case, they no longer suffer through hours of insomnia.

Consider some ideas for resting your body and write them down to commit that you will incorporate them into your life.

Exercising the Body

We all know exercise is essential for health. Aside from the obvious benefits of relaxation and alertness, everyday heroes use their exercise periods as opportunities to practice different perspectives or imagine outrageously successful scenarios. In effect, you can combine your meditation with exercising.

Practice what's called *walking meditation,* in which you walk slowly, with complete awareness of the present moment and everything that comes into your consciousness. This is great to do out in the country, where you won't be disturbed. Your challenge is then to bring present moment awareness into all you do.

Another approach is to let the rhythmic motion of your exercise put you into a semitrance, so that you are not thinking at all about the movements you are making, or the work that is waiting for you, or the person you really don't want to deal with today. Your mind becomes empty, and you become simply a body, feeling the air or water. You experience a state of grace.

If you are working at your desk, reading, or involved in sedentary pursuits, it is good to give yourself a thirty-second shot of physical energy every hour. Stop what you are doing, stand up, jump up and down, wave your arms vigorously, shake your legs and jiggle your head around. Let noises come from your mouth. Shake the cobwebs out of your brain by overstimulating it like this for thirty seconds. Try it now. Stand up and Just Do It! You will be amazed at the difference in your alertness and energy level. Jean Houston and Robert Masters, at the Foundation for Mind Research, believe that this radically alters the firing of the neurons in your brain and contributes to your creativity.

Write down ideas for exercising your body that you can incorporate into your life.

Nourishing the Body

As with exercise, we all know we are supposed to eat healthfully to maintain optimum mental and physical health. But to what extent do you actually do this? Studies have shown that proteins increase alertness, and fats and simple carbohydrates slow it down. The beneficial effects of an overall pattern of healthy eating may not show up instantaneously in measurable ways, but you will eventually notice them.

You can also nourish your body by loving it. Treat it nicely with warm baths, a massage, and regular rest and relaxation, and it will be your faithful ally.

Write down ideas for nourishing your body that you can incorporate into your life.

Nourishing the Soul

It's not just your body that needs to be nourished on your path to be an everyday hero who creatively meets the challenge of living stress-free in the here and now. Don't forget to nourish your creative essence—your soul. What is it that nourishes your soul? Is it reading inspirational books or poetry? Listening to particular kinds of music? Being in the beauty of nature? Playing with children? Talking to sage individuals? What fills you with a feeling that it's grand to be alive?

Write down ideas for nourishing your soul that you can incorporate into your life.

THE RETURN

TO LIVE STRESS-FREE IN THE HERE AND NOW

Now that you have traveled this path, what do you know? How does grace, like the touch of Kalisha in the story, manifest itself in your life? How have you, like Ivor, become godlike? What wisdom do you have now for living stress-free in the here and now?

Make your hero's declaration now to affirm your transformed relationship to time and stress. Complete the statements and use colors to make a visual declaration.

No one really knows enough to be a pessimist.

Norman Cousins

HERO'S DECLARATION

Because I am in a state of grace, I

The visual image to honor my completion of this quest is

ONE DAY AT A TIME

Now that you have made an affirmation of your commitment, your challenge is to flow with time and events on a daily basis so that you are totally present and able to function at your peak level at all times. Ivor was able to transcend panic and being overwhelmed by remembering that there is much more to life, and that what matters is living now and Just Doing It! The test of your travels on this path is to change the approach you have for dealing with time and stress.

Begin by living just one day fully in the present in all that you do, going beyond the small, daily concerns and allowing your creative source to fully express itself in all of your being. Start this exercise when you have a fairly normal day ahead of you, and you know you will be able to get back to this book in twenty-four hours.

In the space below, jot down what you now know about being in a state of grace and its effects on your experience of time and stress.

This sounds like a simple instruction. You just did something like this on the preceding page, didn't you? This time, however, approach the challenge in a qualitatively different manner. Don't intellectually think of what it means to live stress-free in the here and now. Let a feeling or knowing about the wisdom of grace emerge intuitively, then write this down or draw a symbol for it. It may help you to take a few moments to close your eyes and remember the still, quiet place inside you.

To Live Stress-free in the Here and Now

Now, do whatever you ordinarily would do for the next twenty-four hours. Just Do It! At this time tomorrow, open your workbook to this page again, and take a few minutes to again remember the still, quiet place inside you. Reflect on how you lived the last twenty-four hours.

What Happened?

What things did you do and what attitudes did you have that freed you from the constraints of time and stress? How much did you consciously pay attention to your experience of the vast present moment in these twenty-four hours? How much were you on automatic pilot?

Jot down your observations of your day below or in the margin. Be sure to include any notes to yourself about significant differences you noticed, and situations that caused you to forget about grace.

Observations on Just Doing It! for One Day

FOLLOW-UP: MAPPING YOUR PATH
TO STRESS-FREE LIVING

Now you are ready to complete new visual and verbal logs of your travels. How are you different in terms of where you are now on your own everyday hero's path toward living stress-free in the here and now?

Don't look back yet to the logs you first made when you started this chapter. Recall that the visual log is an intuitive sort of mapping of where you are now on your path toward resolving the challenge of living within time and without stress. The verbal log is a chance to characterize this challenge in terms of the six stages of the hero's journey: innocence, the call, initiation, allies, breakthrough, and celebration.

You can prepare the outline of the visual log and the six headings for the verbal log yourself, in your journal or on separate sheets of paper. Once your logs are ready, your task is to depict your current situation regarding time and stress (including the events of the past week), first visually and then verbally. What happened for you?

Prepare yourself by taking a few moments to breathe and be still. Allow a sense of your journey over the last week to come into focus. Use colors to draw a figure or other symbols to represent yourself on your path in the expressive pictorial log.

After you have completed the visual log, take some time to contemplate it. What are your drawings and colors telling you about your time and stress search now? What does it remind you about your journey on this challenge? When you are ready, make notes about where you are regarding the six stages of the creative quest in your written log.

Once you are satisfied with your new visual and verbal logs and how they relate to each other, you can compare them to the ones you did earlier in the chapter and see what insights you can gain.

REFLECTIONS ON YOUR PATH

Now that you've completed this chapter and have worked on the time and stress challenge for a week or so, write a letter to yourself about your experiences of this quest. This can serve to consolidate and legitimize your experience so far.

That which was not, came.

That which came must go.

Muktananda, remain calm
and steady

in the midst of all that comes
and goes.

Swami Muktananda

You should keep this letter or statement as tangible evidence of your journey to this point. Then, if you feel the need to do more work on this challenge in the future, or just want a boost regarding your ability to live stress-free, you can go back to this review of your accomplishment.

CELEBRATE!

How are you celebrating your completion of this path? What are you doing to reward yourself for your successful journey? How are you making a public statement of your private changes? Make sure that in the days ahead you continue to acknowledge and celebrate your mastery of time and stress.

Achieving Personal and Professional Balance

A student was interviewing for a job with a prestigious firm in the line of work that most interested him. He mentioned that he was about to get married. One of the interviewers mentioned that he was about to get married, too, and he didn't know if he'd have enough time.

"Time for what?" the student asked. "The wedding or the marriage?"

"Both," said the interviewer, and laughed. But our student didn't think it was very funny. He had been brought face-to-face with the issue of personal and professional balance.

Tom Peters and Nancy Austin, in their book *A Passion for Excellence,* take a dismal perspective as well. Their words in the margin suggest you cannot have a richly balanced life.

But we know many people who do. They have it all by mindfully traveling their path, not trying to live up to some set of inappropriate outside standards. And in nourishing themselves they are better able to nourish others through their work.

Anne is a psychotherapist who teaches occasionally at two local colleges. She also loves to paint, and has a studio behind her little wooden cottage. This cottage is on a grassy hill at the edge of the Pacific, overlooking three miles of white, sandy beach.

"I almost don't believe my life," Anne told us. "I spend half my week reading all the books I love and just playing in my studio, and the other half I work intimately with people. Every evening I run on the

We are frequently asked if it is possible to "have it all"—a full and satisfying personal life and a full and satisfying, hard-working professional one. Our answer is: No.

Tom Peters and
Nancy Austin

beach and then eat supper watching a marvelous sunset. And they even *pay me* to live like this!"

Anne has put together her part-time jobs in such a way that she loves her work, yet still has time for a rich and fulfilling personal life. Her parents and brothers were against her unorthodox choice of lifestyle; they would have preferred her either to get married or to find a stable full-time job, for the sake of security.

"But the thing is," said Anne, "I'm so happy this way. I have everything, even though they don't see it! You just have to choose what's important to you, and go for it."

Choice: choosing a balance of personal and professional time during your week that works well for you. It is the same whether you are single or married, female or male, on a fast-track career or just trying to get along. You have to make choices, big ones in a lifetime and little ones every day. If you pay attention to your journey, you soon learn that the goal isn't a static equilibrium in which your personal and professional lives are always somehow perfect and unchanging. That would be unrealistic and uninteresting. There would be no opportunity for self-development in either realm.

You need to make choices about what you do so that there is a dynamic interplay between the two. Give full attention to work if it demands that—temporarily. In addition to professional success, you need to relax, take care of yourself, and have relationships. You need to get back in balance if you find yourself off balance. In fact, the best state of all is probably one of synergy between the personal and professional aspects of your life, such that each aspect seems enriched by the other. This is how you can have it all.

Most people, when asked to think of a time when they had balance in their lives, almost always report something other than the sense of stability that might be conjured up by the world *balance*. It is almost like the beginning of a new love affair. They speak of intensity, of flowing, of everything in their life working well, of there being synergy and stimulation between all parts of their life.

Surprisingly, the great majority report that they experienced a sense of balance in their lives in situations that, by outside standards, would seem to be chaotic—a new job, moving from one part of the country to the other, expecting a baby, starting a new educational experience, buying and settling into the first home, or all of these. These critical events in our lives seem to force us to make choices in the heat

It's not easy taking my problems one at a time when they refuse to get in line.

Ashleigh Brilliant

of the battle. The real challenge, however, is to continue this sort of balance or synergy every day.

In this chapter, the ancient myth of Theseus, told and retold for twenty-five hundred years, shows a hero who chooses to give more attention to the professional, rather than the personal side of his life. We see the consequences of this, as well as the result of his brief attempt to redress that imbalance.

As you read the story, imagine yourself as Theseus. How does he make choices? Think about your life—your work and personal time. How do you have these aspects in balance? In what ways are they out of balance? What could you do differently?

——— PREPARATION ———

Theseus and the Minotaur

Theseus was a brave little boy who grew up not knowing his father, in the Greek city of Troezen. When he was sixteen, his mother told him the meaning of his name, "a person or thing that is deposited." She also showed him a large rock, and told him that his father, King Aegeus of Athens, had secretly deposited his own sword and sandals underneath it.

"If you are able to move the rock, you will find that the sandals fit you, and the sword is the right size for you. Your father would like you to be a good and brave hero," she said.

Theseus easily moved the rock, and didn't question the idea that he was to become a hero. What better profession for a Greek youth who discovers, in adolescence, that he is of royal birth?

King Aegeus had also left a ship for Theseus so that he could sail easily back to Athens, but in Theseus's zeal to carry out his mission, and in his desire to emulate his famous cousin, Heracles, he chose to go the more dangerous route—following, on foot, the coast road to Athens.

"Don't worry about my safety. I'll carry on the family tradition in the most heroic way," the youth exclaimed. "Like my cousin, I won't go looking for trouble, but I'll set things right. There are many bandits here and I'll handle any who accost me by turning the tables on them! That's the kind of hero to be."

Starting out for Athens, Theseus first encountered Periphetes, a ferocious savage who used a huge iron club to bludgeon people to death, and who was the terror of everyone who tried to travel that road. When he raised his club to Theseus, the boy wrestled it out of Periphetes' hands, and hit him over the head.

"Well, old fellow, have a taste of your own medicine," he called. The club felt just right in his own hands, so he carried it with him, bearing it as a token of his first victory.

Further along the road lived Sinis, known as Pine-Bender. He would bend down the tops of two tall pine trees so that they almost touched. His trick was to ask passers-by to assist him, whereupon he would tie one of their arms to each pine tree, and then release the trees. The trees would spring upright, tearing his victims in half.

Sinis saw Theseus coming, and pulled down the tops of two pines in his usual way.

"Please help me with my task, young man. You look strong, and I am so old and weak," Sinis begged.

Theseus, who knew with whom he was dealing, in a trice had tied Sinis himself to the trees and let them go, sending pieces of the bandit flying everywhere.

"This is so easy," he thought. "Being a hero is the life for me. I won't waste my time with anything else."

Continuing his journey, Theseus grew more courageous and was able to rid the countryside of the dangerous people and animals that had been terrorizing local folk and travelers alike. He used Periphetes' club to destroy a gigantic, wild sow that had been eating people as they tried to plough their fields. Now farmers would be able to grow crops again, and their families would be healthy once more.

Theseus continued on, with no thought for anything but being a fair and brave hero for the people.

The coast road wound around the edge of sheer cliffs, and there Theseus encountered a man who sat blocking the road. The man ordered him to wash his feet. Knowing that this fellow kicked people over the cliffs, to be gobbled up by a savage sea turtle, Theseus knelt down as if to do his bidding and, in a feat of great strength, shoved the man over the cliff, into the turtle's mouth.

"This is going pretty well," thought the young hero to himself. "I like this line of work."

A stocky man jumped in the middle of the road and challenged Theseus to wrestle with him. Aware of his own great strength, Theseus asked him, "What if I don't want to?"

"You must," the man laughed. "Everyone must." He sported in

squeezing the life out of his victims with his bare hands, and this youth looked like an easy mark.

"If you insist," sighed Theseus. Quick as lightning, he picked the man up and threw him head first to the ground. That was the end of him and the end of Theseus's adventures on the coast road. He had arrived, finally, in Athens.

The way to Athens was now safe for travel. Theseus was acknowledged as a hero whose mission was to make things better for ordinary people. He headed for his father's palace.

His father, Aegeus, had never met his son, and knew nothing of his son's adventures. Aegeus had since married, and his wife wanted her sons to be heirs to the throne. When Theseus arrived, she convinced Aegeus that this hero was really a villain. She invited him to the palace and asked Aegeus to give him a goblet of poisoned wine. Then, just as Theseus was about to drink, Aegeus recognized his own sword. He grabbed the glass out of his son's hand.

There was much rejoicing at their meeting. Aegeus embraced his son, and made it known how proud he was of his work. "How happy I am that you have come home, son," he said, with tears in his eyes. "Now you can rest from your great deeds. Stay by my side now and we will make up for all those lost years when we were apart."

But this was not to be. Theseus had no interest in spending time with his father. He was committed to his life's work, and felt compelled to continue on with the next adventure.

"I'm at the prime of my strength, father," he responded. "I can't sit around here. What other heroic deeds need to be done?"

Aegeus sighed sadly. He was very proud of his son. He also knew he couldn't keep him when Theseus was so driven to be successful. He thought of an unfortunate situation that needed resolving, and told Theseus about King Minos.

Many years earlier, the handsome son of King Minos had been killed in Athens. Minos's second son—really his wife's son, from a love affair with Minos's prize bull—had the body of a man, the head of a bull, and was extremely vicious. Minos had taken over the island of Crete to hide this son, called the Minotaur, in a labyrinth built deep underground, from which it was impossible to find one's way out. To avenge the death of his other son, Minos demanded that seven virgin youths and seven virgin maidens be sent to the Minotaur every year. They were sent into the labyrinth and devoured by the Minotaur.

It was now time for this sacrifice and, of course, Theseus wanted to volunteer as one of the seven virgin youths so that he could slay the Minotaur and free Athens from this annual tribute to Minos. Aegeus was quite distressed, and told Theseus that many youths had gone before him, each more heroic than the last, and each thinking he would be the one to slay the Minotaur. None had returned. And every year fourteen more of the best of Athens's young people were sacrificed to the awful Minotaur.

Theseus paid no heed to his father's pleas. He was determined. With a heavy heart, Aegeus helped him procure provisions and took him down to the ship to sail to Crete with the other youths. The ship's sail was black—it was a ship of doom. Aegeus gave Theseus a white sail and said, "I will watch for your return across the sea. If you are victorious, hoist the white sail before you set sail for Athens, so that I may prepare to celebrate your victory."

Before setting sail, Theseus made a sacrifice to the goddess of love, Aphrodite, to be his guide on this voyage. And then the ship made its way to Crete.

Minos met the ship and noticed Theseus as the most beautiful and strongest of the seven virgin youths. He immediately challenged him to prove himself by retrieving a gold ring, which Minos tossed into the sea. Though this was not the task he had come to accomplish, Theseus dived in and, helped by dolphins, retrieved not only the ring, but a golden crown that Aphrodite had once given as a wedding present to an undersea being.

Minos's beautiful daughter, Ariadne, watched this, and couldn't help falling in love with Theseus. He, too, noticed her, the first woman for whom he had ever felt any emotion.

"How can I defeat the Minotaur?" he wondered aloud.

She whispered to him, "If you'll take me back to Athens with you and marry me, I'll help you slay my half-brother, the Minotaur."

Theseus pledged to marry her. Ariadne then brought out a magic ball of thread that the builder of the labyrinth had given to her. Whenever she went to visit the Minotaur, she simply tied one end of the thread to the door and it unwound itself and rolled along the many twisting, turning passageways, leading her to the Minotaur. To return, she would rewind the thread, following it back to the door.

"You can follow this thread to my half-brother and back again quite safely," Ariadne told Theseus.

Theseus's heart was slightly a flutter, perhaps from his love for Ariadne, perhaps because this was the first time he had ever needed and accepted help from another. He volunteered to be the first to go into the labyrinth. With one last glance at Ariadne, who stood silhouetted in the doorway, he set off into the cold, dank darkness.

If it weren't for the thread, he would have been lost in the maze of passageways. Instead, it led him to the Minotaur, who was asleep. Theseus crept up to him and beat him to death with his bare hands. He then followed Ariadne's thread back to her and to daylight.

The couple embraced, and stole away to the ship, taking the other youths with them, and set sail for Athens before King Minos could figure out what had happened. There was much rejoicing on the ship, and Ariadne happily looked forward to marrying Theseus.

However, the ship stopped at an island on the way back, and after making passionate love there, Theseus left Ariadne and sailed back to Athens without her, anticipating the praise and glory to be bestowed upon him for his great deed.

But in his excitement, Theseus forgot to hoist the white sail. Aegeus waited for days at the top of the cliff, looking over the sea for the return of the ship. When it finally came into view, he saw that the sail was black, not white. He thought that his beloved son had failed, and had been killed by the Minotaur. In his grief, he threw himself off the cliff, to drown in the sea.

On Theseus's return, he was honored for slaying the Minotaur, and was made king of Athens. Modeling himself after his cousin, Heracles, he was a wise and good king who brought democracy to the people of Athens.

However, the story continues in a different vein. Although his heroic deeds continued to be successful, after Theseus abandoned Ariadne, all his relationships were unsuccessful—with his father, as we have seen, with women, and with a son he later had. He did find a good friend with whom to adventure, but their heroic quests almost cost Theseus his life. It seems that while Theseus's exploits were indeed heroic, his narrow focus on achievement was a curse that led him to have an unhappy life in his older years.

THE MANY MEANINGS OF THESEUS AND THE MINOTAUR

Many of us remember the tale of Theseus from our childhood. We may even recall that somehow a piece of string helps the youth destroy the Minotaur and thus become a hero, and that Theseus is paired with Ariadne, and that he is known for many other heroic deeds. He stays in our mind as a model of heroic valor, and we seldom recognize how this very one-sidedness of his life is the defect that ultimately leads to his ruin.

We aim to be like Theseus. We strive to have a life with purpose, and to do good for other people through our work. These are indeed commendable traits—up to a point.

Remember,
every stick has two ends.

G. I. Gurdjieff

As the story of Theseus demonstrates, allowing our work to take such a hold that we don't nourish ourselves personally, or remember to cherish our relationships, can result in tragic imbalance. Of course, there is also the imbalance that occurs when we become so wrapped up in our personal life that it encroaches on our professional life. Either way, we aren't allowing the various parts of our life to sustain one another.

How did Theseus's life get out of balance? He failed to *ask penetrating questions* when he discovered that his father wanted him to be a hero. King Aegeus has his son's professional track planned from birth—a similar job to his cousin's. Theseus just went along with the family plan. This is certainly one way to let your life get out of balance. But when Theseus does ask a question, when he admits that he isn't sure how to kill the Minotaur, Ariadne enters, symbolizing personal relationships.

Similarly, Theseus's skill of *precise observation* is, at first, rather limited. A handsome and virile youth, he only wishes to rid the land of bandits. He appears not to see the value in developing his personal life, and he is not even aware of his father's deep love for him. When Theseus notices Ariadne, we see his symbolic development from a partial person, living in the land of "masculine" actions, to a whole person, integrating the "feminine" attributes of caring. The union, though temporary, is further symbolized by his connection to her via the thread, as he succeeds in slaying the Minotaur. It is the wholeness, the balance of work and relationship, that allows him to be successful.

But he quickly slides back into his habitual way of being and loses the relationship. His personal life is rudely forgotten for the glory of his successful work. He loses the ability for precise observation and reverts to his tunnel vision.

If you are to be able to successfully balance your personal and professional life, and not let either side take over, it is important to observe what is taking your attention and energy, and to notice what you can do about this.

Both early in the story, and later, Theseus's *judgment* is that the correct or best components of life are the actions of a hero. He is strongly motivated to act in the way he believes to be right. It is interesting to note that his father, King Aegeus, had casually forsaken Theseus's mother and then returned to his own kingdom, giving the young man a model of what life and accomplishment are all about. Many of us adopt our inner voice of expectation, blame, and criticism, our voice of judgment, from our parents. There is no room in this narrow definition of correct living for any deviation. Yet it is when he deviates from this, when he shows *absence of this judgment* and accepts assistance from the woman, Ariadne, that Theseus succeeds in his challenge with the Minotaur. But then the lure of heroism beckons him when they are on the island, and his old judgments return. He loses his relationship as a result, and this, as we see, sets up a domino effect of failed relationships.

Theseus does show *faith in his own creativity* when he sets out to rid the road to Athens of its dangers, but there is a catch. His faith is not based on anything internal; it is blind faith based on his desire to please his father and be a great hero. Later, before he sets out for Crete, he takes action to ensure that he will have full creativity—he asks the goddess of love to be his guide. When he dives into the sea and retrieves not only Minos's ring but Aphrodite's crown, this is an omen that she is truly protecting him, and he can rise to the most impossible challenges.

The Work Alibi:
When It's Harder to Go Home
Harvard Business Review
article title

YOUR PATH TO BALANCE

Now review the myth of Theseus as a story that says something quite profound about your path through life. Put yourself in the role of Theseus, but see that role enacted in the legend of your life. Then write an answer to each of the following questions.

1. Which aspect of the story of Theseus most parallels your life journey? What issue about balance does this bring up? What are the similarities to Theseus's situation? What did or could you do differently?

2. Theseus's name means "a person or thing that is deposited." His father, by leaving the sword and sandals under the rock, also gave Theseus his profession. What professional or personal expectations have been left for you? By whom? How were they laid down? How do these judgments and expectations get in the way of finding balance in your life?

Executive Guilt:
Who's Taking Care of the
Children?

Fortune
article title

3. On the road to Athens, Theseus has several encounters that require him to do his hero's work. In your life, what analogous situations must you confront that threaten to tear you in two, devour you, throw you over a precipice, or squeeze you to death?

4. Theseus did not seem to realize how much his father or Ariadne cared about him. Have you ever not noticed that someone cared deeply for you, because you were caught up in your work? What happened? Is there a situation in your life like that now? If so, describe it.

5. Theseus didn't ask questions about the appropriateness of his professional path, he just followed it. What questions do you need to ask about your work?

6. One's personal life consists of various relationships, leisure activities, hobbies, self-development goals, or other pursuits. Theseus's relationship with Ariadne enhanced his professional life. What aspects of your personal life enhance your professional life?

7. When your personal and professional lives becomes unbalanced, what things that nourish you personally do you tend to leave out? Which are most obviously missing now? What might you do about this?

8. *Theseus was extremely successful at vanquishing bandits, and was seen as a hero for this. What are you most successful at and recognized for? Describe those things in your professional and personal life that you feel are your biggest successes. Describe what other people consider to be your great successes. In what ways are these the same or different? What is the impact of other people's opinions on the way you live your life?*

9. *Theseus asked the goddess of love to be his guide. What sort of person or quality would you ask for as a guide to help you live a balanced life now? Describe who you would ask, and why you would ask that person. In what way could they best guide you?*

10. *Theseus's most creative time, when there was synergy between his personal and professional lives, was when he was in Crete, in love with Ariadne, slaying the Minotaur, and opening up the possibility for a new life for himself. Take a moment and think of a time when you had this sort of synergy in your life. What were the circumstances? What was your experience of this? If you found yourself out of balance, as Theseus did, what caused this? How did you, or how could you, get back in balance?*

11. *The story of Theseus is an allegory that can be interpreted on a surface level and more deeply. Aided by Ariadne's thread, Theseus went into the dark labyrinth to confront and conquer the dreadful Minotaur. Is there a Minotaur in your life now? What is the maze you would have to enter to find it? What is the thread that you would need to protect you?*

The answers to these questions begin to paint a picture of your own path toward balance. You might notice themes that have been playing out in both aspects of your life, and some directions for you to explore as you bring things more into balance.

MAPPING YOUR PATH TO BALANCE

Visual Log

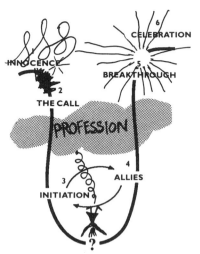

In Melissa's visual log, she expressed that she was overwhelmed by her work. She felt as if she had lost touch with the thread that kept her on track, and had fallen into the bottomless pit of too-much-to-do. Unlike Theseus, she did not feel at all heroic about her work. In fact, she described the large, black cloud as "full of things I have to accomplish, and it's cutting me off from my wisdom about taking time for myself and my relationships and things I love to do."

Melissa's drawing is simple: it shows a stick figure representing herself. You will probably draw a quite different picture from Melissa. Allow your intuition to draw. The more childlike and unplanned it is, the better.

A Visual Travel Log

Where I am at the start of this journey

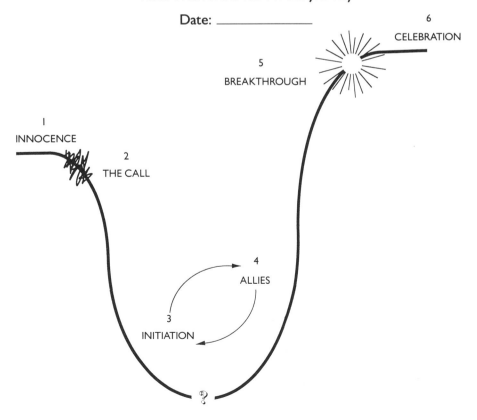

Verbal Log

Melissa's verbal log clarifies the images she portrayed in her visual log.

INNOCENCE (Feeling comfortable with my situation)

> Excited about all my projects at work.
> Loving my husband.
> Thinking I can easily do it all!

THE CALL TO ADVENTURE (Identifying and recognizing my challenge)

> Things take too long.
> Deadlines approaching!
> Machine doesn't work!!!!

INITIATION (Really being tested)

> Panic!
> No way to finish.
> No time for sleep, let alone relationships, hiking.

ALLIES (Finding strength and help)

> Knowledge of how to meditate (not an ally right now).
> Stewart.

BREAKTHROUGH (Reaching new awareness or resolution)

> Time for everything.
> Breathe to relax (I need to remember to do this!)

CELEBRATION (Returning home and being different)

> Time off to play/love/hike.
> Project a resounding success.
> (I can have these as my vision right now, the thread to know about, and try to
> catch hold of!)

All the wonders you seek are within yourself.

Sir Thomas Browne

This challenge is one that Melissa has yet to resolve. Even though she feels stuck in the initiation phase, she was able to jot down some ideas for the three following phases. "At least I know what I have to do now. I think if I call on my ally of meditation, this will change my mindset and get me out of the hole I feel I'm in right now," she said.

A helmsman does not need the same resources to wreck his ship as he does to save it. If he just turns it a little too far to the wind, he is lost, and if he does it not deliberately but from mere lack of attention, he is lost all the same. . . .
So keep awake.

Epictetus

Melissa looked at her visual log after she wrote in her verbal log, and said, "Oh, I need to redraw it so the thread reaches through the cloud, and loops through my hand, and up to the celebration side. Then I need to draw a pulley of some sort that will pull up the thread with me hanging onto it." She thought for a while and added, "Or perhaps the other end of the thread comes back down into my free hand so that I can be my own pulley and by pulling on the right-hand end of the thread I can pull myself out of the pit!"

She did not actually redraw the thread, but the insight about pulling herself out of the pit of being overwhelmed by her work showed her a way in which she might restore the balance that she felt was lacking.

Melissa's example can show you how ideas can come to you when you complete this self-assessment. You don't need to figure out anything to do. Just look at what you've drawn and written and see what's there.

Before doing your verbal log, take a few minutes to consider your life. Notice how it is like Theseus's, with people who care about you, wonderful lands to explore, and your work to be done.

Now do as Melissa did, and write your response to each of the phases of the hero's journey. You may write one word or a whole paragraph. Don't censor what you write. Just let the words just flow out. This is your private log and nobody needs to see it unless you show it to them.

Once you have completed the verbal log, look at what you have drawn and written without judgment to find out where you are on this particular path. You will find it interesting to compare them and see what difference you notice in yourself after completing the exercises in the chapter.

RECOGNIZE YOUR DECISION NOW!

Often, a major reason that we allow our work to take over is that we don't stop and ask ourselves, "Do I really want to do this? Is this something that will benefit *both* myself and other people?" We simply go ahead with the task because we are expected to, or because it doesn't occur to us that we might have another option. Like Theseus, we follow the path laid out for us by someone else, or even one that we have selected ourselves, but which we have not questioned.

A Verbal Travel Log

Where I am at the start of this journey

Date: _____

INNOCENCE (Feeling comfortable with my situation)

It is impossible to enjoy idling thoroughly unless one has plenty of work to do.

Jerome K. Jerome

THE CALL TO ADVENTURE (Identifying and recognizing my challenge)

INITIATION (Really being tested)

ALLIES (Finding strength and help)

BREAKTHROUGH (Reaching new awareness or resolution)

CELEBRATION (Returning home and being different)

Work is a four-letter word. It's up to us to decide whether that four-letter word reads "drag" or "love." Most work is a drag because it doesn't nourish our souls. The key is to trust your heart to move where your talents can flourish. This old world will really spin when work becomes a joyous expression of the soul.

Al Sacharov

We may even believe that we really love doing what we are doing. Then we wake up one day and ask, "Where's my soul? Who's important in my life? When did I last have a chance to play?" These are the times that we realize that we might have been somewhat on automatic pilot as we charted our course through life. We might have forgotten to pay attention to our wisdom and intuition when we made some of our most important decisions. We might have forgotten that it is actually healthy not to be professional and responsible all the time.

If you want balance or synergy in your life, you have to make choices or decisions that are absolutely right for you in every situation you face. The problem that you probably have, however, is that you're often not seeing clearly enough to recognize the decision you already have made within yourself. So, for the next week or so, live by the motto Recognize Your Decision Now! Whenever you consider doing anything, ask yourself this question: Is it a *yes* or a *no*? And *notice* which decision you've already made inside.

Don't let yourself off with a *maybe*. Recognize that when it comes down to it, everything in life is either a *yes* or a *no*. Notice how balance often falls out of your life when you agonize over small decisions that could be made instantly—should we go out to eat or stay at home? Should I go now or work an hour more? Chocolate or pistachio ice cream?

Start with these small decisions, and let your intuition come out. Recognize that within you you have already made the decision. Notice your own natural intuition. The more you do, the more it will be at your service.

Don't stop with the small decisions. Notice how you also make the large, life-changing decisions with which you may be grappling. Should I move to Seattle? Do I want to quit my job? Is this the person with whom I want to spend the rest of my life?

We sometimes get stuck thinking we have to make the right decision. But what is the right decision? How can we know? No matter how many facts we have gathered, it is not until we see what life brings that we can know the results of our decisions. In fact, there are no right or wrong decisions. There are only *choices* and *consequences*. Therefore, listen to your inner voice of wisdom to see what choice it's suggesting you make. Recognize Your Decision Now! and then be an everyday hero—make that choice and see what adventures the consequences bring you. Below are some specific things you might do.

- Allow yourself a short quiet period (ten to thirty minutes) each day to tune into your essence, and especially your intuition. Walk or meditate during this time.
- Eliminate the words *maybe* and *perhaps* and the phrase *I'm not sure* from your vocabulary for a week. Make decisions without agonizing over the *what ifs*. Notice how you feel; notice what happens.
- Make all of your everyday decisions on an intuitive yes or no basis.
- Make at least one major decision that is very significant to your life on an intuitive yes or no basis.
- Before you go to sleep, write down a question for which you'd like your dreams to provide insight. Write down your dream or thoughts or feelings upon awakening, and then examine them to see what they may say in answer to your question.

It's important to live with this motto consistently. Keep it in the back of your mind all the time. Write it down and keep it in a prominent place as a reminder. Every day pick a time to review the last twenty-four hours. How have you done balancing you personal and professional life? What have you been deciding to do? How has it been to Recognize Your Decision Now! instead of slipping along on automatic?

As you review each day, write brief notes to yourself in the margins of this book or in your journal. Record any feelings or events that have something to do with your path to personal and professional balance. Draw doodles to capture how you feel or what has happened. Let this be fun. Let it be a *yes*. Find ways to play. And Recognize Your Decision Now!

> *Recognize*
> *Your*
> *Decision*
> *Now*

——— THE JOURNEY ———

You have set out on your path to personal and professional balance by reflecting on the parallels between the story of your life and the story of Theseus and the Minotaur. You have constructed visual and verbal logs of where you are on this journey right now, and you have begun to live with this chapter's motto. In effect, you have moved out of the state of innocence and answered the call to adventure. You have answered yes to the challenge to explore the possibility of greater synergy between your personal and professional lives.

LOOKING AT WHAT YOU DO

The things with which we fill our lives are significant for a number of reasons. Some eat huge amounts of time out of our day. Some are important but take very little time. Driving out to a nearby park and hiking to the top of a hill to watch the sunset could be quite time-consuming, but watching the sunset as you drive home may take no extra time at all.

Some of them are essential. For example, eating is essential. If you are a bus driver, driving is essential. You may like or dislike these things, but they are an essential part of your personal or professional life.

Some of what we do, we do only out of a sense of duty or responsibility. If you have no interest in plants, but routinely care for some plants that your neighbor gave you, this might be something that you do not particularly want to do, but you do it because you feel you should do it. This also may be the case if you stay late after work returning phone calls because no one else did.

There are some aspects of our personal and professional life that make us feel good about ourselves: running a mile without feeling tired, making a successful business deal, helping someone.

What are the key activities you choose to fill your life with and how do they fit into each of the categories of time consuming, essential, done out of duty, and makes you feel good? Jot down your key personal or professional activities below in what you feel are the appropriate categories. Some of your activities will appear in more than one category. That's natural.

Look at the activities you have listed as personal and which are professional. Draw a circle around those that are professional and notice the pattern across the four categories. Begin to see the characteristics of your choices. If you feel that your choices relate to other characteristics than these four, use the space at the end of the exercise to write in characteristics and activities that relate to them. What does this tell you about what determines the kind of balance in your life?

Take Time

Essential

Done out of Duty

Make Me Feel Good About Me

What does your life look like when you put all this together? You've summarized this using words on the last couple of pages. How do your personal and professional lives balance? Which takes up more time and energy? Which is more pleasurable? Which aspects of each are most rewarding? Which aspects might you like to eliminate?

Read the instructions below and take a few minutes to carry them out, pausing at this sign (....). Listen to what your intuition tells you about your personal and professional life. There isn't any one correct way to do the exercise. You may have actual visual images or you may simply have an intuitive sense of the balance. Notice what happens.

THE BALANCE

Sit comfortably and close your eyes. Take a deep breath and breathe it all the way out. Feel the air coming in and filling you right up (....) Hold it for a couple of seconds, (....) and then feel it emptying out of your lungs and dispersing. Do this four or five times. (....)

Think about your personal life. What scenes, people, and situations come to mind? (....) How do you feel? Just notice the feelings and mental images you have. (....)

Now, think about your professional life. What scenes, people, and situations come to mind? (....) Now, how are you feeling? (....)

Imagine a giant scale—the kind with two trays, each hanging from an arm. Imagine that all the images and feelings you just experienced are on or near to this scale. (....) What happens? What is on the scale and what is not? Which side is heavier? (....)

Sit with this visual image for a few moments. (....) Then open your eyes and bring yourself back to this book.

Think of the illustration of the balance scale as the balance of your life: What would be on each side? Use colored markers or pencils to draw what is on your own personal balance scale. Be as fanciful as you like. Try to capture the images and feelings you had with your eyes closed. Don't worry if your drawing doesn't look like great art! The important thing is that you capture your intuitive sense of things.

What did you discover as you completed this activity? How does your scale balance? Which sort of things weighed it down? Which side was lighter? Write down your impressions from your drawings in the margin or in your journal.

Now try this. Look at your picture as if someone else had drawn it, and you are seeing it for the first time. Pretend you know absolutely nothing about the person who drew the images, and nothing about what they might mean to that person. What do you see? What life-choices does the artist seem to be making? What story do these pictures tell? Write your answers below or in your journal.

WHAT IS YOUR DECISION NOW?

Remember, the goal of achieving personal and professional balance is not necessarily to have the scale sitting still with both sides equally full. It is to have a scale that can tip one way or the other as the situation demands, so you don't become stuck, as Theseus did, with one side of your life consistently dominating the other.

Your challenge isn't to simply cut out whatever it is that throws things out of whack. That isn't really dealing with the issue. Your challenge is to reestablish a dynamic equilibrium that will energize you, allow you to jump into your work when that is necessary and to be fully involved in your personal or leisure life at other times.

You may have some ideas about things that could be different. For instance, you might have some ideas about reorganizing the things that take an inordinate amount of time. You may reconsider whether some of the things you believe to be essential really are so. You might want to stop giving so much attention to those things that you do or people that you spend time with out of a sense of duty, and see if there's another way of handling them. You might decide to include more things that make you feel good about yourself in your work or personal life.

It's often easier to *have* an idea than to actually act on it. It all comes down to making decisions. Pick one issue that is very important to you but that you haven't been able to resolve. Spend a few minutes right now clarifying this significant choice that you might make about your life. The more drastic your idea, the better. What needs to change? How can you make this change?

Write your idea or issue as a question to yourself in the space below, starting with the words, Should I . . .? Write it as a question that can be answered with either of two alternatives such as, Should I stay at my present job? Yes or No? or Should I take job A or job B? or Should I do this or that?

Well, what do you think? Should you? You may feel as if you don't know whether or not to make the decision or take the action you wrote about.

There is a way to make it easier. Toss a coin.

That's right. That's what we said.

"Wait," you say. "Come on now, don't suddenly boil my life down to a game of chance. I thought this book was full of psychologically sound approaches to my path through life. What's with this 'toss a coin' suggestion?"

Be patient and trust us. Find a coin and hold it in your hands for a moment as you review your question. This is an important question that you've had trouble resolving; commit yourself now to abiding by the flip of a coin. You will do whatever the coin flip says. Commit to this now.

Now, decide whether heads or tails will be a yes (one alternative), and which will be a no (the other alternative).

Flip your coin and see what you get. Write down which came up, heads or tails, under the coin in the margin.

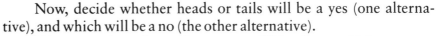

Consider the possibility of actually going with the answer you got. Are you ready to go with that decision? Or would you like to go for the best two out of three tosses?

Don't toss just yet. Recognize Your Decision Now! In fact, we don't want you to toss your coin again. This was a trick question. The key isn't how the coin falls. It isn't even that you should do what the coin says. The point is—what was your reaction when we suggested you might toss again and try for two out of three tosses? That tells you what decision you already have within you.

If you felt satisfied with the possibility of acting on the yes or no that you got, that suggests that your intuition is telling you that this idea is something you could actually carry off. If, on the other hand, you wanted to try tossing the coin again, what does that say to you? It suggests that you weren't 100 percent satisfied with your suggestion. If you were, why would you have wanted to risk messing up your decision by the possibility of getting two of the opposite side of the coin for your other two tosses? You probably had some hesitations about putting it into practice. You might not have consciously known this, but your intuition knew.

Reflect on what you experienced just now, and how you can act on what your intuition has told you about the decision that you already have within you. Know that, no matter what the decision is, it is always in you in some form. Keep making decisions and paying attention. You won't even have to flip a coin to know your own answer immediately.

SYNERGY OF YOUR PERSONAL AND PROFESSIONAL LIVES

The word *synergy* is a literal translation of a Greek word meaning "working together." At one point in the story Theseus's personal and professional lives work together so that each is enhanced by the other. Ariadne falls in love with him because of his heroic nature, and he can be heroic because she is supporting him. When one sees the relationship of one's personal and professional lives in this light, the issue is no longer of, "I'm working too hard. I have to stop so I can have a personal life, because I know I can't have both." Instead, each part of your life can add to or enhance the others. The result is a life in which everything seems to fit together and in which the more one has a fulfilling personal life, the more one has a fulfilling professional life.

In Chinese philosophy, the idea of interrelationship and mutual synergy is part of what's known as Tao, or "the way." The way to have a satisfying life is to live in such a manner that the various parts of one's life flow naturally from each other, and are not compartmentalized or at odds with each other as they vie for our attention.

This is represented by the symbol of two complementary oppo-

Train a fig-tree in the way it should go, and when you are old, sit under the shade of it.

Charles Dickens

sites interrelated in such a way that both together are necessary to form a whole. You have probably seen this symbol of the union of the Yin and the Yang many times.

The black (Yin) represents the mystery, the realm of receptivity and depth, the symbolic realm of the female. The white (Yang) represents the realm of bright light where things are known and clear, the realm of activity and achievement, the symbolic realm of the male. Together they form a circle, the symbol of fullness and infinity. They are not two alien entities; within each one is a perfect circle of the opposite. What a powerful symbol for the balance of your professional and personal lives! This is definitely not the balance of static, separate, clearly defined, unrelated aspects of life; this is a dynamic and fluid balance where the two are inextricably related, and therein lies their power.

This is a very different way of looking at the relationship of your personal and professional life than the balancing of the scales. Try looking from this Yin and Yang perspective, and in the symbol we've provided, use colors or words to indicate how your work and leisure are, or could be, related synergistically.

What do you see in your diagram? Contemplate it and make notes in your journal.

Another Way to Find the Synergy

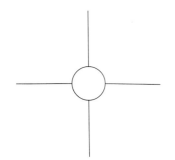

Here is another way to play with the elements of your decision. In your journal or elsewhere, divide a blank page into four sections with a circle in the middle. (See the example in the margin.) You will draw a picture or symbols in each section and allow your intuition to make your decision for you; play Sherlock Holmes as you do this.

This time, the pictures will be about balancing the personal and professional sides of your life, but you can adapt this process for virtually any decision you have to make. Play some wordless music that is at least twenty minutes long while you are doing this activity. Something romantically classical is most effective. It's important to have the music playing until you've completed four drawings, as you will see. Take a moment to find a tape or record or radio station.

1. Pick up a colored marker or pencil in a color that appeals to you and draw a quick symbol for your personal life in one of the four main sections of the figure. It doesn't matter if it's not realistic.

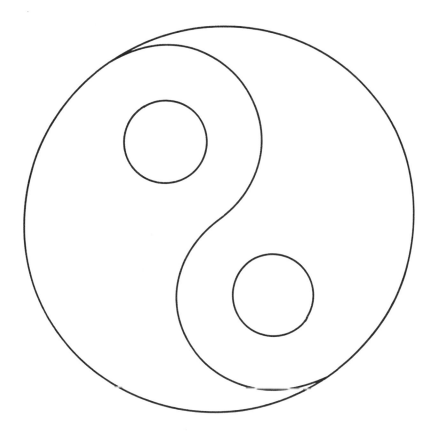

2. In the next section, draw a quick symbol for your professional life. Again, just let your hand draw something, not your mind.

3. In the third space, draw a more complex picture. Draw the two symbols together in this space to illustrate their relationship to each other in your life right now. You may just redraw the two symbols, or you may change the size or color, or a few lines. Or you may draw something entirely different, as long as you metaphorically put your personal and professional life together in the same space and see how they coexist.

4. Now look at the symbols in your third picture. Just notice them on the page. Wipe any thoughts out of your mind. Just notice your symbols. Listen to the music and imagine the symbols dancing with each other to the rhythm of the music. Imagine them flowing and changing to the music. After a minute or so, close

your eyes and keep imagining the symbols dancing harmoniously to the music.

5. In the fourth section, draw what you observed above, to show how the symbols changed and became harmonious with the music. Just draw the colors and shapes.

6. Look at your last picture. How is it different from the third one? What colors, sizes, shapes are different? What new images appeared? What does that suggest to you about a different relationship between your personal and professional lives? Brainstorm; look for all the associations you can from your drawing; pay special attention to the changes in your images that might be seen as metaphorical changes you could effect in your life.

7. Now that you've seen a more harmonious configuration of your personal and professional lives, the last step is to bring this into being. What are you going to do? What new way will you look at things? In the circle in the middle, write down a word or phrase that sums up your own personal wisdom about how to achieve that balance you seek. Write your own motto!

MEET YOUR GUIDE

Are you recognizing your decisions more quickly and efficiently? Is this efficient and appropriate decision-making leading to more balance and synergy in your life? Whether your answers are yes or no, you can become more skilled in recognizing your decisions to have a concrete way to talk to your intuition. The following exercise lets you give your intuition a form, and hear what it has to say. If you already have a sense of an inner guide, the activity can be easy and fun. If you do not, it might provide you with some interesting insights.

In order to meet your intuition, you need to be relaxed and receptive. Unplug your phone, and make sure that you won't be bothered for the next twenty minutes.

Read over the instructions two or three times and then close your eyes and proceed with the meditation. Or read them slowly into a tape recorder and play them back. If you do this, pause at the three dots to allow enough time so that you can be relaxed and see the images described. Or, you might ask a friend to read the instructions to you.

After the meditation, both write down and draw a colored picture of what happened. (Make sure you have your pencils out now so you don't have to break your relaxed state.)

Sit comfortably with your back straight and supported, and close your eyes. Notice how you feel. Notice your back against its support, and those parts of you that are supported by the floor. (....) Notice your head at the top of your neck, and imagine that an invisible thread coming out of the top of your head is effortlessly holding it up straight. (....)

Notice your brain. Feel it sitting in the center of your head. If thoughts and chatter enter it, watch them but don't hold onto them. Let them pass through. (....)

Notice your breathing. Watch your breath as it comes into your throat and lungs. Sense the air coming in and filling you up, filling your lungs, so you can breathe deep down into your abdomen and your belly rises and falls. (....) Rises and falls. (....) Imagine the air filling all the area inside your skin, so you are a being of air, sitting quietly, breathing. Being. (....)

Now, imagine that you are walking on a path through a sunny meadow. The path leads to some woods off in the distance. Picture or sense this as vividly as you can, noticing what you see, what you hear, what the grass feels like, and what you smell. You might even pick a berry and taste it. (....)

As you enter the woods, you notice a cave. The inside of the cave is lit with hundreds of candles. (....) A very wise being is in the cave, waiting for you. Take a moment to walk into the cave and see what's inside it. Notice what the being looks like, and say hello. (....)

This very wise being cares about you and your journey in life. Ask this wise being any questions you wish to, and listen to the answers. Know that you will remember them later when you leave the cave. (....)

The very wise being has a gift for you, something from the cave. Accept it with thanks, for it is valuable. (....)

It's now time to say goodbye to the very wise being. Know that you can come and visit this being any time, and that the being may visit you, even without your knowing. Say goodbye and follow the path back out into the meadow. (....)

Take a deep breath to breathe in the air of here and now in this room, and open your eyes when you are ready. (....)

*When a man's busy, why,
  leisure
Strikes him as wonderful
  pleasure:
Faith, and at leisure once is he?
Straightway he wants to be
  busy.*

Robert Browning

What happened? Jot a few notes in the margin or in your journal to record the highlights of your meeting. Then use colors to capture the essence of your experience. Your picture doesn't have to look like anything recognizable to anyone else. It simply needs to have significance for you.

CONCENTRATING AND LETTING YOUR INTUITION LOOSE

One clue that your personal and professional lives are in balance is that you are able to be involved in what you do with your full attention and energy. As we mentioned earlier, you may be so completely absorbed in your work that, to an outsider, it may seem as if your life is not in balance. But then, if you can become absorbed in a leisure activity with as much concentration, the balance is there. In dynamic balance you experience an overall sense of fulfillment. One mark of this is the ability to be fully alive in the present, whatever it may be.

In fact, if you can experience this concentration, you may find that a concern or question you have in the back of your mind about something else will suddenly resolve itself.

We ask that you practice this sense of absorption in a particular way. Recall the question that you wrote down for the coin toss or, if it has been answered, think of another meaningful question you have about your life. Think of something you have been grappling with for a while, and write down that question in the box in the margin.

Now that it's safely in its box, forget about it for a while. This may be hard to do, but the fact that you wrote it down means that you don't need to keep it inside your head. You can get rid of it here on this page, and then come back to it later.

Now you're going to be challenged to do something very hard.

In the next twenty-four hours, find something that you want to do, and put yourself 150 percent into it. It can be something such as concentrating on eating a food you especially like, playing a particular game that engages you, washing dishes, or walking or sitting in a place that activates all of your senses. Do something that will be completely involving for you. Concentrate on your activity so that you are truly there with it in the present. If you can't think of anything that you want to be that absorbed in, this is a double challenge for you!

All you have to do is to become deeply involved in some activity in either your personal or professional life. Then right after you have completed that engaging activity, reread the question you wrote in the box, pick up a pen or pencil, and start writing about it in this book or in your journal. Don't stop to think or analyze. Simply come back to your issue and write. Let your wise intuition guide your writing. Keep writing for at least a couple of minutes. Then read over what was written, and see what new angle or perspective might emerge.

Now you have had some adventures on your path to balance the personal and professional sides of your life. Perhaps you started out somewhere like Theseus, and were involved in your professional life so much that your personal life was nonexistent. Or perhaps you felt like you were on a wild seesaw. Or maybe your life is fairly well balanced most of the time, and you chose this challenge to see if you could achieve balance virtually all the time!

By now you have probably identified those aspects of your life that you would like to increase, and those that could be removed from center stage. You've spent some time asking your intuition to be your ally here—an ally that Theseus didn't use very often on his adventure.

What's left now is to celebrate your newly rebalanced life. This celebration is part of the hero's return. As an everyday hero, you are about to return home to your everyday personal and professional lives with greater wisdom as to how to live them in synergistic balance and harmony.

THE RETURN

TO ACHIEVE PERSONAL AND PROFESSIONAL BALANCE

As you have probably recognized over the course of following your path to achieve personal and professional balance, your inner wisdom, in the form of your intuition, holds the key for bringing these two aspects of your life into harmony. You've learned from Theseus's experience that it is not the things you do to show your greatness that will bring you success in this realm; true success comes from accepting and following the thread that connects you to your intuition.

Now you are asked to make your hero's declaration, and identify further ways in which you might remember your thread. How are you going to put into practice the wisdom you now have? And what visual image captures the best sense of balance in your life? What would it be like to live a life of personal and professional harmony and balance? Incorporate your responses to these questions in your hero's declaration.

HERO'S DECLARATION

Perfect personal and professional balance in my life would consist of

The visual image that captures this essence of synergistic balance is

Specific things that I will do to remember the thread that connects me to my inner wisdom are

ONE DAY AT A TIME

Now that you have described what your balanced life looks like, and have identified specific steps you could take to stay in touch with your intuitive wisdom, your challenge is to live in balance on a daily basis.

Theseus lived in balance for a short while, and then chose to discard it. Seeing how easy this is, even when you know better, the test of your travels on this path is the opportunity to be different in the way you live your life each day with balance.

This exercise asks you to live just one day—fully in touch with your inner guide during all that you do—so that this day contributes to a profound and harmonious sense of dynamic balance in your life. Do this when you have a fairly normal day ahead of you, and you know you will be able to get back to your book in twenty-four hours.

Before you begin your day, jot down or draw below what you need to know about balance in your life.

This sounds like a simple instruction. You just did this, didn't you? This time, however, you are asked to approach the task in a qualitatively different manner. You are not to think about it intellectually, as you probably did before. Just let a sense of feeling or knowing emerge intuitively.

It will help for you to close your eyes and remember the still, quiet place inside you. Take a few moments to do this before drawing or writing about your personal and professional balance.

Balance in My Life

Now, do whatever you ordinarily would for the next twenty-four hours, without forgetting about balance. At this time tomorrow, open your workbook to this page again, and take a few minutes to again remember the still, quiet place inside you. Reflect on how you lived the last twenty-four hours.

What Happened?

What things did you do and what attitudes did you have that encouraged life? How much did you consciously pay attention to balance in these twenty-four hours? How much were you on automatic pilot?

Jot down your observations of your day in the space provided or in your journal. Be sure to include any notes to yourself about significant differences you noticed, and situations that caused you to forget about balance.

Observations on Living in Balance for One Day

FOLLOW-UP: MAPPING YOUR PATH TO BALANCE

Now, you are to complete another visual log and verbal log of your travels. How are you different now? How are you different in terms of where you are on your everyday hero's path toward achieving a dynamic, synergistic balance between the personal and professional aspects of your life?

Don't look back yet to your initial logs you made when you started this chapter. Recall that the visual log is an intuitive sort of mapping of where you are now in your path toward resolving the challenge of achieving personal and professional balance. The verbal log is a chance to characterize this challenge in your life right now in terms of a hero's journey. How do real events and people in your life parallel aspects of this metaphor?

Prepare the visual and verbal logs in your journal or on separate sheets of paper. Take a few moments to be still and pay attention to your breath. Allow an awareness of your journey over the last week to come into focus. Use colors to draw a figure or other symbols to represent yourself on your path in the expressive pictorial log. Then make notes about where you are with regard to the stages of this challenge in your written log.

REFLECTIONS ON YOUR PATH

Now that you've completed this chapter and have worked on the balance challenge for a week or so, write a letter to yourself about your experiences on this path. This can serve to consolidate and legitimize your experience so far.

You can keep this letter or statement as tangible evidence of your journey to this point. Then, if you feel you need to do some specific work on this challenge in the future or just want a boost to your ability to achieve balance in your life, you can go back to this review of what you just accomplished.

CELEBRATE!

How are you celebrating your completion of this challenge? What are you doing to reward yourself for your successful journey? How are you making a public statement of your private changes? Make sure that in the days ahead you continue to acknowledge and celebrate your journey and the synergistic balance in your life.

9

Finding Your Way to Prosperity

All the wonders you seek are within yourself.

Sir Thomas Browne

Achieving the conventional external successes of money, power, and recognition doesn't seem to be all we think it should be. The moment we think we've won the prize, something comes up in another part of our lives to make us feel we have hit bottom. Then, seemingly out of nowhere, we find that life has taken an upswing again.

What is constant within all of this change? What allows us to keep leaving that state of innocence and answer the call, to jump into the pit of initiation and find allies to help us come up to the breakthrough and celebration—over and over again?

Only one answer comes down through the ages: the need to know, become, and fulfill your true self, your inner essence, your inner creative resource. The sages keep telling us to "Know thyself," yet we continually shy away from that, hoping that a little more money, or becoming the son or daughter our parents always wanted us to be, or even eating an especially good meal, will fill the bill instead.

And yet knowing yourself is not impossible. You just have to draw upon your inner resource of compassion. By this we don't mean the mushiness of do-gooders, but a loving kindness, first for yourself and then for others. This compassion is an unspoken affirmation that you have unlimited creativity within you and that others have it too. And it is also an affirmation that you are a channel or instrument for a larger creativity—so you can be unattached to all the rewards you get just by reveling in being your true self. When you have this compassion, you indeed have prosperity.

You may be surprised at the story we've chosen to illustrate these truths: Cinderella. When you reread this timeless story (which has been told in countless forms all over the world), you can get much more from it than you could when you were a child. Now you will see that you have aspects of *all* of the characters. Just like Cinderella's stepsisters, there is a part of you that keeps grasping for one thing after another. Just like the Prince, you have an aspect that appreciates the goodness and lack of pretension represented by a Cinderella. Just like her father, you can sometimes be oblivious to all these aspects of yourself as you strive to survive day to day. Just like her Fairy Godmother, you have the power to turn ordinary, everyday things into something special. And just like Cinderella herself, you are able to live from your essential nature and have not only the satisfaction of self-worth but all the external rewards.

Go forth on your everyday hero's path and have fun as you discover what the nature of true prosperity is for you, who your allies are, and how you can experience it.

<hr>

PREPARATION

Cinderella

Once upon a time, there lived in the forest a poor but happy family. There was a hardworking woodcutter, his loving wife, and their beautiful daughter Ella, who loved to play in the woods, making toys out of pine cones and small rocks and long wispy grasses.

One winter, the snows were especially heavy, and winds howled through the chinks of the cottage walls. The woodcutter's wife became very ill. Ella nursed her tenderly. She made broth to nourish her, and sang songs to cheer her. But the winter was too long, her illness too dire, and one night the woodcutter's wife died. Ella whispered a prayer for her mother so that her soul would find peace. She grieved in the traditional custom, by rubbing ashes from the fire into her own hair.

The woodcutter was also very sad and, after a time, became extremely lonely. But by and by, he chanced to meet a fine lady with two daughters who had come into the forest. He married the fine lady, and brought her home to be Ella's stepmother, hoping to bring happiness back into his cottage.

However, the fine lady's daughters were not accustomed to living in the style of the woodcutter. Nor did they bring happiness with them. They laughed at Ella. "Look at you!" they taunted her. "Taking cinders from the fire and dirtying yourself with them. What's the point of that?" And they teased her. "Cinder-Ella," they called her. "Cinderella! Cinderella!" And so she became known as Cinderella. Cinderella's stepsisters, Farra and Drulla by name, were discontented with the simple life they now led.

"Why can't we have fancy clothes," they would complain. "This porridge is slop. Why can't we eat sweet cakes with sugar icing off silver plates? This is a useless, pointless life. Who will ever want to marry us if all we have are raggedy clothes? Why don't you give us fine silks and brocades? Then we'll really be worth something!"

The woodcutter tried very hard to teach Farra and Drulla what his dear wife had taught to Ella. He tried to teach them compassion for all living things, integrity, and honesty. He tried to teach them that real beauty is more than skin deep, and to show them the wonders of the forest. But Farra and Drulla didn't care. They became sullen and angry.

"Don't try to fool us," snapped Farra. "We're just shabby nobodies out here."

"Who cares about dumb old wildflowers?" whined Drulla. "I want silk slippers for my feet."

The years went by and the stepsisters became more and more dissatisfied. Farra said, "See! Just shabby nobodies. If you'd go into the town and bring us fur blankets and golden dishes, things would be different."

"Yes," complained Drulla. "And if only you'd take us into town to meet the society ladies, somebody would give us silk slippers and money, and we could marry nobles and princes, and we wouldn't have to live out here in this rundown little cottage."

While the stepsisters complained, longing for luxury and scheming how to find nobles and princes to marry, Cinderella worked from dawn to dusk, and kept the fire going. She washed clothes and scrubbed the floor. She cooked meals for her stepsisters, her stepmother, and her sad old father. She did the mending, and in the Spring planted flowers around the house. Although her heart was filled with grief for her mother, it was also full of love, and sometimes this love came out in snatches of song.

Farra and Drulla shook their heads and said, "Our stepsister doesn't know what's important."

Now, as Spring was turning to summer, the stepsisters heard that the Prince was going to have a magnificent ball. All the gentlemen and all the ladies from all the counties in the kingdom would be there.

"We have to go to find ourselves noblemen to marry," said Farra.

"Yes," replied Drulla. "Cinderella, you'll have to make dresses for us. The best you can. And they'd better be beautiful!"

"What shall I make them from?" asked Cinderella.

"We don't know, but you better make them fast." And the stepsisters kicked Cinderella to show her they meant business. "And don't forget to make our supper and mend our boots and wash our shawls," they reminded her.

Cinderella wanted to go to the ball, too. She dreamed of dancing to beautiful music in the arms of a young man. He wouldn't have to be a prince, just a kind person. But time was short, and she didn't even know how she was going to sew clothes for her stepsisters, let alone herself.

She sat and looked out at the night, wondering what to do. She saw the trees gently swaying in the night breeze and the moonlight, and she had an idea. She gathered up some moonlight, wove it, and sewed it into two beautiful dresses for Farra and Drulla, dresses that shimmered and seemed to dance by themselves.

It was past dawn when she finished, and was going to go to sleep when her stepsisters woke up and shouted, "Where's our breakfast, Cinderella?"

So Cinderella put the porridge on the fire, and while it was cooking, she showed her stepsisters the dresses she had made. They were amazed and delighted at the beauty of the dresses, though of course they didn't tell that to Cinderella. They didn't even thank her. Then Cinderella said to her stepsisters, "You know, I think I'll make myself a dress like yours and go to the ball, too."

"You!?" shrilled Farra. Farra and Drulla laughed. "You have ashes all over you. No one would be interested in you!"

"And besides," chimed Drulla, "there won't be time to gather more moonbeams before tonight. Anyway, we need you to fit our dresses and make us lunch and comb our hair and paint our faces."

Cinderella sighed. She knew there would be no time to gather moonbeams. She knew her stepsisters were making great demands on her, too. "But they are unhappy and don't know it," she said to herself. "If I can give them a little pleasure, perhaps they will be kind. Perhaps they will learn to love and be loved." And Cinderella set about her tasks.

That evening, Farra and Drulla went off to the ball. Their dresses were truly beautiful, but there was something strange about them, too. Cinderella saw that her stepsisters didn't look beautiful, but she couldn't put her finger on why. After they had left, and the moon came out, she looked out at the trees and sighed.

"There's no time to sew a moonbeam dress now. And I do so wish I could go to the ball."

Suddenly, a sphere of light appeared! With a whirring sound it spun around in front of Cinderella, growing larger and larger, and with a little "poof" a beautiful being suddenly stood where the light had been.

"Who are you?" asked Cinderella, somewhat taken aback.

"I'm your Fairy Godmother and have come to grant your wish. Not only will you go to the ball, but you will have a beautiful dress to wear and a horse-drawn carriage to ride in."

"But . . . I don't need . . . ," stammered Cinderella.

"Never mind that!" said the Fairy Godmother and pointed her wand at the moonbeams. With a flash, the moonbeams gathered themselves up and wrapped themselves around Cinderella so that she was wearing a dress a hundred times more beautiful than those of her stepsisters. Then the moonbeam wrapped itself around her feet so that, instead of her ragged sandals, she had slippers that shone like the night sky. They looked like magic glass and felt as soft as cobwebs to her feet.

"But there's nothing even like a carriage here," protested Cinderella, "and certainly no horses or footmen to guide it. Why, there's only . . ." and she looked around. "There are only mice and that old pumpkin."

In an instant, six mice were transformed into six magnificent white horses, and the pumpkin grew, quick as a flash, into a beautiful golden carriage, complete with a footman.

"There you are," said her Fairy Godmother. "Now hop in and stop dithering, child. But remember, the magic wears off at midnight. You *must* be home by midnight!"

With that, the Fairy Godmother disappeared in a bright cloud. Cinderella climbed into the pumpkin carriage, and the horses trotted off and took her to the ball.

Cinderella had a wonderful time at the ball. A handsome young man asked her to dance, and they waltzed as if in a dream. As they waltzed, Cinderella told the man about her life, and how much she loved the woods. She told him that her mother had died, and that this was her first time out of the forest since her mother's death. She told him about caring for her stepsisters. The man asked Cinderella to dance again. And again. And again.

Suddenly, the grandfather clock in the corner began to strike twelve.

"Oh, my goodness!" gasped Cinderella. "I must go!" And she pulled herself from the young man's arms.

"Wait!" shouted the Prince, for that is who he was. "Don't leave! Who are you?"

But Cinderella was gone. She raced into the carriage, which sped away faster than light, arriving back at the woodcutter's cottage on the last stroke of twelve.

As the clock's chimes faded into silence, Cinderella found herself alone, by the fireplace, dressed in her old, torn dress. She pinched herself and asked, "Was this a dream?" But no, she felt too full and happy inside to have dreamed about the young man with whom she had danced. She turned back to the fire and put another log on it. "I may not be rich and important, but this night is one I'll remember always. I am happy and rich in memories."

Then she noticed that she was wearing only one sandal. "Where can my other shoe be?" she wondered. She looked everywhere for it. No sandal. "I must have lost it when I ran out of the ball," she thought. "Well, I can make myself another one tomorrow."

The next day, Farra and Drulla wouldn't stop talking about the ball. "Ooh, the one with the golden diamond ring and the velvet jacket danced with me," preened Farra.

"Well," returned Drulla, "the one with sixteen stallions and a hundred peacocks danced with me!"

"And did you have fun dancing with the poker from the fireplace?" they asked Cinderella. And they laughed. They had no idea that the beautiful young woman who had captivated the Prince was their stepsister. Cinderella said nothing, for she knew she would only be teased. Besides, she wanted to keep her precious memories a secret. They nourished her as she went about her tasks.

A few days later Farra said to Drulla, "Did you hear? The Prince fell in love with someone who ran away from him at midnight. And she dropped her glass slipper. So he's searching the kingdom for the owner of the slipper. He's trying it on all the young women, and when he finds the one it fits, he'll marry her!"

"Oh," gasped Drulla. "That would be even better than marrying the one with the stallions and peacocks. Let's try on the slipper."

They didn't have long to wait. The very next day the Prince's carriage arrived at their cottage. The Prince was sad and weary. He had been trying the slipper on all the young women's feet in the kingdom, and this was the last, the poorest, and the most distant cottage of all. He was tired of hearing, "Ooh, it fits. It's me, it's me," when he could easily see that their feet were too big or too small or too long or too short. Besides, none of the young ladies had the grace and gentleness and warmth of the lady he had held in his arms.

"Hullo, Hullo," said the Prince's footman, jumping down from the carriage and striding to the cottage door. "Any young ladies in this house?"

"Oh yes, there are two of us," said Farra and Drulla. "And we both loved dancing with the Prince at the ball." (Which was untrue, as neither one had danced with the Prince.)

"It must be me he's searching for," said Farra, eyeing the gold on the carriage.

"No, no, it's me, of course," interrupted Drulla, looking at the beautiful horses.

The footman said, "Well, let's try you." He tried to place the slipper on Farra's foot, but it was much too big and almost broke the slipper.

"Wait a moment. It must have swollen from all that dancing, you know," Farra exclaimed. "Let me try again." And she pushed her foot harder into the shoe, so that her skin was scraped and bruised.

"Oh, I want that gold so much," she sighed, oblivious to the pain.

"Sorry, lady," said the footman at last, pulling off the slipper. "Doesn't look like a fit." Farra sat on the ground and began to cry.

"Well, since I'm the last young lady, it must be me," Drulla breathed in her sexiest voice. "Why don't we just forget about the old shoe. I'll just get into the carriage pulled by those handsome horses."

"No, lady. You have to try the slipper," said the footman. "Prince's orders."

So Drulla put her foot into the slipper, but her foot was much too skinny. "Oh, I danced so hard with the Prince that night that I must have worn the flesh off my foot!" she said.

The footman did not believe her. "Sorry, miss. It doesn't fit." He turned from Drulla and went back to the carriage to talk to the Prince.

After a brief, whispered conversation, he came back to Drulla. "Are you *sure* there are no other young ladies here? We've searched the whole kingdom and the one who owns this slipper has to be somewhere. Are you sure there's no one else?"

"Absolutely no one," snapped Drulla. "It's me, I tell you."

Just then, Cinderella came out of the cottage to fetch some water at the well.

"Who's that?" asked the footman.

"That? Oh, she's nobody," Drulla quickly replied. "Just our stepsister. She's not who you're looking for."

"Got to try her," returned the footman. "Prince's orders."

He called to Cinderella, and tried the slipper on her foot before Cinderella was quite aware of what was happening. The slipper fit like a glove. Cinderella felt full and wonderful inside.

"A perfect fit," cried the footman.

On hearing that, the Prince forgot his gloom and jumped out of his carriage. He gathered Cinderella up in his arms and, humming a waltz, waltzed around the carriage with her.

"Stop! Stop!" shouted Cinderella. "I can't go with you."

"Why not?" the Prince asked, but set her down on the ground.

"Because I don't have riches and land and servants. I am not a fine lady of the court. I don't have money or gold. I'm a poor woodcutter's daughter still grieving for my mother and trying to take care of my father and stepsisters. You won't want me."

"That's right!" chorused Farra and Drulla.

"Nonsense," said the Prince. "That's the reason I do want you. I'm not looking for wealth and courtly bearing. I'm tired of all that. I'm looking for a true soul who knows how to love and be loved. I'm looking for a real human being with whom to share my life. Someone with compassion, integrity, and honesty. I'm looking for you."

So saying, he knelt down on one knee and took Cinderella's hand. "Oh, one of inner beauty, will you marry me? It's you with whom I wish to spend my life. You who can sing songs of moonbeams and bring sunlight into my heart."

"Well," began Cinderella, "what about my father and stepsisters and stepmother?"

"Bring them to the palace, too," replied the Prince.

"Then, yes," said Cinderella, "I will marry you."

And Cinderella and the Prince climbed into the carriage, and rode off toward the most spectacular sunset that has ever been seen.

THE MANY MEANINGS OF CINDERELLA

Even though Cinderella is a European story, it embodies many of the truths of the East. Cinderella's way of being shows the Eastern tradition of *dharma*—of righteous living without attachment to the results of doing your "life-purpose." Further, the story is permeated by the Western and Christian concept of the "true soul who knows how to love and be loved," as the Prince says. Cinderella shows us the essence of compassion.

Unlike our other heroes, Cinderella uses all four of the tools for creativity without faltering. As such, she is an exemplar, someone who masters the seeming conflict between money (and all external goals) and a rich feeling of inner self-worth. She just *is*. She does her work without complaint, even when it is very difficult, and manages to keep up her spirits. She embodies the very seeds of true prosperity, which come to bloom when the Prince reflects the value of her inner qualities back to her.

Cinderella exhibits *faith in her own creativity* with her devotion to her mother and her ability to make a breakthrough, when she makes her stepsisters' dresses. The Fairy Godmother, who appears as her ally, is one of the great literary symbols of the creative resource we all have within us. The Godmother symbolizes Cinderella's power to find true prosperity, and reminds us that we always have the answer, the potential, and power to meet our challenges. Our inner essence has the qualities of intuition, will, joy, strength, and—most importantly—compassion. It is the Fairy Godmother's loving kindness that catches our hearts, because we have always wanted that unconditional support from someone—our parents, our teachers, our lovers, our friends, our spouse. The message of Cinderella is that this loving kindness is always there, inside us. We need only be clear-sighted enough to see it.

How does Cinderella get that clarity? She shows a total *absence of judgment.* Never do we hear her criticizing her stepsisters, even though we can easily see their faults. She observes them and does what needs to be done. The only time her voice of judgment even comes close to making a statement is when she says to the Prince, "You won't want me." That inner blame and criticism makes a last-ditch effort just as she is about to reach a breakthrough.

However, the Prince recognizes Cinderella's inner beauty and doesn't pay attention to her self-doubts: He whisks her away so they can marry. His role is to show us how love can pull us past the barriers that the voice of judgment erects.

Throughout the world of mythology and fairy tale, marriage represents a sacred union of complementary aspects of humanness, which must both be present if we are to live creative and fulfilling lives. This union may be interpreted in many sumbolic unions: external and internal prosperity, as in the story of Cinderella; professional and personal life; intellect and heart; and assertiveness and receptivity, to name but a few. This union is not easily achieved. We see that Cinderella could not have married the Prince had she not first gone through the initiation of her mother's death and her stepsisters' callousness.

The Prince is the main representative of *precise observation* in the

Cinderella tale. Cinderella sees everything quite clearly because she has virtually no voice of judgment. She even understands that talking about her night at the ball is fruitless, so she holds her joy inside. The Prince, however, is able to see beyond the surface into Cinderella's true worth. Although his is a romantic love in the story, his marriage to Cinderella is a metaphor for our own ability to marry that keenly observant aspect of our inner self with that external self that acts in the world. It is a metaphor for our coming into our own inner wisdom, joy, courage, and compassion.

If you can observe even the simplest thing in a pure way, energy wells up; this is the experience of self-worth. And, of course, when you have a profound sense of your own value as a human being, then this is prosperity; for even in outwardly hard times, your inner value cannot be diminished.

Cinderella asks a number of *penetrating questions*, even though her questions seem quite simple on first reading. She asks the Fairy Godmother who she is, reflecting our own desire to know the source of our creativity and power. She asks herself where her missing shoe is, which is, ultimately, the key to her prosperity. Of course, she doesn't know this, but she doesn't worry about what cannot be retrieved. Instead, she simply has faith that she will be able to replace it.

The Prince, quite significantly, asks who and where Cinderella is as he scours the countryside searching for the owner of the glass slipper. He is searching for the qualities that will make him whole; he needs her as much as she needs him.

The stepsisters ask questions, too, but they do not ask *penetrating* questions; because they do not want answers. Their questions are simply a way of expressing their dissatisfaction with their lives. Their questions stand in contrast to really powerful and penetrating questions, which can show us our inner power.

Cinderella's most penetrating questions come in the form of wishes. Her strongest inner questions are answered when she wishes. She seems to go into a trance when she makes the dresses for her stepsisters, when she has the idea to make them out of moonbeams. She wonders about going to the ball herself and, when she wishes, her Fairy Godmother, an embodiment of creative spirit, suddenly appears. A question of wonder can be a connection to your inner creativity.

You are probably not alone if you are thinking that this is all well and good, but your life isn't a fairy tale. You may feel sometimes that

"Ashes" and "Cinders" in fairy tales are code words for the ashy, sooty, depressed, "out of it" time.

Robert Bly

you have more of the wicked stepsisters or woodcutter in you than you have aspects of Cinderella, her Fairy Godmother, or the Prince. You're not really human unless you have some concerns about money, some hidden competitive thoughts, and some desires that get in the way of feeling a rich flow of self-worth.

You have the basis of your inner essence, and particularly its aspect of compassion, that can help you to deal with the challenge of identifying and finding true prosperity. But, like many of us, your voice of judgment is probably still active regarding money and external rewards. On one hand, you may feel that you can only be successful if you attain a certain material level of success. On the other hand, you may feel that somehow it's not "right" to go after money, and that you'd be better off avoiding it. Your challenge might be to come to terms with these opposing views.

YOUR PATH
TO TRUE PROSPERITY

A story such as Cinderella's endures because it says something essential about aspects of the human condition. Like a particularly powerful dream, this story can remind you of your strengths and your weapons for dealing with the challenge of money versus self-worth, which is at the root of the search for prosperity. At the same time, it can show the specific nature of that challenge for you.

Now, reread the story as if you are all the characters, in all their richness. The scenery, the objects, and the storyteller are also parts of you and your life. Then answer each of the questions below.

Use the space below or your journal. Remember, the best approach is to go with whatever comes to your mind first, even if later you decide to elaborate. Trust your intuition.

1. Even though Cinderella has good qualities and prevails in the end, she has a difficult life during most of the story. Do you remember how you felt about her situation—her mother dying, being forced to do menial work for two demanding stepsisters—when you first heard the story? Have you felt that in your own life? Can you relate to this feeling now? Describe a time when you felt like Cinderella.

2. Imagine that right now you are in the situation you described above. How do you feel? What emotions do you have? What physical sensations? Where are they in your body? What kind of thoughts are going through your mind?

Success rests with the courage, endurance, and, above all, the will to become the person you are, however peculiar that may be. . . . Then you will be able to say, "I have found my hero and he is me."

George Sheehan

3. Cinderella's idea to make the stepsisters' dresses out of moonbeams is a magical moment of discovery. You, too, may have had moments like this, which had magic in their own way. Recall one of your own such moments of discovery, and write about it in terms of its magic.

4. The wicked stepsisters can be seen as representing your shadow side—the side of you that you don't particularly like or want other people to see. What aspects do you have that may cause you shame? (Remember that these aspects could be fabrications of your voice of judgment; they might not be part of your true self or essence.)

5. The Fairy Godmother is the compassion of your own inner essence. Who has supported you or admired you in such a way that you could glimpse your essence? What is it like to be around such a person? What does this tell you about your true self?

6. At several points in the story, Cinderella falters. She doesn't immediately accept the external rewards (the Fairy Godmother, the Prince) that have come from her connection to her true self. Think about a time when you believe you may have not accepted a gift that was offered to you. Describe. What would you do in that situation today?

7. *Several relationships to money or external symbols of prosperity are represented. The wicked stepsisters don't feel they have enough and always want more. The Prince has so much that he is only looking for a true soul. Cinderella seems not to notice money and external rewards. When she dreams of dancing at the ball, she doesn't desire a prince for a dancing partner, just a kind person. Which of these perspectives is most like yours? What is your relationship to money?*

8. *The Fairy Godmother turns ordinary things—mice, a pumpkin—into magnificent ones. What aspects of your life seem ordinary but are really quite precious to you?*

9. *Is there a missing glass slipper in your life; some aspect of you that you are ignoring but will provide the key to your own deep sense of prosperity? What is it? Who or what would be most likely to be searching for the real you—who or what will give you a sense of wholeness when they find that the shoe fits?*

Now that you've answered these questions, what have you learned about your own story? What aspects of your self became clearer? These questions should help clarify the nature of your own path to true prosperity, and the qualities of yourself or situations in your life that help or hinder you in achieving this.

You may not have the same concerns about prosperity as another reader. You may have identified with the poor woodcutter who works so hard to survive, or with the Prince who has everything, but yearns for genuine union with another person, or even the Fairy Godmother or the stepsisters, as representatives of qualities you would like to develop or diminish.

Seeing yourself reflected in this timeless story is the starting point for this path. The exercises in this chapter let you undertake your own journey of self-discovery. It is the riches within you that can give you an abiding sense of prosperity, regardless of the external contingencies of your life.

MAPPING YOUR PATH TO PROSPERITY

Visual Log

Melissa's visual log is interesting. In a sense, her challenge to find her true prosperity was the complement to the journey presented in the Cinderella story.

"My stage of innocence was when I was a sixties flower-child," she told us. "I thought money was bad. Period. And love was good. And you couldn't have both. So I chose to be a loving person, and really didn't pay any attention to earning a living. I almost pretended that money didn't exist for me. I did feel prosperous, in terms of feeling good about me but, oddly, I felt resentful that I was poor."

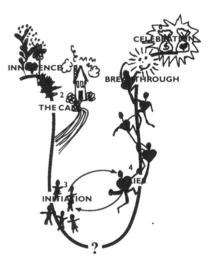

The call, for Melissa, was to be self-sufficient. She drew a house to represent having her own place to live, and pointed out that she realized that she couldn't have this if she didn't also allow material prosperity to be a part of her life. Her initiation consisted of several years in which she held a number of part-time jobs, all working with people, so that she could earn money *and* feel good about herself. "I guess I had a challenge opposite to that of many people," she said. "I had to learn that material prosperity was okay. But maybe the reason I didn't think it was okay was that I wasn't sure I deserved it."

Melissa drew a smiling face in the center of the breakthrough, to show that she needn't feel bad about herself if she lives well. "I learned about right livelihood from knowing several people who are making it in the world *and* are compassionate human souls." She drew these figures as her allies.

Melissa's celebration, which she feels she has almost reached, shows how she can feel good about prosperity and abundance in her life.

Now draw your visual log. Remember that you will probably draw a very different picture than Melissa's. Just play with your picture. Allow your intuition to draw it—the more childlike and unplanned it is, the better. Don't worry if you don't know what it means. The point is to just do it.

A Visual Travel Log

Where I am at the start of this journey

Date: _____

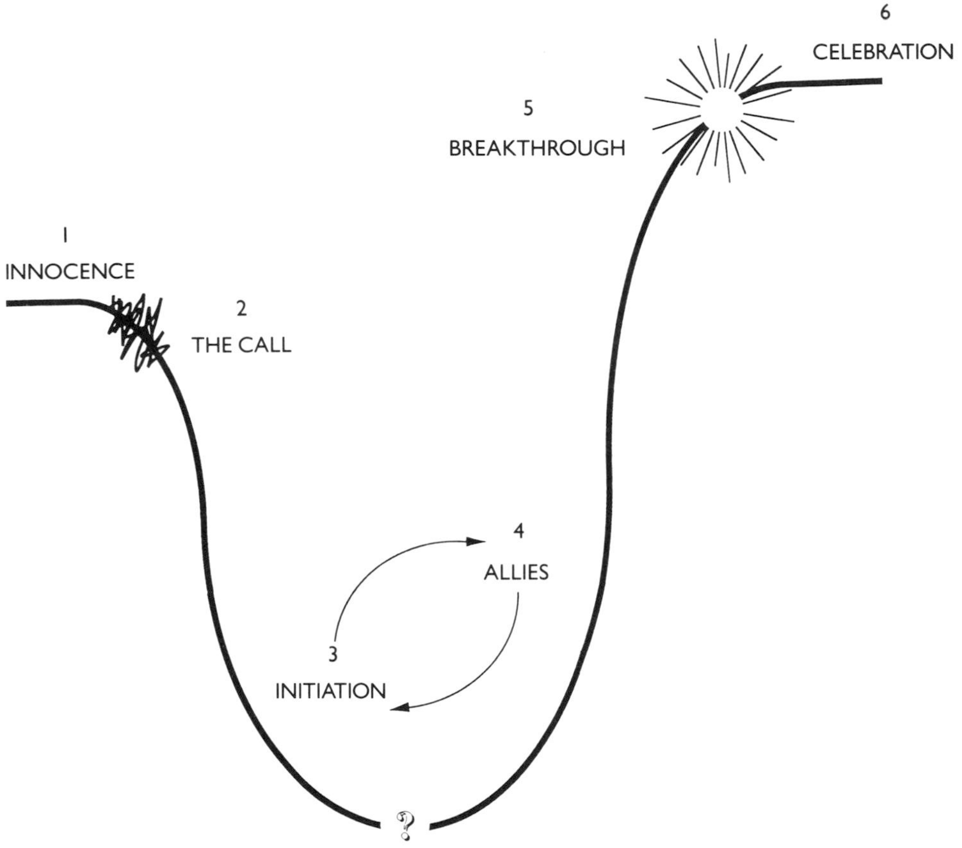

Verbal Log

Melissa's notes in her verbal log clarify the images she portrayed in her visual log.

INNOCENCE (Feeling comfortable with my situation)

> Hippie flower-child.
> Love is good. Money is bad.
> My worth depends on quality of loving.

THE CALL TO ADVENTURE (Identifying and recognizing my challenge)

> Being out in the world on my own, having to earn my living!

INITIATION (Really being tested)

> Trying to live righteously.
> Felt I was going in all directions, working really hard and not earning much, even though I was doing morally correct work.

ALLIES (Finding strength and help)

> People I knew who were compassionate human souls who also had *things* in life.

BREAKTHROUGH (Reaching new awareness or resolution)

> Here I am! I am a good person. If I take care of me I can be even more loving for other people.

CELEBRATION (Returning home and being different)

> When I know this 100 percent.
> Realizing and living in a way that acknowledges it.

Melissa's issues with money and self-worth could be very different from yours. Often, people are struggling with the notion that self-worth can be seen as prosperity, and for the first time are seriously considering the more inner-oriented ways in which they feel very rich and full. In either case, the realization that prosperity can mean inner *and* outer value, if you are living with compassion and acting from your creative essence, can be a liberating and rewarding shift of perspective.

Now write your response to each of the phases of the hero's journey. Don't censor what you write. Let the words just flow. This is your private workbook and nobody needs to see it unless you show it to them.

The value of completing this self-assessment is to start probing, questioning, and observing without judgment just where you are on this particular path.

A Verbal Travel Log

Where I am at the start of this journey

Date: _____

We should find perfect existence through imperfect existence.

Shunryu Suzuki

INNOCENCE (Feeling comfortable with my situation)

THE CALL TO ADVENTURE (Identifying and recognizing my challenge)

INITIATION (Really being tested)

ALLIES (Finding strength and help)

BREAKTHROUGH (Reaching new awareness or resolution)

CELEBRATION (Returning home and being different)

BE YOUR SELF

Cinderella gives us a model of someone who lives from her inner essence. Even when she is in an unpleasant situation, she doesn't change her way of being. She doesn't become alienated and put herself down. She doesn't believe she is better than other people. Her ideal comes from inside; she doesn't try to copy what someone else does.

The motto for this chapter is, Be Your Self. When you live by it, you can have an experience of living like Cinderella; being your self in the highest possible sense. This is true prosperity. The suggestion this motto makes is to let go of your outer pretensions, of any inflation or alienation you might feel. After you shed all this, you are simply yourself, and you can work hard, accomplish much, and do so with joy. Then you will truly experience prosperity in its fullest, richest sense.

Of course, it's not easy to Be Your Self right away. First you have to let go of anxious striving. Stop masterminding the results. Experience what it means not to have to improve, to accept yourself just as you are and live from the power of that realization.

During the time you are working with this chapter on the challenge of experiencing true prosperity, approach all of your tasks and activities in the following ways:

Seek no approval from others. Try to live up to your own high standards for your work without the compulsion to please others. If you find yourself seeking approval, say to yourself, "Seek no approval," and get on with what you are doing.

Make no comparisons of yourself or your work to others. If you find yourself feeling superior to or inferior to someone else, say to yourself, "Make no comparisons," and get on with what you are doing.

Seek no recognition or reward. Do your work and live life well because it pleases you to do it well. If you find yourself motivated primarily by recognition or reward, say to yourself, "Seek no recognition or reward," and get on with things. This is not to suggest that you reject recognition and reward when it comes your way—as it inevitably will. Just try not to strive for it.

Work hard and do your best for its own sake. To Be Your Self is to live up to your own internal standards, regardless of what the rest of the world thinks. Take pleasure in the process of doing your work to the

The mainspring of creativity appears to be . . . [one's] tendency to actualize himself, to become his potentialities.

Carl Rogers

The almighty dollar, that great object of universal devotion throughout our land, seems to have no genuine devotees in these peculiar villages.

Washington Irving

best of your ability. If you find yourself thinking or worrying about what others will think, just say to yourself, "Do your best," and then get on with your life.

Remember, you won't get the benefit of living with this motto unless you stop to observe your experiences. Take some regular time every day (most people find that the evening is best) to reflect on your last twenty-four hours. Make daily notes in the margins of this book or in your journal about how you lived with this motto. What were your experiences? What did you think, feel, and sense? What happened? And through it all, don't forget to *Be Your Self.*

Be
Your
Self

——— THE JOURNEY ———

You may have often realized in your travels that having material wealth is great, but feeling successful in life involves something deeper than that. It involves feeling good about yourself as a human being—a human being who is a very ordinary human soul like millions of other people and, at the same time, a very worthwhile and valuable being on the planet.

On this journey, you can be like a modern day Cinderella, exploring your relationship to external and internal wealth. The journey starts with an examination of your relationship to external wealth and moves into an exploration of your feelings about your inner wealth.

We have found that, in our culture, people have a very difficult time talking about money—how much they make, what their aspirations for it are, what they use it for, what their net worth is, how much savings they have, whether and how their checkbook is balanced, how much money they have saved, how much trouble they are in in terms of money owed, and so on. No matter how much money you have or don't have, there is probably something that we've listed in that last sentence that you'd rather not talk about, certainly not to strangers but perhaps even less so to co-workers or people close to you.

People often have more difficulty talking about and contemplating issues related to money than about death, relationships, and religion. It seems that money is an outer representation of their feelings of fear or guilt. When you are not in touch with your self, with your inner essence, money can become the main indicator of who you are.

Therefore, you can put enormous psychic energy into such issues as having too much money, or too little, asking for a raise, or facing the annual income tax work. This emphasis on money pulls away from acknowledgment of self-worth. You forget that there doesn't have to be a conflict between money and all the external rewards and a feeling of self-worth with both inner and outer prosperity.

Every day, in every way, I'm getting better and better.

Émil Coué

WHAT IS MONEY, ANYWAY?

Let's explore your relation to money and external prosperity. Take out a dollar bill—just a simple, green, one-dollar bill. Hold it in your hand.

Sit quietly and see what it feels like between your fingers. Smell it. Look at it for a minute or two. Have you ever inspected a dollar bill this closely before? What do all the pictures on it mean? Why are they there? How much do you know about this piece of paper in your hands?

When you've finished reading this paragraph, close your eyes, and take five minutes to allow images to come to your mind about this dollar bill. Continue to hold the bill. Close your eyes after reading each of the following questions. Open your eyes and write or draw your answer.

I celebrate myself and sing myself.

Walt Whitman

What does this money you are holding in your hand represent?

What are you willing to do for money?

What are you not willing to do for money?

What are you willing to do with money?

What are you not willing to do with money?

Thinking to get at once all the gold that the goose could give, he killed it, and opened it only to find—nothing.

Aesop

What anxieties do you feel as you hold the money?

What energy do you feel as you hold the money?

Look at the back of your dollar bill. You'll see a pyramid, like the great pyramids of Egypt, symbolizing all the ancient mysteries and knowledge of the ages. The pyramid is topped by an eye, reminiscent of what is known as the third eye in some Eastern philosophies. It represents intuitive and spiritual knowing to some people, including past founders and leaders of the United States. That symbol and others on money are reminders that the value of the paper is something entirely different from what we normally ascribe to it. But what does it mean for you? Contemplate this symbol, and draw or write in your journal or in the margin what it might be telling you about your relationship to money.

Now put down the dollar bill and contemplate what you have written or drawn. Write a summary vignette or paragraph about your relationship to money.

THE INHERITANCE

Suppose you were to be notified that a long-lost relative had passed away and left you $10,000, tax-free. Below, write what you would do with the money.

$10,000

Now, suppose you were informed that there had been a mistake, and that your tax-free inheritance was really $1,000,000. What would you do with that money?

$1,000,000

And now, suppose that, miracle of miracles, you were informed that the person managing your relative's estate was really quite bad with numbers, and that your inheritance was actually $10,000,000 (still tax-free). What would you do now?

$10,000,000

i thank you God for most this
amazing
day: for the leaping greenly
spirits of trees
and a blue true dream of sky;
and for everything
which is natural, which is
infinite, which is yes.

e. e. cummings

People have a variety of reactions when they imagine these scenarios. Their reactions often indicate something about the role they ascribe to money and material wealth in their lives. What sort of reactions did you have? Consider the following questions and jot down some responses.

1. What did you notice as you imagined the three situations? Did what you would do with the money change as the amount became higher? If so, in what way did it change?

2. Was there a certain range in which you would spend the money on yourself, and a range in which you would spend it on other people? How did the amount make a difference in this?

3. Was there a point at which you couldn't imagine having this much money? What was that point? What was it like to picture yourself with this much money?

4. Did you have images of yourself living frugally, like Cinderalla in a cottage in the woods, or more opulently, like Cinderella in the Prince's castle? Did you imagine significantly changing the way you live?

YOUR ISSUES ABOUT MONEY AND PROSPERITY

Having thought about the inheritance, notice if you're frugal or indulgent. Do you lust after material wealth, or feel that you don't deserve it, or are you pretty well balanced—able to feel good about the quality of your life, neither too concerned with material wealth nor alienated from it.

Talk with yourself about your issues concerning money. Under *More Money* below list any concerns, judgments, and beliefs you have about material indulgence. You might write something like, "Material wealth is the most important thing to me right now," or "Rich people are selfish." Do the same thing under *Less Money*. You might include, "I don't think of myself as prosperous because no one in my family is," or "It's not right to be paid more than minimum wage."

Concentrate on your attitude to material prosperity. Be specific. Start on this path by clarifying on paper the nature of your issues about money. It's okay if you only write things on one side of the list. It is important to talk to yourself about money issues so you can move away from a voice of judgment perspective on material prosperity and toward an integration of prosperity into your experience of being your self.

More Money   Less Money

KNOWING YOURSELF MORE FULLY

There is story about a young man who wanted to become enlightened. For him, wealth was not measured in dollars or in BMWs, but in knowing everything he could about spiritual philosophies. He read books upon books and studied all the sacred traditions. He had many gurus and teachers. He certainly knew far more about enlightenment than any of his friends. In his terms, he was well on his way to being a very wealthy man.

This young man had a chance to go to Japan to visit a famous Zen master. Upon meeting this teacher, the young man immediately began trying to impress the master with his vast spiritual knowledge. The Zen teacher listened, and offered the young man some tea. The young man nodded to let the master know that he wanted some, and continued talking.

"Oh, Master, there is so much I can learn from you, so much you can give me. And, see, I am already just about your equal. See how much I know. . . ."

The man talked.

The master poured tea into the young man's cup.

The man continued to talk.

The master continued to pour.

The man's words poured out of his mouth, demonstrating his wealth of knowledge. The master was busy with the tea. The man continued to talk.

The tea poured out of the pot and into the cup. It filled the cup and overflowed onto the table and young man's lap. The master continued to pour.

"Hey!" shouted the young man. "Stop!" What are you doing? You can't put any more tea in here!"

"Not," said the master, "unless you empty your cup."

As the Zen master suggests, try to empty your cup of preconceived beliefs about prosperity. Practice being open and ready to receive what might come along. If a part of you identifies even a little bit with the stepsisters and feels that somehow your personal value is tied up with material value, try to disown that perspective right now. Notice what happens to your challenges about money and prosperity when you intentionally empty your cup.

The next several exercises focus on uncovering and discovering the secret treasure that lies within you.

What lies beyond us and what lies before us are tiny matters when compared to what lies within us.

Ralph Waldo Emerson

Who Are You?

Your initial response may be to answer with your name, or to describe your occupation, or some of your roles in life. Perhaps you also add some facts about your background or relationships. This is *some* of who you are, but certainly not all. What about your deepest hopes and fears? Your visions for the fulfillment of your possibilities in life? What does your intuitive voice say about who you are?

Take a few moments to allow your mind to calm down. Just sit still, with your back straight and supported, and your legs and arms uncrossed. Notice your breathing. You might like to read the exercise a few times first before you do it.

As you breathe in, imagine the air is flowing down inside you to a point in the center of your body, somewhere behind your navel. Each breath brings more air into that center space, filling it with light, clear emptiness. As you breathe, imagine the clear empty space in your center growing larger and larger. Each breath brings in more clear, light air inside you.

As you breathe, the center space inside you grows larger and larger until it seems to be filling up your body inside your skin.

Let the clean light air come in and fill up the space inside your skin, so that it fills your body, and comes in with every breath, and flows into your head, too, filling up your head with clear light air.

Feel that stillness and be very, very relaxed as you feel the peace of your center point filling you up.

There is nothing inside you except clear light; nothing but emptiness.

When you feel completely relaxed and still, answer the following questions. Allow your intuition to answer as well as your mind. If you have trouble providing further answers at some point, go back to that calm state by breathing light. Then ask yourself the question again.

Who am I? Ask yourself this question and, in the margin or in your journal, jot down twenty words and phrases that describe who you are. Create as rich a picture as you can with these twenty descriptions. Don't forget to use adjectives and verbs as well as nouns, to use metaphors, to include your toughest challenges as well as your most wonderful successes.

Who was I as a child? Jot down twelve words or phrases in the margins to describe who you used to be when you were a child. Again, allow your intuition to answer this and paint as rich a word picture as you can.

Who will I be in the future? Jot down twelve words or phrases that describe you the way you would like to be ten years from now. Describe your inner world as well as your outer characteristics.

Who does my Fairy Godmother say I am? Imagine that we are offering three wishes to someone who deserves them, and your Fairy Godmother wants you to have the three wishes. How would she describe you? She can only say *true* things about you. Write down twelve things that your Fairy Godmother might tell us.

Who do the wicked stepsisters say I am? Now imagine that we are trying to decide whether to give the three wishes to your two wicked stepsisters or to you, and your stepsisters have the opportunity to tell us twelve *true* things about you to try and convince us not to give you the three wishes. Write down twelve true things that they might say.

Review what you just wrote. What sort of things did you write down? Did you mainly list the roles you play in your life, or did you mainly describe your more private, inner feelings, characteristics, or aspirations? Is there anything you'd like to add? If so, go back and add what you'd like to complete the picture of yourself.

Layers of Your Self

Many people describe the process of exploring themselves as something like peeling an onion. They peel away the outer layer of skin—those aspects they show to the world—to reveal another and yet another layer of themselves. It isn't that the onion has a separate skin that is on the outside, but that the outside is simply one of many layers. If the layer on the surface is peeled away, the underneath is now on the outside.

You can keep finding more layers to yourself until you get to your center. Toward the center, the onion is sweeter and juicier, while the outer layers can be drier.

Think of yourself as this onion for now. What are your layers? Review the lists you made in the previous exercise and then draw or write the most important of these descriptions of yourself on the cross-section of the onion illustration, drawing or writing them in layers that show how close they are to your central core.

Play as you do this. Try using colors and writing in different directions. Try not writing at all, but simply drawing symbolic shapes and colors. You might like to add to the design, and show things that are important to you or influence you in the space around the onion's cross-section.

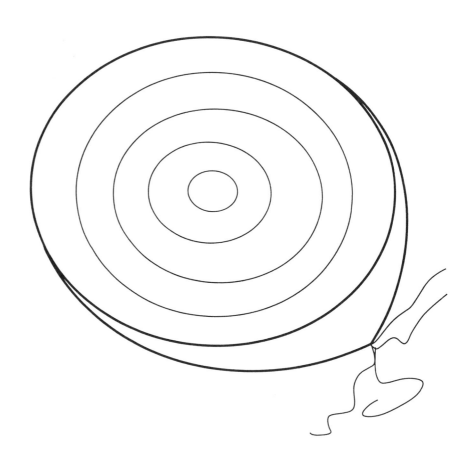

Imagine you are a stranger who found all these responses in a book you'd borrowed. What is your impression of the person who wrote all the lists and completed this drawing of an onion of self.

- What themes emerge?
- What are the values of this person?
- What is the person like?
- What is this person's true humanness?
- What is the person's uniqueness?

Revise any of the lists as needed to make the description even more accurate. Revise your diagram of your self as the layers of an onion to reflect an even more accurate picture.

Collage of My Self

You just revised your description of yourself from the perspective of someone else. How much have you thought about how other people see you? Do they see the real you? How much of the real you do they see? Who is the real you, anyway? What aspects of the real you are kept hidden from many people? What aspects of you do you tend to show people?

Likewise, when you are with other people, to what extent do you truly know and appreciate them, and to what extent is your experience of them colored by judgments based on first impressions or memories of other people you have known?

We constantly see pictures of people in magazines, which communicate us many things to us. Some of our impressions may be accurate, and many may be a product of our own judgments. In magazines we also find lots of pictures representing things we want in life—symbols of the good life.

Look through some magazines and cut out ten to twenty fairly small pictures of people and objects that represent you in some way. Some of these pictures may represent very private, personal dreams, others may represent how you would like to be, or aspects of yourself that you do not like, and some may represent sides of you that you show in certain situations, but not in others. Find pictures that represent the woodcutter, stepsisters, Fairy Godmother, Prince, and Cinderella aspects of you. Find pictures that represent internal and external prosperity.

Consider which of these pictures you would want as illustrations for a magazine article about you. Which ones would you absolutely not have printed?

To make a collage of your self, paste the pictures on a page of your journal or a separate piece of paper. Position the pictures so that their location shows their relationship to each other. You might like to think of the center of the page as representing your inner self, and the edges representing your outer, or public, self. Perhaps you might have one area of the page for the real you, and another for the you that fulfills roles and other people's expectations, or one area might be for your highest ideals and strengths, and another for your less-than-perfect attributes.

Play with your pictures. Make more collages if you have enough pictures. Put them up somewhere where you can look at them daily and see what they reflect about the complex person who is you.

You have now identified many of the qualities you bring with you on your creative journey. Some are helpful and some get in the way. Very often, we don't recognize our strengths and overemphasize or even invent weaknesses. Our self-image often has less to do with reality, and more to do with a fantasy of who we are. Seeing ourselves through clouded lenses distorts our perception of who we are and what we can accomplish.

The following exercises help you clarify your strengths and weaknesses as described earlier by your Fairy Godmother and wicked stepsisters.

"What's Wrong with You Is . . ."

What *is* wrong with you? How do you sabotage your creative journey in life? What have other people actually said to you when they were pointing out your faults? What have you said to yourself when you were pointing out your faults? What wicked stepsister judgments do you now say to yourself? Write some of these things in the balloons in the margin.

PROSPERITY MEANS GETTING RID OF SELF-JUDGMENTS

Read over what you wrote. With things like that buzzing around your head, you probably find it difficult to feel like an internally prosperous person. These petty judgments cut away at your sense of self-worth. It is important to realize that they are based on old half-truths about other people's expectations.

Who is saying or has said each thing to you? Next to each quote, write down the name of the person whose voice is speaking to you through it.

Which of these statements do you say to yourself? Write your name next to each one. Some may be said by you and several other people. Which of these do you believe? Put a B next to these. Which of these is false, an exaggeration, or is otherwise not entirely accurate? Put a big F next to these. If you wrote nasty comments here, you will probably have a lot of Fs. Which one is not simply an observation, but contains an element of negative judgment? Put a big J next to each of these. Which cause you to feel angry with yourself or in some way bad about yourself? Put an A next to these. Which help you feel powerful and happy about yourself and your life? Draw a heart around these.

Look at the page now. Which of these quotes contribute to your creativity? Which get in the way? How do they get in the way? You can see that none of these quotes is helpful, no matter how close to the truth they may be. Your natural creativity will have a much easier time flourishing if these quotes are banished from your repertoire.

As an affirmation of your intent to rid yourself of the power of these judgments, read each one aloud, and then draw the international *no* sign over it. Actually say something like "No more will I listen to you!" or "Begone!"

BANISHING FUTURE JUDGMENTS

We are often not aware how pervasive our judgments are. One student who had never thought of himself as particularly judgmental decided to count the number of times he made judgments during a day. Before the day was out, he counted over seventy-eight judgments! That's a lot for someone who has never considered himself judgmental. Other students have been similarly surprised.

You can stop these self-judgments from exerting their insidious power by catching them when they come out. Whenever you hear yourself saying or thinking one of these things, just *stop*, and substitute a statement that is more conducive to the development of your creativity. It may take some practice to be able to do this.

Character is what you know
you are, not what others think
you are.

Marva Collins and
Civia Tamarkin

For example, if you catch yourself thinking, "You idiot! You should have known better," stop and say something like, "I tried my best, but had some really weird, unexpected results this time," or "I'm an experimenter creating the perfect life." Be careful to avoid statements of alienation and inflation, and to concentrate on true statements of empowerment.

Keep a tally each time you notice yourself saying something unhelpful or alienating about yourself. Carry some paper with you and make a mark each time you catch yourself. The more marks on your tally sheet, the more you are destroying the things that sabotage your creative expression, and thus the more you are allowing your feelings of self-worth to flourish.

If you really want to stomp out the judgments that squelch your feelings of self-worth and inner prosperity, note down the situation that triggers each judgment, jot down the statement, and write down *and say aloud* an alternative self-affirming statement that comes from your inner essence.

NEW WAYS TO UTILIZE YOUR STRENGTHS

You have looked at your attitudes about the limitations that interfere with your creativity. What are your real strengths? What are the qualities that your Fairy Godmother attributed to you? How do you feel about these? Do you believe them and have an inner sense of self-worth and prosperity when you think of these things? Do you doubt yourself?

If you sometimes doubt yourself, when do you doubt yourself the most? Which of the judgmental quotes is most effective in getting you to doubt yourself? True creativity in life asks you not just to squelch your judgments, but to recognize and use your strengths. As an everyday hero you often find yourself facing a particularly tough challenge in which you are called on to use your strengths in new ways or in a new context.

Think of a problem or issue that you are currently confronting. How might you use your greatest strengths to meet and overcome this? You need not use them directly. For instance, if one of your strengths is your ability to express your love by cooking nourishing, delicious meals for people, perhaps you might make something nice for yourself as both an expression of loving yourself, and so you feel energized and ready to deal with your critical issue.

Write down your current issue or problem on the top of a page in your journal or elsewhere. Then use your creativity to come up with ways to use *every one* of the strengths mentioned by your Fairy Godmother to meet and overcome this problem. Write down how you will use each strength. Play as you do this, and see what wonderful things you can come up with.

The wealth of the world lies in peace.

Inscription on

Japanese temple

REFLECTIONS ON THE TREASURES WITHIN YOU

How do you feel now? Did you feel pretty depressed when you were looking at your judgments? Did you feel better when you called upon your creative inner resources to come up with ways to use your strengths to deal with a current issue?

Having a sense of inner prosperity doesn't mean that you never have any self-doubts or qualities that you don't like. It does mean that you are appreciative of your strengths, and can capitalize on them to offset the less-than-wonderful aspects of yourself. This is what being your self is about. This is why we asked you to think of *all* the characters in Cinderella's story as aspects of you.

Each of us, on our path towards being the hero of our own life, has and discovers personal assets and liabilities. That is human. Our assets are those things we consider our strengths or treasure. Our liabilities are those things we consider to be our weaknesses. The point about being your self is to realize this and not become inflated by your assets or alienated by your liabilities.

In your work you may have put together profit-and-loss statements. You may have listed the pros and cons of two people applying for a job, or two projects you were considering becoming involved in. Perhaps you have analyzed the advantages and disadvantages of a particular career move. The idea of a balance sheet is probably not new.

Your most precious resource is a human resource; it is your self. Use the nonfinancial personal balance sheet to record your human assets and liabilities. You might think of and write down some of the most important items from your stepsister and Fairy Godmother lists. And don't forget your network of friends and acquaintances and the allies from your visual and verbal travel logs!

Human Liabilities | Human Assets

As you look at your balance sheet, ask, "How can I make the most of my assets (or develop new ones) and minimize my liabilities (or change them into assets)?" There are a few things you might do.

QUESTION YOUR LIABILITIES

Review your list and ask yourself whether your liabilities are truly liabilities, or inaccurate self-judgments? For instance, if you wrote that you were too pushy or not intelligent, or lazy, ask yourself whether you *truly* are that way. Choose three of your liabilities, and answer these questions silently in your mind or write here or in your journal.

What does (liability) mean?

In what situations are you (liability)?

When is (liability) useful for you?

What would happen if you weren't (liability)?

HOW MUCH ARE YOUR ASSETS AND LIABILITIES WORTH?

Most profit-and-loss statements attach a numerical value to all the items on the list, so you can see at a glance how they stack up against each other. It would be arbitrary to give personal characteristics numerical values. However, there is another way for you to identify the relative value of your assets and liabilities. Look at your list. Imagine that the space separating the two sections represents neutrality. Consider that the left edge represents extremely high liability; the right edge represents extremely valuable assets.

Under each item on the lists, draw an arrow from the center line (neutral) out towards the edge (extreme) of the page. Let the length of the arrow indicate the strength of each liability and each asset. Thus, under each liability, you would draw an arrow that starts at the center line, and goes to the left. Those things that are minimal liabilities would have fairly short arrows under them. Those that are awful liabilities would have longer arrows. Under each asset, you'd draw an arrow starting from the center line and pointing to the right. Longer arrows would indicate your stronger assets. These arrows give you a picture that shows you at a glance the balance of your human liabilities and assets.

When we examine the line lengths in the sample balance sheet in the margin, we see that this person considers the liability at the top of the list to be quite serious, while the bottom one on the list isn't so bad. Similarly, the person's first two assets seem to be of medium value, while the third is very significant and the fourth is smaller.

REDUCING LIABILITIES AND CAPITALIZING ON ASSETS

Once you've drawn arrows indicating the strength of your human liabilities and assets, look at your nonfinancial balance sheet again. There is one more thing to do.

Which things on the liabilities side could you do away with or have less of? Which things on the assets side could you expand upon or have more of?

Using a different colored pen or marker, now edit your balance sheet to show those liabilities that you realistically could get rid of or reduce, and those assets that you realistically could develop.

Retrace each arrow with your second color, but this time the length of the arrow indicates changes you will make to improve the balance of your human liabilities and assets. A shorter arrow pointing to the left indicates a liability that you can do something about, so that it becomes less of a liability. A longer arrow pointing to the right indicates an asset that you can make even stronger. Some of the arrows you draw with your second color may be the same length as the first arrows. Some may be a different length.

Humans have an unparalleled capability to become many things.

Albert Bandura

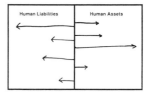

INTENTIONS BASED ON SELF-AWARENESS

Now be practical. Exactly what assets and liabilities will you change? What things will you do differently? What is your intention here? Sometimes just identifying something about yourself results in changes in your life. It is as if having greater personal clarity somehow results in being slightly different in ways that have profound results.

Sometimes, you need a gentle prod to move from simply seeing more clearly who you are, and who you might be as you experience true prosperity, to taking action and making definite strides toward being prosperous. What can you actually do on your path to find your way to prosperity, to your destination of having a rich feeling of self-worth?

Look at the arrows you have drawn, especially those cases where the second arrow under a liability was significantly shorter or longer than the first. Use the space below to jot down statements of intent about five liabilities or assets. What *specific* differences in attitude or behavior would you be willing to make? Allow your inner essence to suggest action you will take to minimize your liabilities and increase your assets. Write these below.

The world is too much with us, late and soon. Getting and spending, we lay waste our powers.

John Milton

——— RETURN ———

TO FIND YOUR WAY TO TRUE PROSPERITY

On your path to prosperity you've had many adventures. You have examined your relationship to money and material wealth. You've dug up the riches and treasure within you, and have demolished some of the negative self-judgments that have been keeping this treasure hidden. You've experienced the creative essence at the core of your real self and you've acknowledged that true prosperity is yours if you are receptive to the forms in which it might come.

The final thing to do is to acknowledge and affirm the prosperity that is already in your life. Who is this wealthy self? What makes it wealthy? Complete this statement in your hero's declaration, and then draw a precious jewel to represent all that is abundant in your life. Let it represent everything you like about yourself. Let it symbolize your richest dreams.

A great antidote to greed is generosity. . . . Give, even if it requires a conscious effort to do so. By sharing whatever you have, your greed will diminish.

Laurence and Barbara Tarlo

——— HERO'S DECLARATION ———

My self is my truest wealth because

This jewel represents my true prosperity

ONE DAY AT A TIME

Now that you have made a statement of your self and your prosperity, your challenge is to be your self and feel a rich sense of self-worth on a daily basis. Cinderella managed to do this through all of her hard times, and the Prince had true prosperity by valuing that quality in her. The test of your travels is the opportunity to be both Cinderella and the Prince, and especially to be your own Fairy Godmother, and so find your way to prosperity. This starts with living just one day with a rich sense of self-worth and of all the wealth in your life.

Start the next exercise when you have a fairly normal day ahead of you, and you know you will be able to get back to your workbook in twenty-four hours.

In the space below jot down what prosperity is in your life.

This sounds like a simple instruction. You just did this on a preceding page, didn't you? This time, however, you are asked to approach the task in a qualitatively different manner. You are not to *intellectually* think of prosperity and then write it down, as you probably did on the last page. You are to let a sense of feeling or knowing your prosperity emerge *intuitively*. It will help for you to close your eyes and remember the still, quiet place inside you.

Take a few moments to do this before describing or drawing a symbol for your prosperity below.

My Prosperity, My Self

> The other great antidote to greed is gratitude. If you contemplate all that you have, and all the blessings you have been given, gratitude will arise and drive greed out.
>
> Laurence and Barbara Tarlo

Now go do whatever you do for the next twenty-four hours, without forgetting to really be your self. At this time tomorrow, open your workbook to this page again, and take a few minutes to again remember the still, quiet place inside you. Reflect on how you lived the last twenty-four hours.

What Happened?

- What things did you do and attitudes did you have that gave you a sense of inner wealth?
- How much did you consciously pay attention to being your self in these twenty-four hours?
- How much were you on automatic pilot?

What shall it profit a man, if he shall gain the whole world, and lose his own soul?

Mark 8:36

Now jot down your observations of your day. Be sure to include any notes to yourself about significant differences you noticed, and situations that caused you to forget about your wealthy self.

Observations on Living One Day as My Wealthy Self

FOLLOW-UP: MAPPING YOUR PATH TO PROSPERITY

The last part of this chapter, as with each of the challenges, is to complete another visual log and verbal log of your travels. How are you different now? How are you different in terms of where you are on your own Hero's journey toward recognizing and experiencing true prosperity?

Don't look back yet to the logs you first made when you started this chapter. Recall that the visual log is an intuitive mapping of where you are now in your creative quest for recognizing and experiencing true prosperity. The verbal log is a chance to characterize this challenge in your life right now in terms of a hero's journey. How do real events and people in your life parallel aspects of this metaphor?

Prepare your outline of the visual log and take a few moments to be still and pay attention to your breath. Allow a sense of your journey over the last week to come into focus. Use colors to draw a figure or other symbols to represent yourself on your path in the expressive pictorial log. Then make notes about where you are regarding the six stages of the journey in your written log.

REFLECTIONS ON YOUR PATH

Now that you've completed this chapter and have worked on the prosperity challenge for a week or so, write about your experience of this quest. This can serve to consolidate and legitimate your experience so far. Write it as a letter to yourself (or to us or some friend or relative), so that you can get into its informal, reporting style.

You can keep this letter or statement as tangible evidence of your journey to this point. Then, if you feel the need to do some more specific work on this challenge in the future or just want a boost regarding recognizing and experiencing true prosperity, you can go back to this review of what you just accomplished.

CELEBRATE!

How are you celebrating your completion of this journey? What are you doing to reward yourself for your successful journey? How are you making a public statement of your private changes? Make sure that in the days ahead you continue to acknowledge and celebrate your journey and the profound prosperity in your life.

Living Your Own Myth

The path of the everyday hero leads you to break boundaries—the boundaries of your assumptions about what you can and can't do, the boundaries that have kept you within a small, safe country, while the whole vast world lay waiting for discovery all around you. In this book you have examined the myth of the hero's journey in many forms, but there has always been one act that lay at the center of each story: the act of personal transformation. Sleeping Beauty and her Prince, Perceval, Beauty and the Beast, The Peasant Who Married a Goddess, Theseus, Ariadne, and Cinderella each represent aspects of your inner self as you met challenges. The path of the everyday hero is grounded in trust; the trust to leap into the unknown and pursue your highest ideals even when your doubt of the outcome is most profound.

How do you feel about yourself and the way you've dealt with the challenges in this book? We hope that you have found a new energy, not only for the five challenges in this book but for other challenges as well. If there is one truth in all this, it is that you have to embark upon your hero's journeys over and over again in your life. Challenges will appear, persist, and reappear in new forms. But as an everyday hero, you will more easily and effortlessly take the call, leap from innocence and fully enjoy, experience, and learn from each encounter.

SUMMING UP YOUR JOURNEYS

Where are your now on the five challenges of this book? In chapter 2, you answered that by drawing stick figures on the five paths representing stages of the creative process, or hero's journey. Take a moment now to depict visually where you are today on these challenges by

Our highest business is our daily life.

John Cage

The great path has no gates,
Thousands of roads enter it.
When one passes through this
gateless gate
One walks freely between
heaven and earth.

Mamon Ekai (Zen monk)

again drawing a figure on each path. Celebrate your movement along each path (even if you are still in one of the rather unsettling phases of one or two of the challenges) with bright colors.

Next, write a sentence or two about what you have discovered and what needs to be done next in your life's journey.

YOUR OWN MYTH TO LIVE BY

We hope that, as a result of using this book, you will always walk the path of the everyday hero with strength and wisdom to meet whatever challenges life brings you. When you translate your challenge into a story of the hero's journey, you experience an awakening of a new awareness about the meaning of the challenge and your ability to resolve it. There are always clues, hidden in symbolic form, of your inner resources and the path that transforms your roadblocks into building blocks.

Your final activity is to write your own myth that holds the seeds of your creative spirit and heroic path. It's best to do this with a significant challenge in mind. Consider your biggest challenge right now. It can be one of the five you worked on in this book or another one, such as improving your health or bringing your creativity into an organization. Where have you been on this challenge up to now? Where are you going? What dragons have you fought? Which ones have wounded you? Which have you vanquished and which ones are you still living with?

Think of this challenge in terms of the phases of the hero's journey. What was your state of innocence? The call to adventure? What was or is your initiation, and who have been or might be your allies? What would breakthrough be like? (You may not know this just yet.) Can you imagine a celebration of your resolution of this challenge?

Don't worry if you cannot answer all the questions, but do make sure you have a clear idea of your challenge. Think about the feelings it brings up for you, and remember that out of your pain can arise the strength and wisdom of the hero. In some cultures the healers and wise ones are those who have experienced the deepest loss or the greatest wounds. For example, when Oedipus found out that he had inadvertently killed his father and married his mother, he blinded himself in despair. But after this tragedy he became so wise that the people of Athens came to him for inspiration and help. In a more modern view, the Velveteen Rabbit became "real" after he was rejected and thrown away.

Think of your challenge as a dragon. It is said that there are two ways to catch a dragon. The easy way is to grab it by the tail; however, you can't necessarily tame it this way, and in fact, it can turn around and breathe its fire at you. Alternately, you could grab it by the snout. This is harder, and riskier, but when you have the dragon like this, you can tame it easily. In the same way, there are two ways to find your guiding myth, each with its benefits and its pitfalls.

The easy way, but not necessarily the most effective, is to think of the myth or story that means the most to you right now. If one does not come to mind, review the list on page 33 in chapter 4. Once you have a story in mind, reflect on the following questions:

- How is the hero of that myth like you? In what ways do the hero's struggles parallel your own?
- How did the hero's state of innocence parallel your initial state of innocence?
- What elements of your call to adventure do you see?
- In what ways does the hero's initiation speak to your own trials?
- Who are your allies in your life?
- What sparks the hero's breakthrough? Can you draw parallels to your life?
- How is the hero transformed in the final phase of celebration? What clues does this give you about transforming your own situation?
- If you were to sum up how this story reflects your own creative spirit in one easy sentence, what would that sentence be?

Just as a dream can provide you with inspiration as you reflect on it for several days or weeks, so too can the story you chose. Carry it around in your consciousness and notice as other meanings come to you. However, while you are the author, actor, and producer of your dreams, someone *else* created this story. Thus there may be some aspects of this tale that resonate in you, and others that do not.

The wonder is that the characteristic efficacy to touch and inspire deep creative centers dwells in the smallest nursery fairy tale— as the flavor of the ocean is contained in a droplet or the whole mystery of life within the egg of a flea. For the symbols of mythology are . . . spontaneous productions of the psyche, and each bears within it, undamaged, the germ power of its source.

Joseph Campbell

Draw your chair up close to the edge of the precipice and I'll tell you a story.

F. Scott Fitzgerald

Some years ago, one of us, Lorna, had strongly identified with the Greek myth of Eros and Psyche during pursuit of her Ph.D. Psyche has four impossible tasks to accomplish before her transformation, but at the last minute makes an error that results in the seeming negation of all she had accomplished. (All turns out well in the end, however.) Lorna had identified so closely with many aspects of this story that it was almost no surprise when after her final dissertation defense, a computer glitch destroyed the dissertation and back-up copy, meaning the whole thing had to be retyped. To what extent did she invite that by identifying with a myth with a built-in trip-wire at the end? Might the "dragon" not have turned on her if she had lived by a more appropriate myth of her own creation? Since then she has returned to her own myths.

Telling and living by your own personal myth is the second way of resolving your challenge, and is like catching a dragon by its snout. You will achieve a better fit this way. People sometimes find this hard at first, but the images and plots that your intuition comes up with tend to have an immediacy and power that illuminate new ways through your challenge. Take Douglas, for example.

Douglas was lonely and did not do well with relationships. He felt like a round peg in a square hole at work, and always felt different from his colleagues. Although he didn't fully know it, this problem with relationships started when he was in junior high school. His family was moving from the rural Midwest to New York City, and Douglas was heartbroken about having to leave. On the East coast, he was teased as a country hick by the children at his new school. He turned to antisocial behavior that, in one way or another, remained his hallmark into his mid-twenties.

The story he told to illuminate his relationship challenge was about a seed ripped from a field of flowers by a storm and buried in ground that was rained out of nutrients. Or so it appeared. In reality, the seed germinated from the rains, and eventually sprouted, growing not into a flower, but into a beautiful, large oak tree providing shelter for little animals and picnickers.

Douglas didn't plan to have his story to turn out the way it did. When he heard himself tell the ending, he had a profound realization that he was, metaphorically, like that seed—indirectly nourished by the storms in his life, not destined to be a flower, but in his own time to become strong and worthwhile. This mythologizing of his life allowed Douglas to break through and trust that there was a way out.

To mythologize your life, and elevate it from your local story to the level of what Jean Houston calls the great story of transformation, you need to start with a clear sense of your challenge and then retell it as a myth. Give your intuition full permission to make up a story. You do not have to know how it will turn out. In fact, it does not have to be obviously about the challenge at all. Begin with "Once upon a time . . ." and proceed from there. Let the characters be royalty, fairies, animals, objects, anything except the literal people involved in your challenge. Tell your myth through all six phases of the hero's journey, even if your challenge has not yet been fully resolved in real life. We suggest that you write down your story. If it is easier for you, you may wish to recite it out loud into a tape recorder and transcribe it later. Whichever method you choose, it is important to let the story tell itself, and to put it in writing.

As in most of the exercises in this book, make sure you will not be interrupted, and take a few moments before you start to sit still, close your eyes, and notice your breathing. Make sure you are comfortable. In this relaxed state of mind, become aware of what seems to be the most powerful challenge in your life, knowing that you are about to transform it. Remember to include in your myth all the elements of the hero's journey, even if your challenge has not yet been resolved in real life. These elements are:

- an initial state of innocence;
- an event or situation that calls the hero to adventure;
- a period of initiation, a major test of the hero's resourcefulness;
- allies that help the hero discover his or her creative spirit;
- breakthrough to a new awareness or healing situation; and
- celebration of the transformation and recognition of the hero's path.

You might find it useful to generate your story or enrich it with the story elements below. Either select one item from each category or come up with your own, but try to weave all twelve components into your myth. If you would like to use a more random method to choose the elements of the story, you might roll dice. Now, select one item from each category to include in your story.

There is only one journey. Going inside yourself.

Rainer Maria Rilke

Never mistake knowledge for wisdom. One helps you make a living; the other helps you make a life.

Sandra Carey

Do not reject what is of Heaven, do not neglect what is of man, and you will be close to the attainment of Truth.

Chuang-tsu

THE PATH OF THE EVERYDAY HERO

One is not a hero who defeats a mighty army. The true hero is the one who crosses the ocean known as the mind and the senses.

Yoga Vasishtha

A wise person experiences whatever comes before him: whether it appears to be good or bad, he faces it. When you become the master of your mind, nothing is good or bad, as such. All that is, is your destiny.

Gurumayi Chidvilasananda

Location: (1) city, (2) sunlit meadow, (3) forest, (4) cave, (5) underwater, (6) _____

Male Character: (1) king, (2) god, (3) prince, (4) warrior, (5) magician, (6) _____

Female Character: (1) queen, (2) goddess, (3) princess, (4) healer, (5) witch, (6) _____

Ally: (1) wise being, (2) child, (3) dark stranger, (4) snake, (5) songbird, (6) _____

Enemy: (1) thief, (2) liar, (3) murderer, (4) evil goblin, (5) dragon, (6) _____

Relation: (1) mother, (2) father, (3) sister, (4) brother, (5) long-lost cousin, (6) _____

Role: (1) teacher, (2) cook, (3) beggar, (4) lover, (5) trickster, (6) _____

Precious Object: (1) mirror, (2) seed, (3) jewel, (4) sword, (5) goblet, (6) _____

Food: (1) fruit of the earth, (2) cooked meats, (3) wine, (4) bread, (5) honey, (6) _____

Plant: (1) rose, (2) oak tree, (3) aloe vera cactus, (4) deadly nightshade, (5) mushroom, (6) _____

Magic Maker: (1) crystal, (2) wand, (3) glitter dust, (4) amulet, (5) sacred song, (6) _____

Hero's Tools: (1) invisible ink, (2) seven-league boots, (3) cloak of darkness, (4) healing ointment, (5) time machine, (6) _____

In our workshops we sometimes put on music and ask participants to dance their stories to the music. This deepens the experience, since you do not just think of the myth in words, but feel it in your body. Try that now, even if you are using an existing myth. Play a five-to twenty-minute piece of complex music without words that evokes deep feelings for you. Feel your story in your soul. Use body language and movement to express your story.

Imagine that your myth will be published, and that it needs a cover design. Draw a full-page illustration of your creative spirit as it

240

is embodied in your myth. Take your time; use colors. Try not to plan what you will draw, or how you will draw it, but let an illustration emerge out of your hand and drawing implements. Tap into the wealth of feelings hidden in your story as you draw.

Once you have created your myth, danced it, and designed a cover, take a break, look at your story with fresh eyes and analyze it in terms of the hero's journey. How do the elements of the hero's journey manifest themselves in your myth? How does your myth parallel your life? What further clues do you see about how you can be an everyday hero like the hero in your story?

Keep your story alive for at least several weeks after your write it. Think about it over this period and see what new insights emerge. Look for chance encounters or objects that have something to do with your story—a person similar to a character in your story, a series of animals or situations like those in your story. People often tell us of amazing coincidences in which their story seems to come to life almost everywhere they look. They say that this reaffirms the power of their myth, their own creative spirit and themselves as an everyday hero.

POSTSCRIPT

When you have finished this book and have written your myth, do not put them away on the bookshelf or in the back of a drawer. Review them now and then to find new meanings and insights about your creative path for solving challenges. We have found that upon reviewing our own journals, we will suddenly recognize what a picture means months after drawing it. Sometimes insight comes from immediately seeing patterns in our drawings and attitudes; sometimes from looking at them later with a fresh eye.

When you face new challenges, review how you met the five challenges in these pages. Is there something about the way you met one of these challenges that you could apply to this new one? Modify the exercises as you follow your path of the everyday hero and bring your creative spirit to your aid as you face the further challenges of life.

And never forget that you are a hero no matter what you do. Here's one final story to illustrate that. It was told often by the late meditation master Swami Muktananda, who called it "The Lord's Club." We've changed the title slightly.

If you can dream, and not
 make dreams your master
If you can think, and not make
 thoughts your aim;
If you can meet with triumph
 and disaster,
And treat these two imposters
 the same . . .

  Rudyard Kipling

The true saint
goes in and out amongst the
 people
and eats and sleeps with them
and buys and sells in the
 market and marries
and takes place in social
 intercourse
and never forgets God
for a single moment.

  Abu Said Ibn Abi-L-Tkayr

The Hero's Club

Zen student: "Master, what is Zen?"

Master: "Zen is eating when you eat, working when you work, and relaxing when you relax."

Student: "But, Master, that is so simple!"

Master: "Yes, but so few people do it."

It seems that a group of heroes from all professions—athletics, mothering, government, military, business, health care, rescue, aviation, exploration, and the arts got together to form a club. They decided that it would be an exclusive club; so exclusive, in fact, that no one other than certified heroes could attend the meetings. But when they all gathered for their first meeting, they saw that they had a problem. There was no one there to serve them or to do the business of the club.

So one of the heroes had a reasonably nonheroic idea. They would put each of the jobs needed to be done on pieces of paper and then draw out the job they would have for that meeting. And someone became the president, another became cook, another served. One guarded the front door, others cleaned bathrooms, washed windows, kept minutes, arranged and performed entertainment, handled finances, and provided transportation.

At the next meeting, the former president drew cooking detail, the janitor from the previous meeting kept minutes. Jobs were switched around and around from meeting to meeting. Everyone was happy. And no one ever forgot that no matter what their job, they were fundamentally a hero and always would be.

Don't you ever forget either.
We wish you luck in all your endeavors. Travel well on your path.

ABOUT THE AUTHORS

Lorna Catford, Ph.D., teaches at Stanford University's Graduate School of Business and is a Professor of Psychology at California State University at Sonoma. She has been conducting international research on creative problem-solving and leading creativity seminars for business, students, and private organizations for more than fifteen years. Dr. Catford is a licensed therapist in private practice, specializing in using the hero's journey as a framework for creative problem-solving. She lives in Forestville, California.

Michael Ray, Ph.D., is the first John G. McCoy-Banc One Corporation Professor of Creativity and Innovation and of Marketing at Stanford University. He is the co-author of *Creativity in Business* and is widely known for his research on creative thinking. Dr. Ray has appeared on several national television programs, including "20/20" and the PBS series "The Creative Spirit." Together with Dr. Catford, he has taught a course on the concepts of the everyday hero to business students, executives, and professionals that has been featured in such publications as *Time, Fortune,* and the *New York Times.* He lives in Santa Cruz, California.